Construction Mastermind – Volume I

Build Better. Litigate Less.
Construction Risk, Process Discipline, and How Claims Actually Begin.

Published by:
Construction Mastermind Press
United States of America

CONTENTS

ABOUT THE AUTHOR

Keith Whitener is a nationally recognized construction executive, expert witness, and claims strategist with more than three decades of field-proven experience managing high-risk infrastructure and vertical construction projects across the United States and Canada. His career spans billion-dollar water and wastewater programs, design-build fabrication facilities, commercial developments, government infrastructure, and mission-critical data centers, all delivered in environments where failure carried real financial and legal consequences.

As founder and chief executive of National Commercial Development Inc., Keith leads a consulting practice focused on construction risk mitigation, contract optimization, and dispute avoidance. His work supports owners, contractors, public agencies, and law firms seeking to resolve disputes and prevent claims before positions harden and litigation becomes inevitable.

Prior to launching NCD, Keith served in senior operational leadership roles, including Vice President of Operations and Chief Operating Officer, overseeing hundreds of professionals and complex programs from preconstruction through closeout and commissioning. In those roles, he did not study claims from a distance. He dealt with them as they unfolded, often after decisions were already made and leverage was lost.

Keith holds a degree in Civil Engineering with a minor in Psychology. That combination shapes his approach to construction risk, which recognizes that claims are rarely caused by drawings alone. They are driven by human behavior, communication breakdowns, and leadership decisions made under pressure.

This book represents the accumulation of lessons learned, disputes defended, and risks that could have been avoided. It is written for professionals who want to build smarter, lead with clarity, and avoid learning these lessons the expensive way.

DEDICATION

To every project manager who stayed late to write a delay log no one asked for.

To every superintendent who refused to move forward without a signed change order.

To every field engineer who caught the mistake before it became a multimillion-dollar claim.

And to every construction professional who learned, often the hard way, that managing risk is not paperwork.

It is leadership under pressure.

This book is for you.

And to the next generation of builders.

May you build smarter, defend better, and never need the lessons we had to learn the hard way.

ACKNOWLEDGMENTS

No book is built alone, especially not one forged from decades of real-world risk, failure, and field-earned wisdom.

To the mentors and veterans who taught me not just how to build, but how to do it with integrity, discipline, and pride, thank you for setting the foundation.

To the teams I have led and the leaders who challenged me, your grit, dedication, and ability to perform under pressure are the reasons this content rings true.

To the attorneys, mediators, and expert witnesses I have partnered with, your legal insights and precision have helped shape the strategic frameworks that now guide others.

To my friends and family, thank you for your patience, sacrifice, and belief, which gave me the time and clarity to complete this work. Your support means everything.

To our clients at NCD Incorporated, your trust turned theory into practice. You did not just hire us; you sharpened us. This book is as much yours as it is mine.

Furthermore, to you, the reader: thank you for choosing to build smarter. You are the reason this book exists. If it helps you lead one project better or avoid one claim, then it has done its job.

FOREWORD

How Construction Claims Begin

The Moments No One Notices

Construction claims rarely begin with dramatic failures. They begin quietly.

They begin when a question goes unanswered.
When a responsibility is assumed instead of confirmed.
When a decision is made in a meeting and never written down.

They begin in the moments no one flags as dangerous.

Across the construction industry, from airports to tunnels to treatment plants, the pattern is the same. Projects do not fail because teams lack intelligence, experience, or effort. They fail because discipline breaks down at the exact moment it matters most.

Risk does not arrive loudly. It arrives disguised as routine.

To understand how claims actually form, look at five of the most studied construction failures in modern history. They differ in scale, geography, and complexity. Yet each followed the same path. Expectations were implied instead of documented. Ownership was blurred instead of assigned. Warnings existed, but no one connected them.

The Sydney Opera House

A Landmark Defined by Scope Drift and Silent Assumptions

The Sydney Opera House is one of the most recognizable structures in the world. It is also one of the most cited examples of how construction claims originate long before contracts harden and lawyers arrive.

Construction began with incomplete designs. Political pressure demanded early mobilization. Architectural ambition raced ahead of engineering certainty. Rather than pause and resolve the gaps, the project moved forward on assumptions.

Design decisions changed after construction had already begun. Structural systems were revised midstream. Cost and schedule baselines shifted repeatedly, but no one recalibrated responsibility as the project evolved.

Each party believed someone else was absorbing the risk.

The architect believed the owner accepted design evolution.
The owner believed the contractor would manage constructability impacts.
The contractor believed changes would be fairly compensated later.

None of those beliefs were clearly documented. None were reconciled contractually.

The result was not a single dispute, but a cascade. Costs escalated more than tenfold. Schedules stretched for years. Relationships collapsed. Claims followed.

The Opera House was not undone by ambition. It was undone by proceeding without disciplined alignment between design maturity, authority, and accountability.

This is how claims begin when scope is allowed to evolve without structure. Not with confrontation, but with optimism.

The Channel Tunnel

When Interfaces Multiply Faster Than Accountability

The Channel Tunnel, linking the United Kingdom and France, was among the most complex infrastructure projects ever attempted. Two countries. Multiple contractors. Different legal systems. Shared risk, at least in theory.

In practice, risk ownership was fragmented.

Design responsibilities crossed borders. Construction packages overlapped. Interface conditions were numerous and poorly governed. When delays occurred, each party traced the cause to a different boundary.

Geotechnical conditions differed between drives. Equipment performance varied. Schedule assumptions proved optimistic. But the real breakdown occurred at the interfaces — where one scope ended and another began.

No single entity owned end-to-end system performance.
No unified mechanism existed to reconcile competing delay narratives.
No early alignment process forced issues into resolution.

Problems were documented. Reports were written. But they were treated as local issues rather than systemic warnings.

By the time disputes crystallized, positions had hardened. Claims exceeded billions. Arbitration and litigation stretched for decades.

The Channel Tunnel did not fail because of engineering difficulty. It failed because coordination complexity outpaced governance discipline.

This is what happens when responsibility is divided without integration.

California High-Speed Rail

A Program Where Early Decisions Locked In Later Claims

California's High-Speed Rail program illustrates how claims can be baked into a project before the first major structure is built.

Early commitments were made before right-of-way acquisition was complete. Utility relocation assumptions were optimistic. Environmental approvals were still evolving. Yet contracts were awarded and schedules were announced.

Design-build teams were mobilized into a landscape that was not ready for construction.

Utility owners were not aligned. Property access lagged. Third-party approvals introduced unpredictable delays. Each issue was documented, but responsibility for resolution was diffuse.

Contractors followed the contract.
The owner followed the program schedule.
Third parties followed their own priorities.

No one owned the convergence of those realities.

As delays mounted, claims became inevitable. The disputes were not about poor workmanship or defective design. They were about access, sequencing, and assumptions that were never validated.

The program struggled not because risk was unknown, but because it was treated as someone else's problem.

This is how mega-program claims begin. Not with bad actors, but with early commitments made without enforceable alignment.

The Big Dig

A Catastrophe Built One Ignored Signal at a Time

In Boston, the Central Artery project known as the Big Dig suffered a fatal ceiling collapse inside a connector tunnel. Heavy panels fell without warning. Lives were lost. Litigation followed for years.

The immediate cause was a failure of epoxy anchors. The deeper cause was far more disturbing.

Concerns had surfaced months earlier. Designers questioned long term load behavior. Inspectors noted inconsistencies. Field personnel raised observations in daily reports and punch lists.

Each warning existed in isolation. No one consolidated them. No one owned the pattern.

Information was present, but it lived in silos. The collapse did not originate from a single mistake. It grew from incremental signals that were never elevated or connected.

This is how construction risk evolves. Not with alarms, but with silence.

Denver International Airport

The System That Had Everything Except Ownership

Denver International Airport attempted to deploy the most advanced automated baggage system ever built. Instead, the project suffered more than a year of delays and hundreds of millions in cost overruns.

Contractors blamed design changes.
The airport blamed coordination failures.
Subcontractors blamed unclear interfaces and late access.

Investigations eventually identified a simpler truth. No single party owned system integration. Design, software, installation, testing, and operational readiness were treated as separate responsibilities.

Handoffs were constant. Ownership was absent.

A project can survive imperfect design. It can survive schedule pressure. What it cannot survive is a lack of accountability for how the pieces fit together.

This failure was not technical. It was managerial.

The Pattern No One Teaches

The lesson across these projects is not complex. Construction risk is predictable. It is visible. It sends signals long before it becomes a claim.

The problem is that risk lives in the gaps between scopes, disciplines, and phases. It lives where teams assume alignment instead of verifying it.

In those moments, discipline matters more than experience.
Clarity matters more than effort.
Documentation matters more than intent.

The strongest builders are not defined by how well they construct. They are defined by how well they manage the moments between construction activities. They confirm assumptions. They define ownership. They document decisions others take for granted.

They give risk structure before it turns into loss.

What This Volume Does

This book exists to show how construction claims actually begin. Not in courtrooms, but on jobsites. Not with disputes, but with silence.

Volume One is about prevention and control. It focuses on how risk emerges across every phase of a project, from bidding through closeout, and how disciplined teams stop claims before they harden into legal positions.

You will learn how claims form, how early warning signs appear, and how systems, culture, and contract administration determine outcomes long before lawyers become involved. This volume connects execution to defensibility and leadership decisions to financial consequences.

Every chapter is practical. Every concept is grounded in real projects. Nothing here is theoretical.

What Comes Next

Volume Two begins where prevention ends.

When risk is not controlled, claims move from jobsite issues to legal outcomes. Courts do not evaluate effort. They evaluate proof. They apply doctrines, tests, and precedent to decide who pays, how much, and why.

Volume Two examines the most common construction claims and the case law that governs them. It shows how courts interpret delay, disruption, payment disputes, terminations, defects, and damages. It is not about how claims should work. It is about how they actually do.

This volume teaches you how to avoid claims.
The next teaches you how claims are judged when avoidance fails.

The Builders Who Win

The builders who consistently succeed do not rely on heroics. They rely on systems. They do not wait for disputes to surface. They prevent them through discipline, clarity, and accountability.

Great construction leaders do not just build projects. They build predictable outcomes.

If your goal is to build better, protect your organization, and litigate less, this book was written for you.

Because in construction, the most valuable claims are not the ones you win.

They are the ones you never have to file.

"Failure is seldom sudden. It is the result of small decisions made over time." **- James Clear**

Part I – Foundations: Risks, Causes, Culture

CHAPTER 1

UNDERSTANDING CONSTRUCTION RISK

Chapter Foreword

Risk is not a possibility in construction. It is a certainty.

From bid day through closeout, every project carries exposure to cost overruns, schedule delays, quality failures, and legal disputes. This is not because people are careless or unskilled. It is because construction is complex, fast moving, and dependent on thousands of decisions made under pressure.

Most claims do not result from a single catastrophic mistake. They grow from patterns. Small gaps in scope. Unanswered questions. Verbal decisions that were never confirmed. Documentation that arrives late or not at all.

This chapter establishes the foundation for understanding construction risk. What it is. Where it comes from. When it appears. And most importantly, how it can be identified and controlled before it turns into a claim.

"In preparing for battle I have always found that plans are useless, but planning is indispensable" — **Dwight D. Eisenhower**

Risk in Construction: It is Not If, It is When

Every construction project contains risk regardless of size, delivery method, or team experience. The question is not whether risk exists. The question is whether it is recognized, assigned, and managed.

Risk emerges because construction relies on coordination between multiple parties working from incomplete information. Designs evolve. Site conditions differ from assumptions. Owners change priorities. Schedules compress. Trades overlap. Decisions are made daily, often without full visibility into downstream impacts.

What causes claims is rarely poor intent or incompetence. It is misalignment.

Expectations differ.

- Responsibilities are unclear.

- Changes occur without process.

- Impacts go undocumented.

When these conditions persist, risk compounds. The longer it goes unmanaged, the more expensive it becomes to correct.

Uncertainty versus Risk

It is critical to distinguish between uncertainty and risk.

Uncertainty is not knowing what might happen.

Risk is knowing what might happen and failing to prepare for it.

- Unknown subsurface conditions are uncertainty.

- Pricing excavation without geotechnical data is risk.

- Unclear permit timelines are uncertainty.

- Building a schedule with no agency float is risk.

Risk can be evaluated, documented, priced, and assigned. Uncertainty becomes risk when teams choose to proceed without mitigation.

Core Categories of Construction Risk

Construction risk typically falls into several recurring categories. Each one appears repeatedly in disputes, claims, and litigation.

Design Risk
Incomplete, conflicting, or late drawings and specifications that lead to changes and rework.

Schedule Risk
Delays caused by late decisions, poor sequencing, access restrictions, or third-party interference.

Financial Risk
Underestimated costs, cash flow strain, unpaid changes, or improper cost controls.

Contract Risk

Ambiguous language, missed notice requirements, or poorly defined responsibilities.

Performance Risk

Defective work, rework, or failure to meet contract standards.

Procurement Risk

Long lead items, vendor default, material escalation, or supply chain failures.

Regulatory Risk

Permitting delays, environmental compliance issues, or labor violations.

Safety Risk

Jobsite incidents, regulatory citations, or inadequate safety planning.

Reputational Risk

Disputes, claims, and litigation that damage client trust and future opportunities.

These risks do not exist in isolation. They interact. A design delay becomes a procurement problem. A procurement failure creates schedule pressure. Schedule pressure leads to quality defects. Quality defects become warranty claims.

When Risk Shows Up: The Project Lifecycle

Risk is not static. It evolves with the project.

Each phase introduces different exposures and requires different controls.

PROJECT LIFE CYCLE

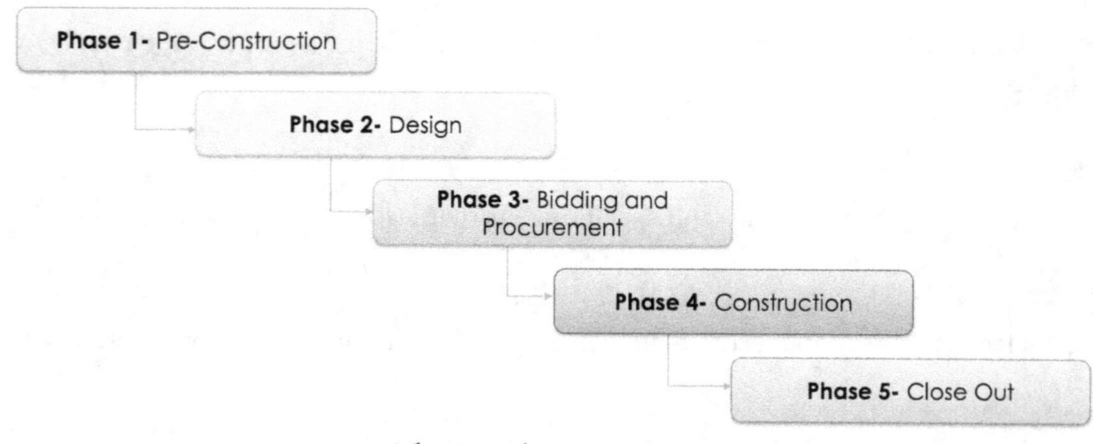

The Five Phases to a Project

Pre-Construction and Design

- **Risk Profile:** Design incompleteness, estimating assumptions, bid errors.

- **Key Controls:** Design reviews, scope matrices, constructability reports, contingency allocation

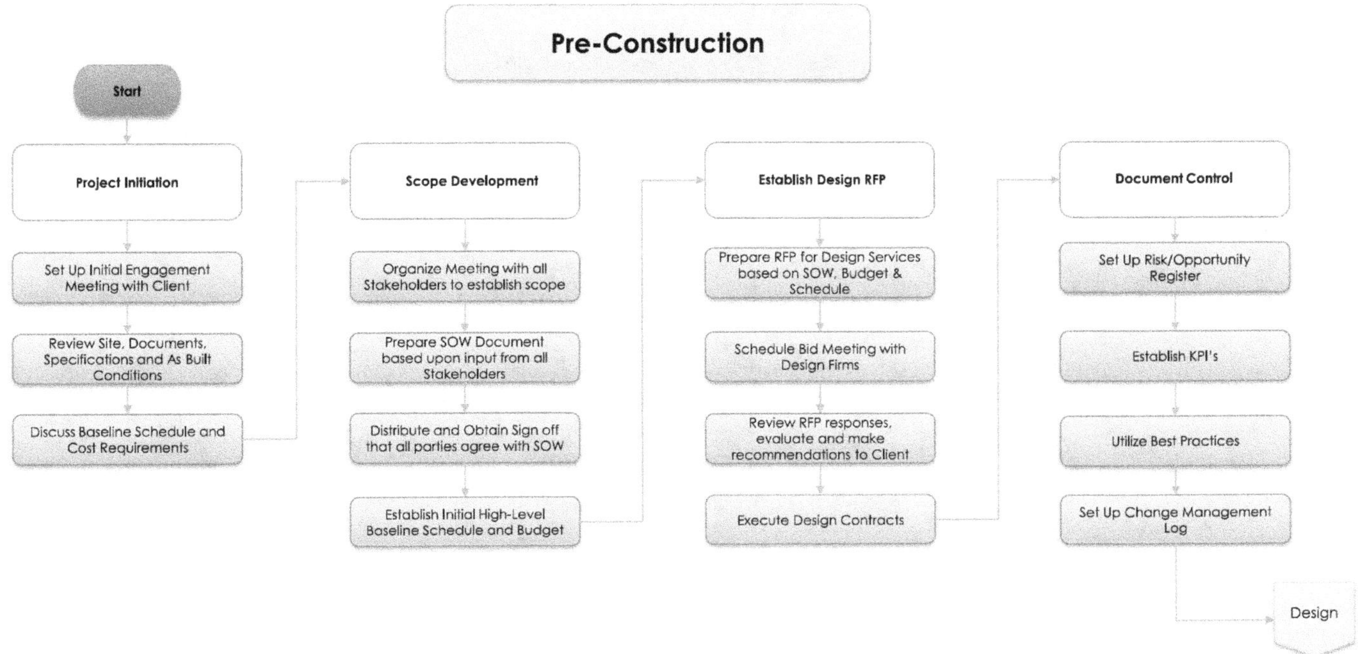

Phase 1 Pre-Construction

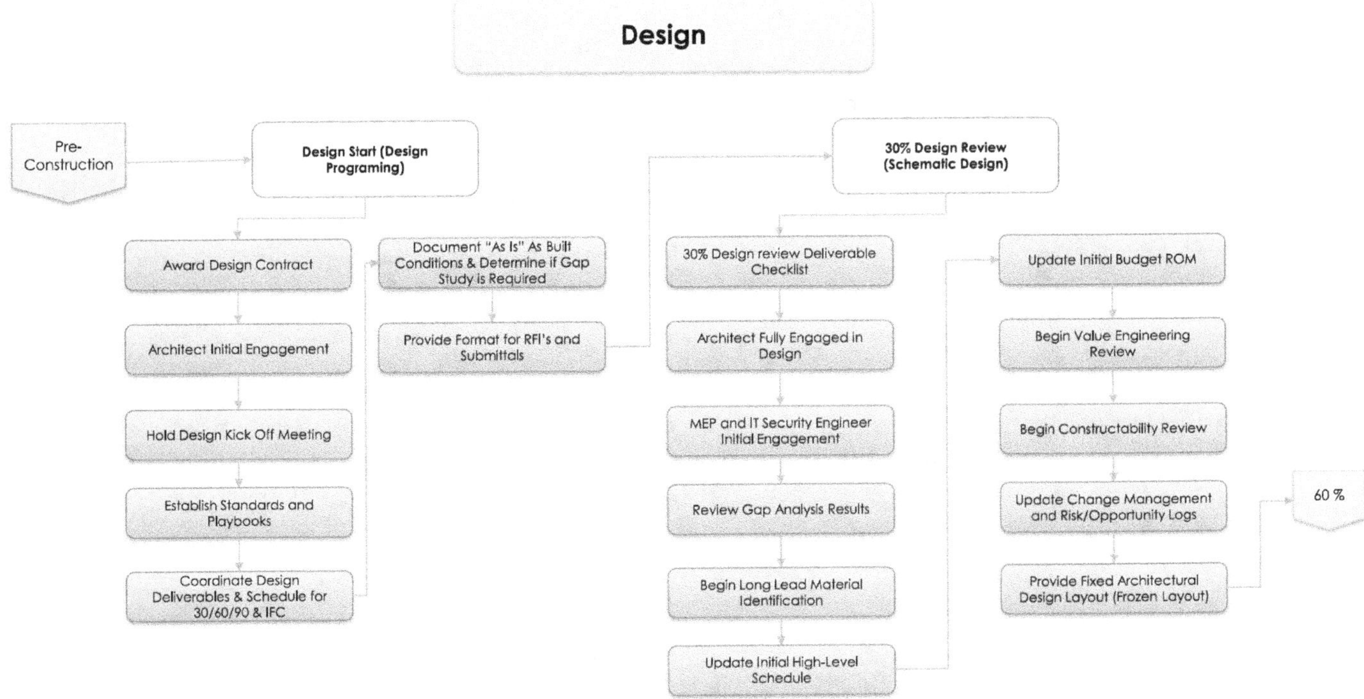

Phase 2 Preliminary Design to 30% Drawings

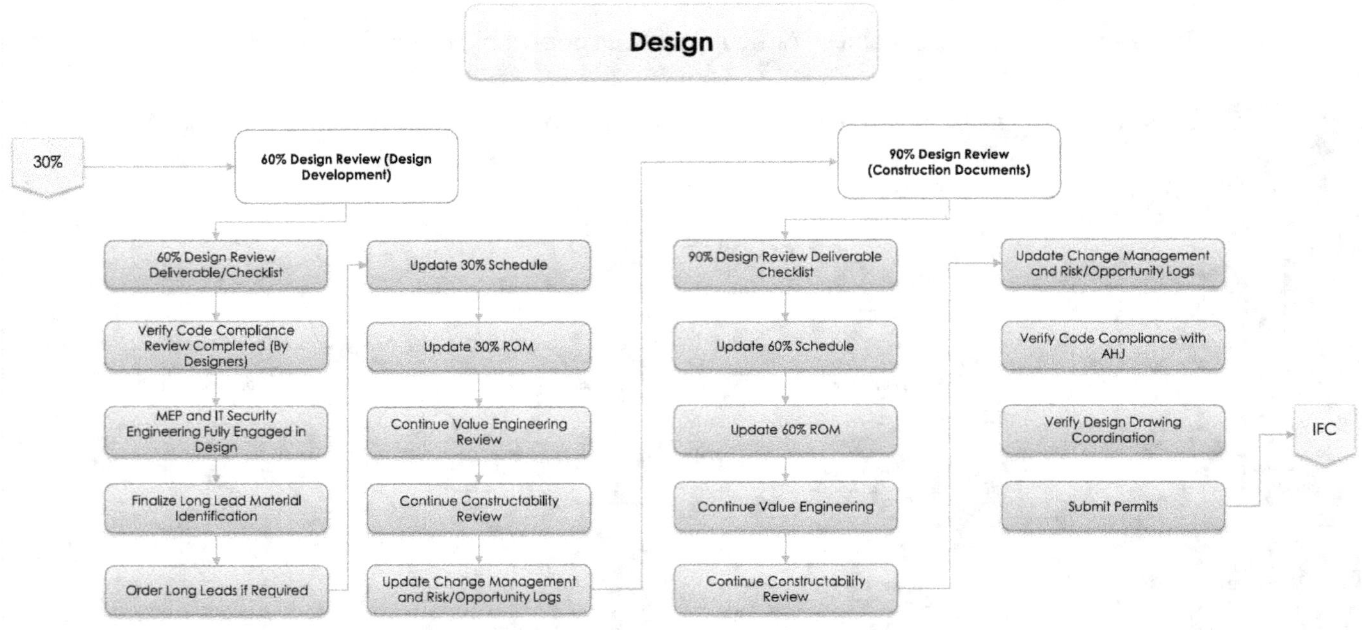

Phase 2 30% Design to 90% Design Drawings

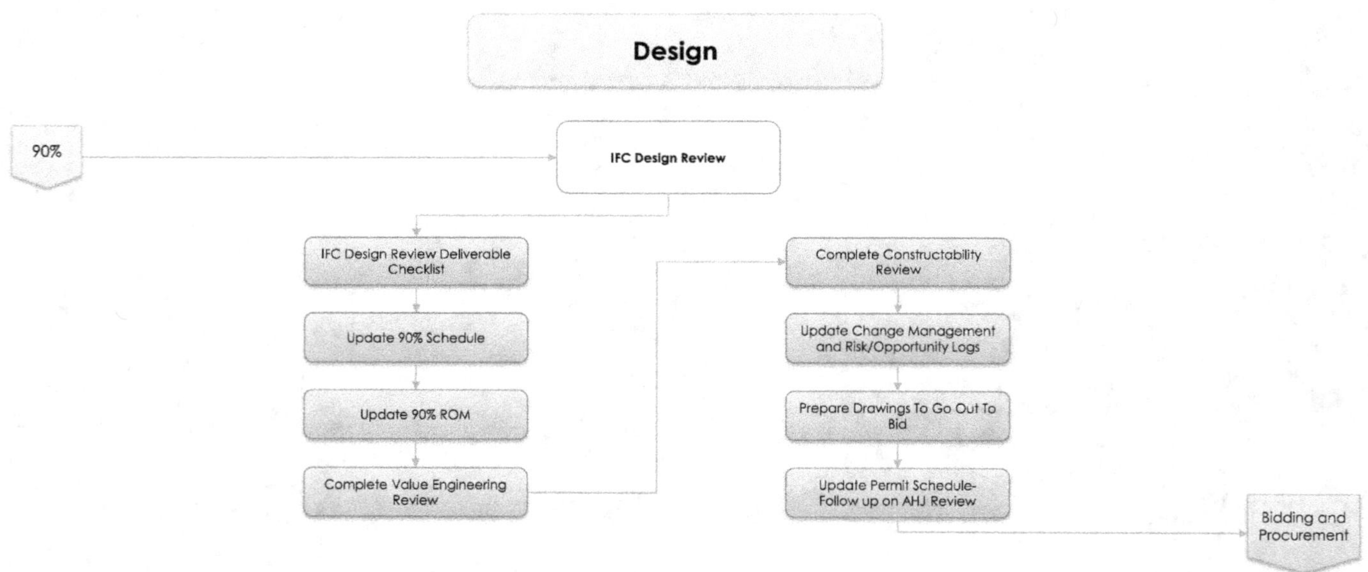

Phase 2 90% Design to IFC Design Drawings

Bidding, Procurement and Construction Phase

- **Risk Profile:** Schedule compression, trade stacking, material availability, and documentation failure.

- **Key Controls**: Realistic updated schedules, daily reports, issue logs, delay notices, and change management workflows.

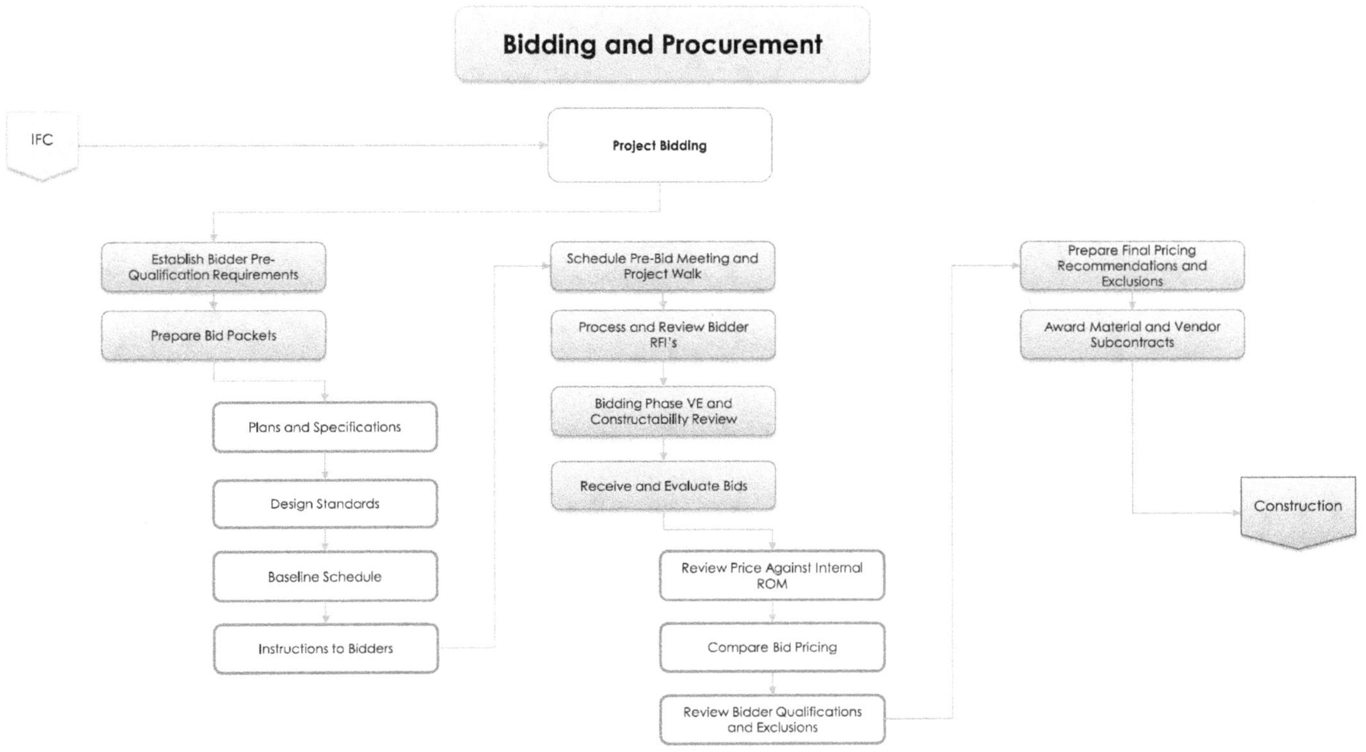

Phase 3 Bidding and Procurement

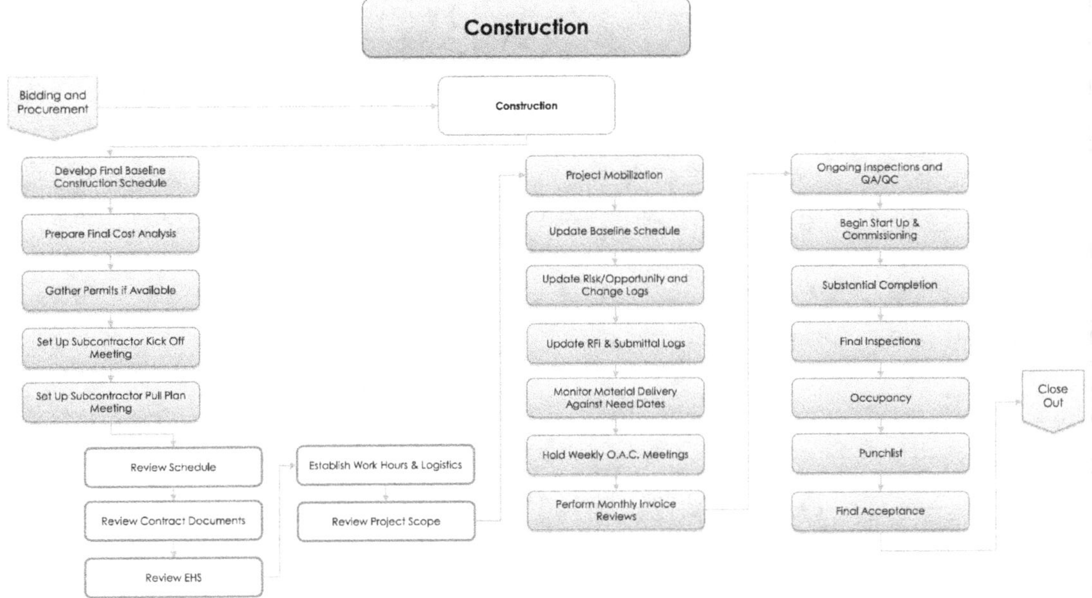

Phase 4 Construction

Closeout and Commissioning

- **Risk Profile:** Unresolved punch list, warranty issues, final payment disputes, lien exposure.

- **Key Controls:** Closeout checklist, substantial completion logs, photo documentation, lien waivers.

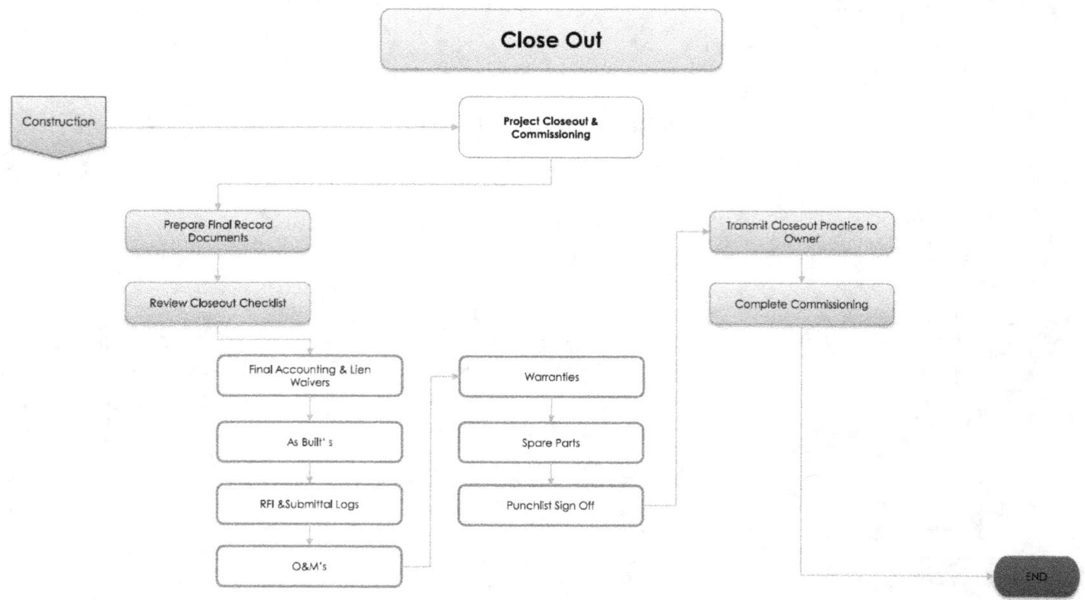

Phase 5 Closeout and Commissioning

Failing to track risks across these phases leaves teams reactive instead of proactive.

Documentation and Handoffs

Most claims do not occur during execution. They occur between tasks.

Handoffs are where responsibility transfers and project lifecycle risk is lost or preserved. From estimator to project manager. From designer to builder. From construction to operations. These moments are where information is lost, assumptions are made, and accountability fades.

Standardizing processes alone is not enough. Teams must define exactly what information must transfer at each handoff and who is responsible for verifying it.

- When expectations are clear, risk declines.

- When expectations are assumed, risk multiplies.

Corporate Handoffs and Processes

Project Documentation Processes and Handoffs			
Departments	**Workflow**	**Process**	**Handoff Documents**
Human Resources	Business process of advertising, hiring, training and termination of employee's.	Recruitment	Employment Application
		Onboarding	Employee Orientation Package
		Training	Employee Roles and Responsibilities
			Disciplinary Warnings and Termination Procedures
		Offboarding	Employee offboarding procedures
			Cobra and HR Termination requirements
Marketing	Business process of marketing to attract new clients.		
Business Development	Business Process of developing new clients.		
Accounting	Accounting Standard operating procedures to process accounts payable, accounts receivable and payroll.	AP	Vendor payable requirements
		AR	Invoicing Format
		Payroll	Employee Payroll setup forms
Safety	Safety plan, rules and regulations.	Safety Plan	Contractor Safety Plan
		Incident Reporting	Contractor OSHA incident reporting form.
		Safety Training	Safety training program.
Legal	Business process of establishing contracts, subcontracts, PO's and avoidance of claims.	Claims Avoidance	Notice requirements and escalation procedures.
		Subcontracts	Standard Subcontract and vendor agreements, terms and conditions.
		Owner Agreements	Standard Owner contract agreement, terms and conditions.

Corporate Handoff's and Processes

Preconstruction and Design Handoff's

Project Documentation Processes and Handoffs			
Departments	**Workflow**	**Process**	**Handoff Documents**
Preconstruction	Project Setup	Initial Scope	Initial Scope of Work
		Initial Budget	Initial project ROM
		Initial Schedule	Project Preconstruction Schedule
	Project Initiation	Initial Client Engagement	Client Engagement Letter
	Establishing Scope of Work	Scope of work by Division	Scope of work by CSI Division
		Qualifications	Project Qualifications and Exclusions
		Risks	Project Risk assessment Checklist
		GAP studies	Project GAP study Checklist
		Preliminary Budget	Preliminary project ROM
		Preliminary Schedule	Preliminary project schedule
		Define Bidding Method	Bid method checklist - Design Build, Progressive Design Build, etc.
		Define Project Goals and KPI's	List of measured performance indicators.
		Setup Project Dashboards	List of project dashboards
Design	Design Request for Proposals	Define Architectural Design Services	A/E services agreement
		Define MEP Engineering Services	MEP services agreement
		Define IT Design Service	IT services agreement
		Define Security Design Services	Security services agreement
		Define Structural Design Services	Structural services agreement
	Design Kickoff	Award Design Contracts	Standard design contracts, terms and conditions.
		Establish Design Schedule	Design schedule of deliverables
		Establish Design Deliverables	Design Services agreements
		Perform GAP Analysis	GAP analysis checklist
		Start Constructability Review	Constructability review checklist
		Start Value Engineering Review	VE Checklist
		Perform Risk Analysis	Risk analysis checklist
		Progressive ROM Analysis	ROM Format and level of accuracy
		Make a Project Plan Meeting Agenda	MAPP Agenda
		Code Compliance Checklist	
	Design 30% Review Requirements	30% design requirements	30% design deliverable Checklist
	Design 60% Review Requirements	60% design requirements	60% design deliverable checklist
		Establish specifications on LL Material	Long Lead deliverable Schedule
	Design 90% Review Requirements	90% design requirements	90% design deliverable checklist
	Design Construction Documents	CD design requirements	CD design deliverable checklist
	Permitting	Permitting Process	
		Permitting Schedule	

Preconstruction and Design Handoff's and Processes

Estimating and Procurement Handoff's and Processes

Project Documentation Processes and Handoffs			
Departments	**Workflow**	**Process**	**Handoff Documents**
Estimating	Business process of estimating the cost of work and providing ROM budget pricing and final contract pricing.	Invitation to Bid	ITB Package and scope requirements
		Bid Package Preparation	Scope breakdown by trade checklist
		Vendor Walk	Jobsite Walk Checklist (Access requirements, hours of operation, etc.)
		Bidding Schedule	Project Baseline Bid Schedule
		Bidding RFI	RFI Log
		Scope of Work	Standard divisional scope of work checklist
		Qualifications and Exclusions	Standard bid qualifications and exclusions.
		Takeoff	Estimate Takeoff Format by CSI division.
	Proposal QA/QC	Vendor Proposal QA/QC	Bid scope QA/QC review checklist
		Vendor Scope Gap Analysis	Bid scope GAP checklist
		Vendor Risk and Best Value Analysis	Bid scope risk checklist
		Pricing Review	QA/QC bid pricing review and pier review.
Procurement	Business process of procuring subcontractors and material suppliers.	Vendor Prequalification	Prequalification checklist (Safety, Corporate Capabilities, Net Worth)
		Subcontracts	Standard Subcontractor Agreement terms and conditions
		Material PO's	Standard PO Agreement terms and conditions
		Insurance Requirements	Insurance requirement checklist
		Bonding Requirements	Bond requirement checklist
		Procurement Limits	Procurement execution plan and procurement spend limits.

Estimating and Procurement Handoff's and Processes

Construction Handoff's and Processes

Project Documentation Processes and Handoffs			
Departments	**Workflow**	**Process**	**Handoff Documents**
Construction	Construction Standard procedures	Project Mobilization	Jobsite Mobilization Checklist
		Establish KPI's	KPI Log
		Jobsite Safety procedures	Safety Plan
		QA/QC inspections	QA/QC Plan
		Pull Plan Meeting	Pull Plan Meeting agenda
		Commissioning requirements	Commissioning Plan
		Long Lead Materials	Long Lead Material List
		Track RFI's	RFI Log
		Project issue escalation	Escalation Procedures
		Track submittals	Submittal Log
		Evaluate project risks	Risk Log
		Establish all project stakeholders	Contact Log
		Weekly client meetings	Construction Meeting Agenda - Client
		Weekly subcontractor meetings	Construction Meeting Agenda - Subcontractor
	Contractor Quality Control Program	QA/QC inspections	QA/QC Plan (Phase 1,2,3)
	3rd Party Inspections	Inspections	Inspections checklist
	Scheduling	Establish Baseline Schedule	Baseline schedule
		Weekly Baseline Schedule Updates	Schedule Updates
		3 Week Schedule Look Ahead	Detailed 3 week micro schedules
	Change Management	Track Change Orders	Change Order Log
		Change order approvals	Change management log
	Badging and Security	Security Requirements	
	Landlord Requirements	Identify Landlord Requirement	

Construction Handoff's and Processes

Commissioning and Closeout Handoff's and Processes

Project Documentation Processes and Handoffs			
Departments	**Workflow**	**Process**	**Handoff Documents**
Project Closeout	Project Closeout Procedures	As-Builts	As-Builts redline requirements
		Commissioning Plan	Commissioning Checklist and sign off form
		Attic Stock	Attic stock turn over form
		Punchlist	Punchlist format and readiness checklist
		Release of Liens	Partial and final release of liens form
		Owner Acceptance	Owner final acceptance sign off
		Final billing	Final billing format (AIA)
		Project Closeout and demobilization	Closeout Checklist

Commissioning and Closeout Handoff's and Processes

Five Essentials for Managing Risk

Know the Contract

Every project leader must understand the contract clauses that affect daily decisions. Risk cannot be managed if the team does not know the rules.

Document Everything

If it is not documented, it cannot be defended. Photos, logs, RFIs, and meeting minutes are not administrative tasks. They are risk controls.

Use a Risk Register

Track risks as living items. Assign ownership. Update mitigation actions. Review regularly.

Conduct Routine Risk Reviews

Monthly internal reviews surface issues early, while leverage still exists.

Engage Legal Early

Legal involvement before disputes form is preventive. Waiting until positions harden is reactive.

Risk Allocation versus Risk Elimination

You cannot eliminate risk in construction, but you can determine who owns it. The purpose of risk allocation is to define who bears the cost, responsibility, and consequences when something goes wrong.

- Who is responsible for unforeseen site conditions?

- Does the owner guarantee permit readiness?

- Who absorbs schedule impacts caused by agency approvals?

Strong contracts answer these questions with clarity. Weak contracts introduce ambiguity, and ambiguity almost always leads to disputes.

Culture versus Paperwork

Risk management is far more than filling out forms or maintaining checklists. It is a discipline, a mindset, and a cultural expectation.

- Do field personnel understand the contract they are working under?

- Does the team rely on written directives, or do they allow verbal approvals to guide construction activities?

- Are delay logs updated each week, or only when litigation appears on the horizon?

Organizations with strong risk cultures do not simply win more disputes. They avoid most disputes altogether because their teams work with intention, clarity, and accountability.

Case Study

The Verbal Directive

An owner's representative instructed the contractor to install a different type of piping immediately but never followed up with a written change order. The contractor performed the work, submitted a change request, and was denied. The owner argued that the contract required written authorization for changes and none had been issued. The dispute proceeded to arbitration.

The ruling followed well-established construction law principles. Verbal direction did not satisfy the contract's change order requirements, and no waiver was proven. The contractor absorbed the full cost of the work.

Courts and arbitration panels have consistently enforced written change order provisions, holding that contractors proceed at their own risk when they perform extra work without contractual authorization.
(See *Amelco Electric v. City of Thousand Oaks*, 27 Cal.4th 228; *C. Norman Peterson Co. v. Container Corp. of America*, 172 Cal.App.3d 628.)

Lesson: In construction risk management, the issue is rarely what actually happened. The issue is what you can document, prove, and defend.

Chapter Conclusion

You Cannot Eliminate Risk, but You Can Outperform It

Risk is the price of doing business in the construction industry. Yet risk does not have to evolve into disputes or litigation. The firms that consistently excel are not only skilled builders; they are disciplined operators who treat risk management as a professional craft.

They document thoroughly. They forecast issues before they strike. They escalate concerns early rather than react late. They train field staff to understand contractual obligations as well as understanding building plans. Most importantly, they cultivate a culture that protects the team, the project, and the client long before lawyers are ever needed. Many of these risks remain manageable if identified early. When they are ignored, undocumented, or assumed away, they become the root causes of claims examined in Chapter 2.

In construction, success is not defined only by what you build. It is defined by how well you protect what you build.

"Risk comes from not knowing what you are doing." – Warren Buffett

WHY CLAIMS HAPPEN

Chapter Foreword

Claims are not random. They are the result of patterns. Patterns of miscommunication, unclear expectations, undocumented directives, or unchecked assumptions. Behind nearly every construction dispute lies a moment when someone failed to ask the right question, document the correct change, or enforce the relevant clause. As discussed in Chapter 1, risk is not eliminated in construction. It is either managed or ignored. Claims form when ignored risks are allowed to mature without structure or documentation. This chapter examines the root causes of claims and how seemingly minor lapses early in a project can escalate into costly conflicts later on.

"An ounce of prevention is worth a pound of cure." – **Benjamin Franklin**

The Anatomy of a Construction Claim

A construction claim is a formal request for additional time, money, or relief due to a perceived contract breach, changed condition, or event beyond one party's control.

However, most claims do not begin with conflict. They start with confusion. Something that was not addressed early, or that evolved without clear documentation or agreement.

Nearly every claim can be traced to a failure in one or more of the following areas.

- Scope

- Schedule

- Design

- Constructability

- Responsibility

- Communication

- Documentation

- Risk allocation

Where It All Starts: The Early Warning Signs

Claims often begin long before anyone realizes it is happening. Here are the most common "warning signs" that a project is drifting toward a dispute:

- Missing or late submittals

- Unresolved RFIs or design conflicts

- Work proceeding without formal approval

- Repeated verbal directives without written confirmation

- Schedule slips and logic changes without documented justification

- Quantity of change orders occurring

- Cost impacts discussed, but not tracked or priced

These moments are subtle, but they represent a breakdown in the controls that create claims.

Bad Contractors Do Not Cause Most Claims

It is a myth that construction claims happen because someone failed to do their job. More often, claims arise because:

- Expectations were never aligned at the outset

- One or more parties misunderstood contract terms

- Changes were made informally, without proper process

- Stakeholders were not held accountable for timely decisions

- Risks were never discussed, tracked, or documented

In other words, claims are the consequence of missing conversations, not malice.

Common Root Causes of Claims

A Field Example: The Missing RFI

On a public works project, a contractor submitted a structural RFI asking for clarification on beam bearing locations. No response came. After three weeks, the superintendent directed the crew to proceed "as shown." The steel was placed. The owner later issued a design bulletin revising the beam layout and rejected the contractor's claim for the cost to modify the work.

Why did the claim happen?

- The RFI was never escalated.

- No written notice of delay or impact was sent.

- The superintendent acted without a formal response.

Each of these decisions removed the contractor's ability to preserve entitlement.

Result: The contractor incurred $180,000 in rework costs that could have been avoided had the documentation and notice been handled appropriately.

Top Five Project Practices That Breed Claims

1. Relying on verbal directives instead of written change orders

2. Failing to track schedule slippage until it is too late

3. Ignoring contract notice provisions during delays

4. Treating RFIs as paperwork instead of critical risk triggers

5. Not documenting field conditions or delays in real time

Claims Do Not Just Happen – They are Allowed to Happen.

Here is a hard truth:

Most construction claims are entirely preventable with the proper understanding of contracts, effective documentation systems, and a culture of accountability.

It is not just about reacting to change. It is about creating a project environment where everyone is aligned, documentation is second nature, and expectations are clearly defined and explicit.

Chapter Conclusion

Clarity Is the Cure

Claims are a symptom of deeper issues: unclear scope, unchecked changes, and unmanaged risk. Understanding why claims happen is only the first step. Preventing them consistently requires more than knowledge. It requires culture, discipline, and leadership systems, which are addressed in Chapter 3.

The most successful teams do not wait for problems to emerge. They track issues in real-time, align expectations early, and document everything as if they were going to trial. Because in today's construction industry, it just might.

"In the law, facts are stubborn things." – **John Adams**

BUILDING A CLAIMS-RESISTANT COMPANY CULTURE

Chapter Foreword

Most contractors do not lose claims because they build poorly; they lose because they fail to build **defensibly**. Documentation goes missing. Notices arrive late. Field changes stay verbal. Risk is not tracked, and memory fades.

Contracts and templates matter, but they do not work in a vacuum. A claims-resistant company is **disciplined by design**: risk management lives in daily routines, and field staff, PMs, executives, and legal all speak the same language of protection.

Projects end; companies must endure. The difference between surviving and thriving is how you manage risk across operations, leadership, and culture. A risk-resilient firm does not avoid risk; it **absorbs, adapts, and outperforms** through systems and behavior. The behaviors described in this chapter only work when grounded in an understanding of risk and claim formation, as outlined in Chapters 1 and 2.

This chapter will show how to build that culture, so that risk prevention becomes part of your company's DNA.

"Excellence is never an accident. It is always the result of high intention, sincere effort, and intelligent execution." **– Aristotle**

What defines a Claims Resistant Company Culture?

An environment where **risk awareness**, **documentation discipline**, and **proactive communication** are routine, not optional. Top performers are not the flashiest; they are the most prepared. Their edge is habits, not luck.

Claims-Resistant

- Notices sent on time; verbal directives confirmed in writing

- Daily reports with labeled photos

- Risk reviewed weekly; rolling risk registers maintained

- Legal included early (preconstruction, kickoff, OACs)

- Executives trained in contracts; field empowered to document

- Foremen document daily

Claims-Prone

- Notices missed or rushed

- Verbal instructions only

- Risk is ignored until a dispute arises

- Legal looped in post-lawsuit

- Executives removed from contract details

- Field assumes "that is the PM's job"

It is not about intelligence – it is **operational discipline**.

Key Traits of Resilient Firms

- Written and enforced SOPs that guide execution

- Leadership that promotes accountability, not blame

- Early warnings treated as assets, not annoyances

- Lessons learned shared, not buried

- Technology that clarifies decisions, not clutters them

- Consistent process, not crisis-driven chaos

Resilient firms do not just react better; they **learn faster** than their competitors.

Embedding Risk Awareness

Culture is what people do when nobody is watching. Disclaimers and QA checklists will not save a reckless culture.

Warning Signs

- Cutting corners framed as "efficiency"

- Documentation treated as optional

- Problems discouraged or softened

- SOPs dismissed as "extra work"

Cultural Controls

- Start leadership meetings with a **Risk Moment** (like a safety moment)

- Recognize teams that **raise** risks early, not just those who fix them

- Make cross-functional risk reviews a monthly habit

- Publish short **Lessons Learned** after project milestones and distribute company-wide

- Promote leaders who **enforce** protocol rather than sidestep it

Standardization Without Bureaucracy

Standardize what reduces chaos; keep judgment where it belongs.

The goal is not to eliminate judgment, but to remove unnecessary variation.

Standardize

- Cost forecast templates

- Risk assessment forms

- Change-order workflows

- Closeout documentation checklists

- Safety incident logs

- RFI/submittal logs

- Lessons-learned format & storage

Stay Flexible On

- Field staffing and trade pairings

- Client-facing communication style

- Software tools when clients mandate systems

- Recovery strategies for unanticipated risks

Pro Tip: Centralize SOPs, templates, and risk playbooks in SharePoint, Procore Docs, or other industry platforms.

Risk Ownership and the Role of Leadership

Risk management is not a department; it is a **mindset** owned at every level. Assign it explicitly by phase and role.

Assign Risk by Phase

- **Preconstruction:** Estimators, BD, Legal

- **Contracting:** Executives, Contract Admin, Legal

- **Project Start:** PMs, Superintendents, Safety, QA/QC

- **Mid-Project:** PMs, Schedulers, Project Engineers

- **Closeout:** PMs, Project Engineers, Client Liaisons

- **Warranty:** Warranty Lead, Field Ops, PM

Best practice: Put risk duties in **job descriptions**, not just in the Risk Manager's portfolio.

Leveraging Technology (Without Drowning in It)

Technology does not manage risk; **people do**. The right stack creates visibility and action; the wrong one creates noise.

Use Technology For

- Delay tracking (Primavera with analytics, e.g., SmartPM)

- CO dashboards tracking approval aging and owner lag

- Procore (or equivalent) logs for RFIs, inspections, and daily reports

- Safety apps for near-miss reporting and escalation

- QA/QC mobile tools tied to punchlists and material verification

- Predictive alerts for overruns or subcontractor slippage

Warning: Unused or misaligned tools create the **illusion of control**. Pick fewer systems; make them mandatory.

Capturing and Applying Lessons Learned

Learning only counts if it changes behavior.

Process

1. Run structured post-mortems

2. Document failures **and** unexpected wins

3. Analyze root causes, not just symptoms

4. Update SOPs or contract playbooks

5. Assign team AR logs with due dates

6. Distribute to all projects and teams

If your lessons live in a folder, they are regrets, not resources.

The Five Foundations of a Claims-Resistant Culture

1. Executive Ownership of Risk:

CEO/COO chairs monthly risk reviews; claim trends on dashboards; risk metrics in Key Performance Indicators.

2. Contract Training Across Roles:

Contract boot camps for PMs/Superintendents; one-page job-specific contract clause summaries.

3. Legal + Project Integration:

Legal in preconstruction, kickoff, and OACs; legal liaisons on high-risk jobs; quarterly legal-ops health checks.

4. Standardized Documentation Routines:

Daily logs with photos; timely delay notices; RFI/CO tracking with escalations; automatic deadline reminders.

5. Field-Level Empowerment:

T&M tickets signed daily; pre-pour/concealed-condition photos required; verbal directives confirmed in writing.

Five Process Tools That Cement the Culture

1. Pre-Mortem Risk Workshops:

Cross-functional team identifies top 10 risks; assigns mitigations; sets follow-ups.

2. Rolling Risk Registers:

Risk type, probability, $$ exposure, owner, and date due shown next to cost/schedule health in executive reports.

3. Commandments of Claims Prevention: *(Examples)*

- No work without written direction

- All claims must be noticed within 7 days

- No verbal authorizations over $10K

- Daily reports are legal records

- Legal reviews every default letter

4. Post-Claim Closeout Reviews:

Capture missed signals, update SOPs, and checklists.

5. Incentivize Prevention:

PMs scored on documentation quality; executives on resolution timelines; legal on close ratios. Recognize **claim-free projects**.

Metrics That Matter (Monthly Examples)

- Notice timeliness (% within contract window)

- RFI aging (median days open; % >10 days)

- CO cycle time (submit → approve)

- Schedule update compliance (% on time)

- Photo coverage (daily logs with location/time tags)

- Risk register freshness (% items updated this month)

Case Studies

The following examples show how these principles work when applied consistently.

1) Portfolio Recovery (Multi-Project)

Actions: Company-wide Change Event Tracker; monthly Risk Committee; Director of Field Training; response playbooks for design conflicts/field conditions.

Results: CO approval time ↓35%; on-time schedule updates ↑92%; gross margins +3.5% in 18 months; employee confidence in risk reporting +22%.

2) Civic Center Expansion (CMAR, $50M, 28 months)

Actions: Legal at OACs; delay notices triggered by aging RFIs; daily rebar photos; COs tracked by issue date and lag; weekly risk registers to the owner.

Results: 14 COs; 0 formal disputes; finished 22 days early; 2% cost underrun.

Checklist: Are You Risk-Resilient?

- Do all project leaders **know and accept** their risk role?

- Are SOPs **current, accessible, and used**?

- Are lessons learned **integrated** into the process, not just filed?

- Do your tools enable **visibility and follow-through**?

- Is risk escalated **early**, not after failure?

- Do subcontractors/vendors meet the **same documentation standards**?

- Is bad news met with **transparency**, not defensiveness?

From Compliance to Ownership

A risk-aware culture is not built on compliance; it is built on **behavior.**

- A foreman takes photos without being told.

- A PE logs a delay because silence is a risk.

- A PM sends a tough notice because protecting rights beats pleasing people.

These are not tasks; they are **habits** that are driven by leadership, clarity, and accountability.

Chapter Conclusion

Build Culture Before the Claim

Claims prevention is not a legal strategy; it is a **leadership** strategy. Tight contracts and strong counsel can provide defenses in a fight, but only culture helps you **avoid** the fight.

Build the culture. Train the field. Reinforce the process. You cannot buy resilience. It is the product of daily, disciplined habits by people who care about doing things right.

The strongest firms are not the ones that avoid risk; they are the ones built to **absorb it, respond to it, and grow**. Do not wait for the storm to learn how to build a shelter. Be ready. Be resilient. In modern construction, it is not just what you build, it is what you **document, protect, and preserve**.

"Most problems are not failures of effort, but failures of clarity." – *W.* Edward Deming

PART II – CONTRACT ADMINISTRATION AND PROJECT MANAGER BASICS

CHAPTER 4

CHECKLISTS FOR RISK ALLOCATION

Chapter Forward

This chapter is an introductory checklist to bridge the gap between high-level claims strategy and day-to-day contract administration. We introduce a universal Contract Administration Checklist, an approvals clock discipline, and a risk allocation matrix across common standard forms. It also provides a beginner on-ramp; the 'first 30 days on a troubled job' starter pack, with simple flowcharts, and a glossary; so new project managers can get oriented fast. This chapter is intended to be used as a reference, not read straight through. Experienced Project Managers can use as a training guideline for new Project Engineers.

"Leadership is not about being in charge. It is about taking care of those in your charge" – **Simon Sinek**

Contract Administration

The following items address the four most litigated areas of contract administration.

A. RFIs (Request for Information) Field-Ready Checklist

- State the problem in plain English (one issue per RFI).

- Attach a marked-up plan/detail snippet and any photo(s).

- Offer two feasible contractor solutions with pros/cons (cost/time).

- Tag any affected specs/drawings and the schedule activity/ID.

- Set the response-by date per contract (insert your form's period) and flag critical-path impact.

- Route to the proper design discipline; log sent date and recipients.

- Escalate overdue RFIs using the contract's escalation path; capture each chase date.

RFI	TRADE	SUBJECT	ASKED ON	BY WHOM	COMPANY	QUESTION	ANSWERED ON	BY WHOM	COMPANY	OFFICIAL RESPONSE	COST IMPACT	SCHEDULE IMPACT	ATTACHMENT
						CONSTRUCTION PHASE RFI's							
001	Architectura	EXAMPLE	3/25/2024	Bob Smith	ABC Company	Question relating to glass wall systems: 1. What type of swing door would you like? Aluminum framed or frameless? 2. What door hardware would you like us to include for these doors? 3. For the glass walls would you like frameless or framed?	3/25/2024	Tom Smith	Design Tech	1. Doors will be 8'-0 stained wood, painted frames. (confirm in IFC set) 2. Hardware to be finalized in design, prelim is in 65% drawings. 3. Alum Framed. (confirm in IFC set)	NO	NO	NO

Example RFI Log

Request for Information (RFI) Form

Project Name: ___________________________
RFI Number: ___________________________
Date Submitted: ___________________________

Requestor Information

- **Company Name:** ___________________________
- **Contact Name:** ___________________________
- **Phone Number:** ___________________________
- **Email Address:** ___________________________

Recipient Information

- **Company Name:** ___________________________
- **Contact Name:** ___________________________
- **Phone Number:** ___________________________
- **Email Address:** ___________________________

Subject of RFI

- **Title/Topic:** ___________________________
- **Reference Documents (e.g., drawings, specifications):**
  - Document Name: ___________________________
  - Section/Page: ___________________________

Details of Request

- **Description of Information Needed:**
  (Provide a clear and concise explanation of the question or clarification required.)

- **Reason for Request:**
  (Explain why this information is needed and how it impacts the project.)

Proposed Solution (Optional)

- (If applicable, suggest a potential solution or approach.)

____

____

Response Section (For Recipient Use Only)

- **Response Provided By:** _______________________________
- **Date of Response:** _______________________________
- **Response:**

____

____

Attachments (if any)

- List any supporting documents or files attached to this RFI.

Example Format of RFI

B. Submittals & Shop Drawings: Field Primer Introduction

- Keep a register with: Specification section, package ID, revision, date submitted, reviewer, due date, status, returned date, and 'Returned As' code.

- Batch submittals by area/sequence (tie to the schedule WBS).

- Record 'reviewer comments impact': rework, resubmit, or field change; log any direction requiring price/time.

- If returned late, capture days slipped, and if any resequencing is required. Prepare a Time Impact Notice if the submittal, procurement, fabrication, delivery, and installation of the material is, or could become, on the project schedule critical path.

Pro Tip:

Delays by stakeholders between submittal approval and final material installation are among the most common causes of project delay and are frequently undocumented or poorly tracked.

PROJECT SUBMITTAL LOG											
Trade/Submittal	CSI Code	Type	Subcontractor	Contact (person)	Submit By:	Actual Date Submitted	Total Lead Time	Date Needed Onsite	Approved Submittal Dated	Comments / Time Impacts / Cost Impacts:	
Fire Proofing	02_50_00_00	Product Data					2 weeks				
Structural Steel	05_10_00_00	Shop Drawings					2 weeks				
Millwork	06_22_00_00	Shop Drawings					2 weeks				
Millwork	06_22_00_00	Samples					2 weeks				
Doors	08_10_00_00	Product Data					2 weeks				
Doors	08_10_00_00	Shop Drawings					2 weeks				
Doors	08_10_00_00	Schedule					2 weeks				
Hardware	08_10_00_00	Product Data					2 weeks				
Hardware	08_10_00_00	Schedule					2 weeks				
Film	08_80_00_00	Product Data					3 weeks				
Film	08_80_00_00	Shop Drawings					3 weeks				
Drywall	09_20_00_00	Product Data					2-4 weeks				
Metal Stud Framing	09_20_00_00	Product Data					2-4 weeks				
Ceramic Tile/Grout	09_30_13_00	Product Data					2 weeks				
Ceramic Tile/Grout	09_30_13_00	Samples					2 weeks				
Ceilings - ACT	09_50_00_00	Product Data					2-4 weeks				
Ceilings - Grid	09_50_00_00	Samples					2-4 weeks				

Example Submittal Log

Submittals – Field Overview

Before construction starts, several types of submittals must be prepared to verify that all materials, equipment, and systems meet project requirements. These documents ensure the work aligns with the design intent and specifications.

Common preconstruction submittals include:

- **Shop Drawings:** Prepared by subcontractors or vendors. Verify dimensions, connections, and details match the design drawings before submitting.

- **Material Samples:** Supplied by vendors. Check color, texture, and finish against specifications.

- **Engineering Calculations:** Prepared by design engineers or specialty contractors. Confirm calculations are sealed and current.

- **Product Data Sheets (Cut Sheets):** Provided by manufacturers. Confirm the model number, capacity, and performance meet project specs.

- **Mockups:** Built by subcontractors. Review for quality, workmanship, and approval before production work begins.

- **Vendor Information:** Includes contacts, model details, and technical support. Verify completeness and consistency with approved products.

- **Closeout submittals** are required as the project nears completion. These capture the "as-built" condition and ensure the owner receives full documentation for operation and maintenance.

Typical closeout submittals include:

- **As-Built Drawings:** Updated by field staff and subcontractors to show actual field conditions and changes.

- **Operation & Maintenance (O&M) Manuals:** Prepared by vendors and subcontractors. Review for contact information, maintenance schedules, and parts lists.

- **Product Warranties:** Collected from manufacturers. Verify warranty periods and coverage align with contract requirements.

Pro Tip:

Always review submittals before sending them to the Construction Manager or Engineer. Check that all referenced specification sections, drawing numbers, and revision dates are correct. Missing or inaccurate information can cause delays in approval and schedule impacts.

As a matter of construction law, approval of a submittal by the architect does not shift responsibility for specification compliance. Even if a submittal is approved in error, the contractor remains responsible for furnishing and installing materials that strictly conform to the contract documents. Courts consistently hold that submittal approval is a review for general conformance, not a guarantee of compliance, and architects are generally not liable for approving nonconforming submittals.

C. Certifications, Tests, and Inspections – Compliance Log

Missed or undocumented testing is a common basis for nonconformance disputes.

- List required certs/tests by spec section; note lead times and agency involvement.

- For each, track request date, scheduled date, result, retest needs, and cost impact.

- Attach lab reports and inspector sign-offs, link to payment milestones where applicable.

D. Notices Menu: What to Send and When

Late notice defeats otherwise valid claims.

- Potential change/constructive change (scope/design info).

- Delay/Disruption (access, approvals, third-party, late responses).

- Differing site conditions / concealed conditions.

- Suspension/acceleration (directed or constructive).

- Force majeure / extraordinary weather.

- Non-conformance / defective work by others affecting your work.

- For each notice: include event, dates, clause(s), initial impact window, mitigation steps, and a request for direction. Insert your contract-specific notice and substantiation deadlines in the Approvals-Clock table.

Sample Construction Delay Claim Letter

This is a sample framework and must be tailored to your contract

Date: [Insert Date]

To: [Owner / Construction Manager / Engineer Name]

Company: [Owner or CM Firm Name]

Address: [Address]

From: [Contractor Name]

Project: [Project Title / Contract No.]

Subject: Notice of Delay and Request for Time Extension: [Specific Delay Event]

1. Purpose of This Notice

In accordance with the requirements of Section [insert applicable clause, e.g., AIA A201 §8.3.1 or DBIA §8.2], this letter serves as formal notice of a delay event that has affected the Contractor's performance and the overall project schedule.

2. Description of Delay Event

On [insert date], during [describe phase or activity], the Contractor encountered [describe the specific issue, e.g., unforeseen underground obstruction, delayed design approval, late material delivery, etc.]. This event was beyond the Contractor's control and not reasonably foreseeable at the time of bidding. Work on the affected activity was suspended or delayed until [insert date], pending resolution or direction from [Owner/Engineer].

Example:

On August 14, 2025, during excavation for Structure 3B, the Contractor encountered an unmarked 18-inch duct bank not identified in the contract drawings. Work was stopped pending design direction from the Engineer. The design revision was not issued until September 2, 2025, resulting in 19 calendar days of delay.

3. Contractual Basis for Relief

Under Section [insert clause reference], the Contractor is entitled to a time extension for delays caused by conditions beyond its control, including differing site conditions, late design revisions, or force majeure events. Accordingly, this delay qualifies as an excusable (and if applicable, compensable) delay event under the Contract.

4. Impact on Project Schedule

The delay to [activity name] directly impacted the project's critical path, as shown in the attached Time Impact Analysis (TIA). The TIA demonstrates a [number]-calendar-day Extension to the Contract Completion Date. Baseline Schedule: Update #03 (dated [insert date]) Revised Schedule: Update #04 (dated [insert date]) Critical Path Activity: [insert activity ID and description]

5. Mitigation Efforts

- The Contractor took all reasonable steps to mitigate the delay, including:

- Resequencing work in unaffected areas

- Coordinating with the Engineer for expedited review

- Increasing supervision to maintain productivity upon remobilization

Despite these efforts, the delay to the critical path could not be entirely avoided.

6. Cost Impacts (if applicable)

As a result of this delay, the Contractor has incurred extended overhead, equipment standby, and inefficiency costs. Preliminary estimates of these costs are summarized below and will be detailed in a separate submittal once fully quantified:

- Extended supervision and project management: $

- Equipment standby: $

- Labor inefficiency and remobilization: $

Supporting cost records and time sheets are available upon request.

7. Request for Relief

Based on the above, the Contractor respectfully requests the following:

- A non-compensable time extension of [   ] calendar days to the Contract Completion Date; or

- A compensable time extension of [   ] calendar days, plus reimbursement of associated delay costs as permitted under the Contract.

This request is made to maintain compliance with the Contract's notice and claim requirements and to preserve all rights to equitable adjustment.

8. Supporting Documentation

Enclosed for your review:

- Exhibit A – Time Impact Analysis (Baseline vs. Update)

- Exhibit B – Daily Reports and Photos

- Exhibit C – RFI Log and Correspondence

- Exhibit D – Cost Backup Summary

9. Reservation of Rights

The Contractor expressly reserves all rights and remedies under the Contract and applicable law, including the right to supplement this claim, provide additional documentation, and pursue time extensions and compensation as further impacts are identified. Nothing in this correspondence shall be construed as a waiver of any contractual, equitable, or legal rights, defenses, or entitlements.

Respectfully submitted, [Name]

[Company Name] [Email / Phone]

Pro Tip:

Always send delay notices and claims in writing within the contract's required timeframe (often 7–14 days). Even if the event's impact isn't fully known, submit an initial notice to preserve your rights and follow up with a detailed analysis later.

"Who Owns What?" A Risk-Allocation Matrix

A high-level matrix comparing common risks across standard Design – Bid – Build projects.

This matrix highlights where risk typically resides under standard delivery forms.

Risk Topic	AIA (Design–Bid–Build)	ConsensusDocs (200-series)	DBIA (Design-Build)	FIDIC (2017 Red/Yellow/Silver)	NEC4 ECC
Design responsibility	Owner design (AE) unless DB/DI; Spearin-style implied adequacy	Balanced; clarifies roles; owner/fair allocation	Design-builder owns design duty & coordination	Varies by book: Employer/Engineer vs Contractor (Yellow/Silver shift more to Contractor)	Emphasis on 'Works Information'; responsibilities set via Scope; collaborative
Notice periods	Set by A201 and Division 01; strict in some areas	Generally specific notice and time frames	Claims/change clocks defined; early written notices	Formal time bars for claims (strict)	Early Warning & Compensation Events with strict timing
Changes mechanism	Change Orders/CCDs; pricing then CO	Change Directives with pricing paths	Owner direction; design-builder proposals	Engineer's instructions & Variations	Compensation Events manage time/money
Differing site conditions	Typically recognized; Type I/II concepts common	Recognized and process-driven	Recognized; DB still may bear some design investigation risk	Defined; notice and entitlement narrow if late	Handled as Compensation Events; early warnings critical
Float ownership	Often treated as shared unless clause states otherwise	Varies by project; often neutral/shared intent	Typically shared; DB controls sequencing	Not expressly defined; practice varies	Managed collaboratively; early resequencing emphasized
EOT vs money	Excusable vs compensable split; ND4D possible	More balanced compensability drafting	EOT plus cost for employer-risk events	EOT available; cost depends on event/book	Time and money via Compensation Events
Payment/certifier	Architect certifies; pay-apps & retainage rules	Owner's rep certifies; prompt-pay focus	Owner's rep; milestones common	Engineer certifies; IPC/Final Payment	Project Manager administers; periodic assessments
Dispute pathway	IDM → mediation → arbitration/litigation	Tiered ADR; direct-to-DRB options	Tiered ADR; DBIA encourages resolution	DAAB/DB, then arbitration	Adjudication/NEC procedures; then tribunal

D-B-B Risk Matrix by Contract Type

Use this matrix during preconstruction and change discussions to reset expectations.

Beginner On-Ramp - First 30 Days on a Troubled Job (Optional Use)

Days 1–3: Triage

- Freeze the facts: export the last accepted schedule; copy logs; image photo drives.

- Issue placeholder notices for the top three risks (access/info/design).

- Start a Running Narrative with a unique ID and daily entries.

Days 4–10: Stabilize

- Meet with the superintendent, scheduler, and project accountant; agree on a single-source evidence list.

- Create an RFI/Approval Heat Map (what blocks the path first?).

- Stand up the Submittal Register and Approval Clock with all submitted and approval dates.

Days 11–20: Prove

- Pick method: Windows or TIA; draft first fragnet if a discrete delay event exists.

- Start a measured-mile comparison if applicable for any disrupted trades.

- Build Field Office Overhead (FOH) daily burn; list Home Office Overhead (HOOH) prerequisites if applicable.

Days 21–30: Propose & Close Loops

- Draft a one-page executive summary and a cover letter with a decision ask/date.

- Load the Exhibit Index and related documents and supporting data; circulate internally; fix any gaps.

- Prepare propose cost – Change Order (CO) and time impacts – Extension of Time (EOT); include reservation of rights clause.

Simple Claim Flowcharts (Reference Tool)

- Notice →

- Capture (narrative/photos/logs) →

- Analyze (Windows/TIA; measured-mile if disruption) →

- Price (FOH/HOOH/equipment/labor) →

- Proposal (cover letter, CO/EOT draft) →

- Negotiate →

- Close (CO/EOT executed; releases managed)

RFI/Approval Flow

- Issue RFI with options →

- Track due date on Approvals-Clock →

- Chase/escalate if overdue →

- If direction changes scope/time, send notice and price path →

- Update schedule and evidence pack

Glossary: Reference for New PMs

- **AIA** — American Institute of Architects (common contract forms, e.g., A201, A312).

- **BIM** — Building Information Modeling (model-based design/coordination).

- **CCIP** — Contractor Controlled Insurance Program (wrap-up insurance).

- **CDs** — Construction Documents (final drawings/specs).

- **CMAR** — Construction Manager at Risk (delivery method).

- **CO** — Change Order (formal modification to contract).

- **COR** — Change Order Request (proposal for change pricing/time).

- **CPM** — Critical Path Method (schedule logic controlling completion).

- **DB** — Design–Build (delivery method).

- **DBB** — Design–Bid–Build (traditional delivery).

- **DRB** — Dispute Review Board (standing neutrals).

- **EOR** — Engineer of Record (signs/seals the design)

- **FF&E** — Furniture, Fixtures & Equipment (often owner-furnished).

- **GMP** — Guaranteed Maximum Price (cost cap with savings share).

- **HVAC** — Heating, Ventilation, and Air Conditioning.

- **IPD** — Integrated Project Delivery (shared risk/reward).

- **JHA** — Job Hazard Analysis (task-level safety planning).

- **LDs** — Liquidated Damages (pre-agreed daily damages).

- **MEP** — Mechanical, Electrical, and Plumbing.

- **NTP** — Notice to Proceed (authorization to start).

- **O&M** — Operations & Maintenance.

- **OCIP** — Owner Controlled Insurance Program (wrap-up).

- **OSHA** — Occupational Safety and Health Administration.

- **PCO** — Proposed Change Order (pending change).

- **QA** — Quality Assurance (process-based).

- **QC** — Quality Control (verification/testing).

- **RFI** — Request for Information (design clarification).

- **RFP** — Request for Proposals (solicitation).

- **RFQ** — Request for Qualifications (prequal).

- **SWPPP** — Stormwater Pollution Prevention Plan.

- **TIA** — Time Impact Analysis (schedule delay quantification).

- **WBS** — Work Breakdown Structure (scope hierarchy).

Claims for New PMs: An Entry Level Primer

What Counts as a Claim?

A written request for time and/or money based on a contract clause and dated facts: a cause, an effect, a period, and a price.

Your Core Proof Tool kit

- Schedules: accepted updates, before/after shots, logic-change log.

- Records: daily narrative IDs, T&M tickets, photos, delivery, and payroll logs.

- Math: FOH daily burn; extra hours from measured-mile; clean markup application.

Basic Flow Diagram

Clause → Cause → Path → Period → Price → Proposal → Paper (exhibits)

Chapter Conclusion

Contract administration wins disputes before they start.

Clear RFIs, disciplined approvals clocks, and a shared understanding of who owns which risks under your form of contract. For new PMs, a focused on-ramp, the first 30 days, with flowcharts and a glossary, turns confusion into action. Use the checklists and matrices here to keep cause, path, period, and price aligned with your contract language. Pair this operational rigor with your claim's strategy, and you will turn paperwork into provable outcomes.

The checklists in this chapter are most effective when used as part of a broader risk management system. Chapter 5 expands these tools into a structured framework for managing construction risk across the full project lifecycle.

"If you cannot describe what you are doing as a process, you do not know what you are doing." – **W. Edwards Deming**

CONSTRUCTION RISK MANAGEMENT OVERVIEW

Chapter Foreword

Construction is not just about delivering physical assets; it is about navigating uncertainty. Unlike manufacturing or finance, the construction industry operates in an open environment with ever-changing conditions: labor shortages, weather delays, market volatility, scope shifts, and complex regulations. Risk is not an outlier in this environment; it is embedded in every phase, every decision, and every contract.

Despite this, many firms treat risk management as an afterthought, handled only when something goes wrong. This chapter introduces a strategic framework for identifying, controlling, and converting construction risk from a liability into a competitive advantage. The goal is simple: move your company from reactive firefighting to proactive foresight.

"Discipline is the bridge between goals and accomplishment." – **Jim Rohn**

What Is Construction Risk?

Construction risk refers to any uncertainty that can negatively impact a project's **cost, schedule, scope, quality, safety**, or **compliance**. Risks can be tangible (e.g., a material shortage) or intangible (e.g., poor stakeholder alignment). Crucially, risk is not the same as an issue. A **risk** is what could happen. An **issue** is what has already happened.

Key risk characteristics:

- Multidisciplinary; legal, operational, financial, and reputational

- Variable: different risks emerge at each project phase

- Manageable; risks can be anticipated, quantified, and mitigated

The Business Case for Risk Management

Construction firms face razor-thin margins, often between **2% and 4%**. One unmitigated delay, change order, or dispute can erase profit and damage reputation. Consider the data:

- According to **McKinsey**, large construction projects take **20% longer** to build than scheduled and cost **up to 80% more** than planned.

- **80% of claims** stem from repeatable failures: poor design coordination, ambiguous scopes, and delayed documentation.

- Only **30% of firms** have a formal risk log process for projects under $100M.

These statistics are not abstract; they are your competitors' vulnerabilities and your opportunity for leadership.

The Three Pillars of Risk Management

To be effective, risk management must move beyond checklists and become a company-wide discipline rooted in three pillars:

1. Systems

- Risk registers

- Risk scoring models

- KPI dashboards and auto-alerts

- Lessons learned databases

- Pre-task risk assessments

2. Culture

- Normalizing escalation, not heroics

- Incentivizing risk transparency

- Training field and office staff on red flags

3. Executive Commitment

- Monthly executive risk reviews

- Pre-bid risk walkthroughs

- Executive KPIs tied to claim prevention and risk closure

Without all three pillars, risk efforts collapse into reactive damage control.

The Five Core Categories of Construction Risk

1. Design & Scope Risk

- *Example:* A GMP contract is awarded on 60% drawings with no design contingency.

- *Early Signs:* Incomplete drawings, CSI overlaps, vague owner standards.

- *Response:* Clarify scope via addenda, include RFI pricing language, and define design completion thresholds.

2. Contract & Legal Risk

- *Example:* Contract includes a "no damages for delay" clause and broad indemnity.

- *Early Signs:* Unilateral terms, missing flow-down, one-sided remedies.

- *Response:* Redline unfair terms, define time-impact compensation triggers, or walk.

3. Execution & Logistics Risk

- *Example:* No laydown area in an urban infill project; materials must arrive just in time.

- *Early Signs:* Poor site access, compressed durations, late procurement.

- *Response:* Create logistics plans, prefabricated assemblies, and traffic control coordination.

4. Market & Financial Risk

- *Example:* Fuel and steel prices spike post-bid.

- *Early Signs:* Volatile indexes, overseas suppliers, long lead items.

- *Response:* Use price escalation clauses, buy early, and establish contingency ranges.

5. External & Environmental Risk

- *Example:* Heavy rains delay structural pours by 3 weeks.

- *Early Signs:* Wet season overlaps, no weather float, minimal coverage.

- *Response:* Force majeure clause enforcement, schedule float, and Builder's Risk adjustments.

Red Flag Indicators: Know Before You Bleed Margin

Construction projects always signal trouble before claims surface. These signals are rarely dramatic. They appear as small delays, informal decisions, unanswered questions, or work proceeding with incomplete information. Individually, they seem manageable. Collectively, they are early warnings that risk is transitioning into exposure.

Red flag indicators are leading indicators, not hindsight explanations. Teams that are trained to recognize them can intervene early, preserve entitlement, and prevent escalation. Teams that ignore them often discover their significance only after positions harden and disputes form.

The indicators that follow are not theoretical.

They are patterns repeatedly observed on projects that later end in claims.

Red Flag	What It Signals
RFI turnaround slowing	Design coordination failure or unclear accountability
Rework trending upward	Incomplete design or unapproved changes
Float consumption accelerating	Late decisions or sequencing problems
Sub performance lagging	Poor buyout or unclear scope
High staff turnover	Burnout, misalignment, or poor leadership

These are leading indicators; watch them closely.

Embedding Risk into the Project Lifecycle

Risk does not appear all at once, and it cannot be managed in isolation. It evolves as a project moves from concept to closeout. Each phase introduces different exposures, different decision-makers, and different opportunities to either control risk or allow it to grow.

Embedding risk management into the project lifecycle means treating risk as a continuous process, not a one-time exercise. It requires aligning preconstruction assumptions, contract language, field execution, and closeout documentation so that risk is identified, tracked, and addressed at each transition point.

Projects that fail to integrate risk into daily operations tend to manage symptoms instead of causes.

Projects that succeed build risk awareness into every phase, every handoff, and every critical decision.

Phase	Tools
Business Development	Go/No-Go matrix, risk screen.
Preconstruction	Risk register, scope validation
Contracting	Clause tracker, flow-down checklist
Procurement	Long-lead risk matrix, escalation clauses
Construction Execution	Daily risk log, RFI/CO tracker
Closeout	Lessons learned log, final risk audit.

Case Study – Organizational Turnaround via Risk Management

A Fortune 500 utility company was facing:

- Change order rates **above 20%**

- Substantial delays on **70% of projects**

- **Zero** enterprise-wide risk tracking

Over three years, with structured risk systems, new legal reviews, and project team training:

- COs dropped to **6%**

- On-time completions rose to **88%**

- Risk logs, risk-based bidding, and escalation protocols became standard

The transformation was not just procedural, it was cultural.

Chapter Conclusion

Risk Is Not the Enemy. It is the Opportunity.

Construction is not about avoiding risk; it is about managing it better than your competitors. Firms that adopt proactive, system-driven, culturally enforced risk practices do not just prevent claims; they win better work, improve margins, and build resilience.

A proactive risk program only works if teams can see trouble forming in real time. Chapter 6 focuses on the early warning signs that indicate risk is transitioning into a claim.

"The greatest danger in times of turbulence is not the turbulence; it is to act with yesterday's logic." – **Peter Drucker**

EARLY WARNING SIGNS OF CLAIMS: HOW TO SPOT TROUBLE BEFORE IT STARTS

Chapter Foreword

Construction claims do not begin in court. They begin quietly.

A missed RFI. An unlogged verbal directive. A subcontractor warns about the scope. Long before any formal notice is filed, the seeds of a claim are planted in the day-to-day execution of a project. However, they are visible if you know what to watch for.

This chapter teaches you to recognize and act on the early indicators of trouble. These patterns, drawn from hundreds of claims audits, are your frontline defense. When combined with dashboards, documentation, and disciplined escalation, they empower your teams to intercept risk before it escalates.

"Good judgment comes from experience. Experience comes from bad judgment" – **Rita Mae Brown**

The Lifecycle of a Growing Claim

Most claims follow a predictable path. Understanding this timeline allows project teams to intervene before costs mount.

The Six Stages of Claim Development

1. **Trigger Event**: Schedule disruption, unclear spec, or miscommunication.

2. **Event Goes Unnoticed or Undocumented**: Issue not flagged or written down.

3. **Work Proceeds**: Performed out of sequence, under protest, or without CO.

4. **Issue Escalates**: Impacts cost, time, or quality; trust erodes.

5. **Formal Claim Submitted**: Monetized, packaged, and positioned legally.

6. **Resolution Process Begins**: Mediation, arbitration, or litigation.

Intervention Point:

Target Stage 1–2. This is where 80% of claims can still be prevented.

Top Ten Warning Signs That Signal Claim Risk

These project conditions should trigger documentation, escalation, and executive review.

1. RFIs Unanswered More Than 14 Days

- **Why It Matters**: Slows procurement, disrupts critical path

- **Response**: Escalate in writing, link to CPM, issue a delay notice

2. Work Based on Verbal Instruction

- **Why It Matters**: Disputes over scope and entitlement

- **Response**: Use Field Directive Form, confirm via email

3. RFI Volume Spikes Without Clarifying Design

- **Why It Matters**: Indicates coordination or design failure

- **Response**: Review RFI patterns, run doc coordination session

4. Submittals Delayed or Unresolved

- **Why It Matters**: Impacts fabrication and installation

- **Response**: Aging report, escalation meeting with designers

5. Subcontractor Scope Complaints

- **Why It Matters**: Signals an incomplete or unclear bid package

- **Response**: Clarification bulletin, scope workshop

6. Unsigned Change Orders for Work Already Performed

- **Why It Matters**: Creates entitlement disputes and denial risk

- **Response**: Assign CO Expediter, escalate aging COs monthly

7. Schedule Acceleration Plans Lack Added Resources

- **Why It Matters**: Leads to productivity loss claims

- **Response**: Submit TIA, track OT separately, revise completion forecast

8. Frequent Staff Turnover or Leadership Conflict

- **Why It Matters**: Leads to missed notices and dysfunction

- **Response**: Escalate internally, reset project culture

9. Long-Lead Item Decisions Delayed

- **Why It Matters**: Delays procurement and field installation

- **Response**: Flag in owner report, build substitution options

10. Missing Daily Logs or Photo Documentation

- **Why It Matters**: Undermines claim defense

- **Response**: Weekly audits, enforce log/photo uploads

Reactive vs. Proactive Risk Management

Most construction firms believe they manage risk. In reality, many simply respond to it. Reactive risk management begins after impacts are already visible: a missed milestone, a denied change order, a deteriorating relationship, or a schedule that no longer recovers. By that point, leverage is already lost.

Proactive risk management works differently. It focuses on anticipating exposure before it matures into cost, delay, or dispute. Proactive teams identify threats early, assign ownership, document assumptions, and act while options still exist. The difference between reactive and proactive risk management is not sophistication. It is timing.

Projects rarely fail because teams did not work hard enough.

They fail because risk was addressed too late.

Reactive Firms	Proactive Firms
Wait until issues surface.	Anticipate risks early.
Assume someone else is handling risk.	Assign risk owners.
Redline contracts post-award.	Review risks pre-bid.
Track lessons post-mortem.	Integrate risk lessons in the kickoff.
View risk as the legal's job.	View risk as everyone's job.

Real-Time Claim Risk Forecasting Tools

Modern risk management is proactive, not retrospective. Leading firms track live indicators. These tools do not require complex software; they require discipline.

Claim Forecast Dashboard

- **Inputs**: Unresolved RFIs, unsigned COs, schedule float, punchlist size

- **Scoring**: Weighted dashboard showing Yellow/Red status

Claims Precursor Log

KPI Alerts

- RFIs not answered after 10 days

- Change Orders (CO) logged but not submitted within 14 days

- Time impact notices unanswered

- Work underway without signed CO

Building a Claims-Vigilant Project Team

Claims awareness is a team-wide competency. Here is how each role supports early detection:

Foremen & Superintendents

- Flag all verbal directives

- Document idle time, access issues, concealed work

- Submit photos of impacted scopes

PMs & Project Engineers

- Weekly claim risk reviews

- Maintain Claim Precursor Log

- Link RFIs to potential delay

- Escalate COs >$250K

Executives & Legal

- Monthly Yellow/Red project reviews

- Maintain a list of legal-exposure projects

- Legal sits in on $10M+ job reviews

- Model future claims based on historic triggers

Chapter Conclusion

Watch for Smoke Before the Fire

Construction claims rarely come as a surprise if you know what to watch for. Delayed RFIs, vague directives, scope gaps, and missing documentation are not just project inefficiencies. They are flashing warning lights.

By using dashboards, logs, and live metrics, you can spot the embers before the fire spreads. Train your teams to recognize the patterns, escalate with urgency, and document as if they will be cross-examined.

Because claims are not just a legal issue. They are a field visibility issue. Furthermore, the earlier you see them, the more likely you are to win, or better yet, avoid the fight altogether.

Spotting risk early only matters if action follows. Chapter 7 outlines the specific strategies project teams use to avoid claims entirely, mitigate them once in motion, or eliminate them before formal disputes arise.

"Small problems ignored become large problems unmanaged." **– Henry Mintzberg**

AVOIDING, MITIGATING, OR ELIMINATING CONSTRUCTION CLAIMS

Chapter Foreword

Construction claims do not appear out of nowhere. They are the visible consequences of invisible risks: missed emails, unclear scopes, verbal agreements, or delayed responses. However, here is the good news: most construction claims can be avoided entirely, or at the very least mitigated or eliminated, if managed with the right tools, training, and accountability systems.

This chapter provides a high-level strategic overview of how to intercept claims before they form. It is organized around each phase of the construction lifecycle. These concepts are expanded in much greater detail in later chapters, which serve as in-depth guides for each specific phase.

The goal here is to orient you to the key risks, warning signs, and intervention opportunities throughout the project timeline. Think of this chapter as the roadmap; the chapters that follow are your tactical toolkits.

"You cannot escape the responsibility of tomorrow by evading it today" – **Abraham Lincoln**

The Three Lines of Defense

Avoiding claims begins with understanding how they form and how to interrupt the process at multiple levels.

1. Avoid the Claim Entirely

- Spot the risk early

- Document assumptions clearly

- Insert protective contract language

- Decline high-risk work

Example:

Identifying vague specifications and issuing RFIs pre-bid. Walking away from a GMP job with only 30% drawings.

2. Mitigate the Claim

- Manage the risk once it is in play

- Notify parties of time or cost impacts

- Maintain contemporaneous documentation

Example:

Logging daily T&M tickets for out-of-scope work and submitting a Time Impact Analysis for unanswered RFIs.

3. Eliminate the Claim as a Threat

- Ensure compliance with notice provisions

- Resolve disputes at the field level

- Use documented settlements and structured ADR

Example:

Executing bilateral change orders or structured mediation clauses.

Phase-by-Phase Risk Snapshots

Each phase of a construction project introduces unique risks. The following is a summary of the key vulnerabilities and strategic interventions. For deeper coverage, see the corresponding later chapters.

Pre-Bid & Proposal Phase (See Part III) Key Risks:

- Bidding with incomplete or misleading documents

- Overpromising on price or duration

- Accepting one-sided contractual terms

Preview Strategies:

- Go/No-Go analysis

- RFP Risk Screening Checklist

- Pre-bid clarifications log

Owner Contract Award Phase (See Part IV) Key Risks:

- Undefined change order process

- Risky indemnity or termination clauses

- Flow-down issues from prime to subcontracts

Preview Strategies:

- Clause Tracker

- Contract Summary Sheet

- Notice and dispute protocols

Preconstruction and Design Phase (See Part V) Key Risks:

- Design coordination gaps

- Incomplete construction documents

- Schedule issues

Preview Strategies:

- Constructability reviews

- Buyout checklists

- Critical path analysis

Bidding, Procurement and Subcontracting Phase (See Part VI) Key Risks:

- Subcontract Language

- Scope Gaps

- Procurement Delays

Preview Strategies:

- Key subcontract terms and conditions

- Peer review for GAP analysis

- Procurement times included in the schedule

Construction Phase (See Part VII) Key Risks:

- Verbal changes without documentation

- Poor field tracking of extra work

- Safety incidents or sequence delays

Preview Strategies:

- Daily logs with photo evidence

- Field Change Directive enforcement

- RFI delay tracking

Closeout and Commissioning Phase (See Part VIII) Key Risks:

- Unresolved punchlists

- Missing O&M documentation

- Unreleased retention or liens

Preview Strategies:

- Closeout matrix

- Warranty walk-through schedule

- Rolling punchlist tool

Embedding Claim Prevention at the Organizational Level

Claim prevention does not happen by chance; it requires proactive systems and cultural reinforcement.

Risk Log Enforcement

- Live tracking on projects >$1M

- Assign ownership and status

- Reviewed weekly with PM team

Lessons Learned Program

- Post-project debriefs

- Pattern tracking (by claim type or phase)

- Archived resolutions for preconstruction reference

Field-Level Risk Training

- Verbal directive logging

- Submittal/RFI delay impact

- Notice timeframes

Legal Integration

- Legal reviews of all major contracts

- Legal present at kickoffs and quarterly reviews

- Monthly project risk reviews

Pre-Mortem Risk Workshops

- Forecast what could go wrong

- Develop mitigation plans by phase

- Assign accountability and create Project Execution Plans (PEP)

Claims Defense Binder

- Required on all projects

- Includes contract, RFIs, COs, daily reports, photos, and punchlist closeouts

- Risk Registers for each project

Culture Drives Prevention

Even with great systems, **risk culture** makes the difference.

- Stop rewarding last-minute heroics and instead, reward early warnings

- Normalize issue escalation at all levels

- Align legal and field operations

- Celebrate avoided claims just like won projects

Chapter Conclusion

The Roadmap to Claims Resistant Execution

Most claims are not the result of surprise; they are the result of poor planning or ignored early warning signs. By embedding proactive strategies across each phase, aligning your team culturally, and using your contract and documentation as shields, **not afterthoughts,** you prevent most disputes before they form.

In chapters 11 through 24 ahead, we will break down each of these project phases in detail, offering specific mitigation tools, checklists, and case-backed tactics that you can put into practice immediately. Use this chapter as your big-picture guide and refer back to it as you refine your process phase by phase.

"If you cannot describe what you are doing as a process, you do not know what you are doing." – **W. Edwards Deming**

CHAPTER 8

RISK ALLOCATION TECHNIQUES

Chapter Foreword

When Prevention Ends, Allocation Begins

Chapter 7 focused on how construction claims are avoided, mitigated, or eliminated before they take form. It addressed the behaviors, systems, and decisions that stop risk from turning into disputes. When those controls work, claims never materialize.

But not all risk can be prevented.

Construction operates in uncertainty. Designs evolve. Conditions change. Stakeholders act late. When prevention fails or limits are reached, outcomes are no longer shaped by effort or intent. They are shaped by allocation.

That is where this chapter begins.

Risk allocation determines who bears cost, time, and liability when projects deviate from plan. Contracts do not prevent problems. They decide who pays when they occur. Courts do not weigh fairness. They enforce what was agreed to.

This chapter examines the mechanisms that assign risk once avoidance is no longer possible. Indemnities, insurance, notice provisions, and limitation clauses do not manage risk in real time. They govern consequences after the fact.

Chapter 7 showed how claims are stopped.
Chapter 8 explains what controls the outcome when they are not.

Together, they define effective construction risk management.

"The ultimate measure of a man is not where he stands in moments of comfort, but where he stands at times of challenge and controversy" **– Martin Luther King**

The Principles of Smart Risk Allocation

Effective risk allocation requires:

- Assigning risk to the party best able to control or influence it

- Making the allocation clear and contractually enforceable

- Avoiding burdens that are uninsurable or impossible to price

- Aligning incentives across stakeholders to promote cooperation

Equitable risk allocation is not about fairness. It is about capability, clarity, and control.

Insurance as a Risk Allocation Tool (See Chapter 23)

Insurance shifts financial risk to a third party, but only if the right policies are in place and coverage aligns with exposure.

Best Practice: Require Certificate of Insurance (COI) submission and review prior to subcontractor mobilization. Do not assume compliance, verify it.

Bonding: Financial Guarantees for Performance and Payment (See Chapter 24)

Unlike insurance, surety bonds guarantee that obligations will be met. They protect the owner and second-tier parties if the contractor fails.

- **Performance Bond**: Ensures completion if the contractor defaults

- **Payment Bond**: Protects subcontractors and suppliers from non-payment

- **Warranty Bond**: Covers post-completion defect repair during the warranty term

Key Case:

***Perini Corp. v. Greate Bay Hotel & Casino*, 129 N.J. 479 (1992).** An owner recovered millions for project delays; proper bonding could have mitigated risk if the contractor defaulted.

Pro Tip:

Verify the surety's financial strength and reputation before award.

Joint Ventures and Subcontractor Risk (See Chapters 14 and 15)

Joint Ventures (JVs) offer collaboration but create shared liability. Risk allocation should be clearly documented in the JV agreement.

Key JV Clauses:

- Management responsibilities

- Profit/loss sharing

- Dispute resolution

- Bonding and licensing

Subcontractor Risk:

Managed through *flow-down clauses*, which bind subs to prime contract obligations. Common examples:

- Indemnity and insurance

- Schedule compliance

- Safety protocols

- Change order notice requirements

- Liquidated damages pass-through

Pro Tip:

Maintain a **Deviation Log** to track exceptions to standard subcontract language and review regularly with counsel.

Project Delivery Method and Risk Transfer

Your chosen delivery model defines how risk flows through the contract structure.

Project Delivery Methods

Which one is the right choice for your next construction project?

In commercial construction, the project delivery method refers to the overall process chosen to complete a construction project, including the contractual arrangements and the organization of the workflow. The choice of delivery method can significantly impact the project's cost, schedule, and final quality. Here are the main types of commercial construction project delivery methods.

Lump Sum Contract

Also known as a fixed-price contract, this involves a total fixed price for all construction-related activities. It is often used when the scope and schedules are clearly defined.

- **Strengths**: Fixed price offers budget certainty.

- **Weaknesses**: Risk of the contractor cutting corners to maintain profit margins.

- **Strategic Use**: Best when the scope is very clear and changes are unlikely, minimizing the risk of additional costs.

Cost Plus Contract

This contract allows payment to the contractor for actual costs incurred plus a percentage or fixed fee, which is agreed upon at the beginning of the contract. It is suitable when the scope is not clearly defined, and changes are anticipated.

- **Strengths**: Flexibility in design changes; contractor is paid for all incurred costs.

- **Weaknesses**: Less incentive for cost control; potential for higher overall project costs.

- **Strategic Use**: Suitable for projects where scope changes are expected or when precise project details are not known at the outset.

Guaranteed Maximum Price (GMP)

Similar to cost-plus, this contract sets a cap or maximum price that the owner will pay. Any costs exceeding the GMP are typically the contractor's responsibility unless changes are made by the owner.

- **Strengths**: Caps spending; shared savings can incentivize cost-effective management.

- **Weaknesses**: Potential for disputes over scope changes and cost allocations.

- **Strategic Use**: Preferred in projects where the scope may evolve, but the owner wants cost certainty.

Time and Material Contracts (T&M)

Under this contract, payments are based on the contractor's actual costs for labor and materials, plus an added amount for contractor profit. It is preferred when the scope of the project is uncertain.

- **Strengths**: Flexibility for undefined projects.

- **Weaknesses**: Uncertainty in overall project cost; requires diligent oversight.

- **Strategic Use**: Useful when project specifics cannot be accurately estimated in advance, and the owner can closely monitor spending.

Unit Price Contract

This contract is based on estimated quantities of items and agreed-upon unit prices for each item. It is often used for projects where the types of work can be quantified, but the total quantities vary.

- **Strengths**: Fair pricing on variable quantity projects; payment based on actual quantities installed.

- **Weaknesses**: Total cost can escalate if quantities increase significantly.

- **Strategic Use**: Effective for projects like roadwork or utilities where quantities of materials can vary.

Design-Build Contract

In a design-build contract, design and construction services are contracted together from a single party. This simplifies project delivery by having one entity responsible for both designing and building the project.

- **Strengths**: Single point of responsibility; faster completion due to overlapping design and construction phases.

- **Weaknesses**: Potentially less owner control over design details.

- **Strategic Use**: Effective for projects with tight schedules or where quick completion is necessary. Useful when the project scope is not entirely defined from the outset.

Integrated Project Delivery (IPD) Contract

This contract involves a multi-party agreement between the owner, contractor, and architect/engineer. It fosters collaboration from all parties, which can lead to a more efficient and cost-effective project.

- **Strengths**: Enhances collaboration; shared risks and rewards.

- **Weaknesses**: Requires high levels of trust and cooperation; complex contractual relationships.

- **Strategic Use**: Best for complex projects requiring innovative solutions and where all parties are committed to a transparent process.

Public-Private Partnership (P3) Contract

Typically used for large-scale public infrastructure projects, this contract involves a government entity partnering with a private company that handles the design, construction, operation, and maintenance of the project for a specified period.

- **Strengths**: Access to private capital and expertise; risk-sharing between public and private sectors.

- **Weaknesses**: Long-term contractual commitments; complex negotiations.

- **Strategic Use**: Ideal for large-scale infrastructure projects needing significant investment, with benefits spread over extended periods.

Design-Bid-Build Contract

This traditional contract separates design and construction services. The design is completed first, then bids are solicited for the construction phase.

- **Strengths**: Well-defined roles; competitive bidding helps in cost reduction.

- **Weaknesses**: Longer project duration; risk of design and cost discrepancies.

- **Strategic Use**: Suitable when project specifications are precise, and a defined budget is in place. Ideal for projects where changes are unlikely, and the lowest cost is paramount.

Construction Manager at Risk (CMAR) Contract

The construction manager commits to completing the project within a guaranteed maximum price and acts as a consultant during the design phase and as a contractor during the construction phase.

- **Strengths**: Early cost estimation; risk of cost overruns often transferred to the CM.

- **Weaknesses**: Can be more costly if the CMAR fee is high.

- **Strategic Use**: Preferred for complex projects where the owner wants the benefit of early construction input without the full exposure to cost overruns.

Construction Manager as Agent (CMA) Contract

In this arrangement, the construction manager acts as an agent for the owner, providing management services without the risk, and does not perform actual construction.

- **Strengths**: Advisory role without financial risk; flexibility in managing multiple contractors.

- **Weaknesses**: The owner carries the risk of cost overruns.

- **Strategic Use**: Suitable for owners capable of bearing cost overruns but wanting expert management and coordination among various contractors.

Multiple Primes

In this method, the owner contracts directly with multiple prime contractors, each responsible for different segments of the project. The owner takes on the role of managing and coordinating the various prime contractors.

- **Strengths**: Direct control over subcontractors; potential cost savings by eliminating a general contractor's markup.

- **Weaknesses**: The Owner assumes more responsibility for project coordination and risk.

- **Strategic Use**: Works well when the owner has strong construction management capabilities and desires close control over the project.

Each of these contract types offers different benefits and involves varying degrees of risk for the project owner. The choice of contract type is typically based on the project specifics, including complexity, duration, budget, and the owner's appetite for risk.

Risk Strategy Tip:

Choose based on project complexity and owner sophistication, not on habits.

Indemnity and Hold Harmless Clauses

These clauses shift financial responsibility for certain losses or liabilities. Understanding them is critical.

Types of Indemnity:

1. **Broad Form:** Covers even the indemnitee's own negligence (often unenforceable)

2. **Intermediate Form:** Covers shared fault

3. **Limited Form:** Only covers the indemnitor's own negligence

California Note:

Under Civil Code §2782, indemnity for active negligence or willful misconduct is often unenforceable.

Review all indemnity clauses for enforceability under your specific state and local laws.

Real-World Risk Allocation Failures

Case 1: Insurance Gap Leads to $600K Exposure

A subcontractor ruptured a major utility line during excavation. Their insurance lacked a pollution rider. The GC, unable to flow down risk properly, was left holding the bag.

Lesson: Align subcontractor insurance requirements with the actual work performed.

Case 2: Owner Stuck with $2.1M in Change Orders

On a complex DBB healthcare facility, the designer's lack of coordination caused massive change orders. The owner's contract did not assign coordination risk to the designer.

Lesson: Delivery method and contract terms must reflect actual project demands.

Summary Table: Risk Allocation Techniques at a Glance

Checklist: Risk Allocation Readiness

- Have all insurance policies been reviewed and match project exposure?

- Are all subcontractor COIs collected and compliant?

- Are JV roles and risks clearly defined in writing?

- Does the delivery method reflect project complexity and the owner's needs?

- Are indemnity clauses enforceable under local statutes?

Chapter Conclusion

Risk is not avoided – It is assigned

Every construction project carries risk. The difference between profit and dispute, or between success and litigation, often comes down to how that risk was allocated at the contract stage.

Competent contractors do not just manage construction; they manage risk. And that starts by ensuring every dollar, every clause, and every role reflects a rational and enforceable plan to deal with what can go wrong.

Do not leave risk to chance. Assign it early. Define it clearly. Ensure it is appropriate. Then manage it relentlessly.

In Chapter 9, we explore how human behavior, incentives, fear, and cognitive bias drive when claims are asserted, escalated, or resolved, frequently shaping outcomes as much as the contract itself.

"The contract is not a formality; it is the rulebook." **– Justice Antonin Scalia**

THE PSYCHOLOGY OF CLAIMS: WHY OWNERS, CONTRACTORS, AND SUBS DISAGREE

Chapter Foreword

Construction claims rarely begin with legal briefs or contract disputes. More often, they arise from misperceptions, emotional reactions, and cognitive blind spots. These are not legal problems; they are human problems.

Every participant in a construction project operates under different incentives, pressures, and perceptions:

- **Budget, deadlines, and public scrutiny drive owners**.

- **General contractors** juggle coordination, design gaps, and change fatigue.

- **Subcontractors** face tight margins, inconsistent direction, and delayed payment.

Layered with stress, assumptions, and poor communication, this triangle of tension becomes a fertile ground for claims. This chapter unpacks the psychological dynamics behind disputes and provides actionable tools to realign project teams before legal escalation occurs.

"You do not drown by falling in the water. You drown by staying there." – Edwin Louis Cole

Triangular Tension: The Root of Misalignment

Owner Perspective

- "I am paying a premium, why isn't this job running smoother?"

- Focused on cost, delivery dates, and reputational risk.

- Often skeptical of change order pricing and perceived inefficiency.

General Contractor Perspective

- "We are caught between owner demands and subcontractor delays."

- Struggles with scope gaps, delayed approvals, and shifting design.

- Often underappreciated for managing project complexity.

Subcontractor Perspective

- "We get late info, impossible deadlines, and slow pay."

- Feels overexposed to risk with minimal control.

- Suspects others of protecting their own interests at the subcontractor's expense.

These disconnects lead each party to assume the others have more power, more money, and fewer problems. That misbelief fuels distrust, and ultimately, claims.

Cognitive Biases That Fuel Disputes

Understanding how common psychological tendencies shape behavior is critical to resolving issues early.

Attribution Bias

- *"I made an honest mistake. You are just negligent."*

- We blame others more harshly than we blame ourselves.

Anchoring

- *"We agreed to $8 million, so I am not paying $8.7 million, even if it is justified."*

- Early budget estimates distort future judgment, regardless of evolving facts.

Loss Aversion

- *"I would rather fight than accept a perceived loss."*

- People resist settling if it feels like admitting defeat, even if it costs more to litigate.

Confirmation Bias

- *"This delay proves what I already believed about the GC."*

- Negative assumptions color all subsequent interactions.

Cognitive Overload

- *"I will just go with my gut. I do not have time to sort this out."*

- Under pressure, people default to intuition instead of evidence.

Patterns That Precede a Claim

Trust Breakdown

- Escalating email tone

- Missed deadlines with no explanation

- Field-level changes made without documentation

Misaligned Incentives

- Owner's resist added cost

- GCs pursue COs to recapture lost margin

- Subs push for payment with minimal paperwork

Escalation Paralysis

- Field issues linger too long without being resolved or escalated

- PMs try to fix what they cannot authorize

- Legal is brought in when it is already too late

Decision Fatigue

- Slow RFI responses, stalled COs, and design indecision

- Teams begin to "work at risk" just to keep moving

Practical Tools for Reducing Emotional Claims Risk

1. Kickoff Alignment Workshops

Bring all key parties together pre-construction to align expectations:

- Who approves what?

- What is the CO process?

- What are the early risk flags?

2. Monthly Claims Risk Reviews

Hold standing meetings with senior stakeholders:

- Review open RFIs and aging COs

- Surface misalignments before they escalate

- Assign closure accountability

3. Communication Ladder

Establish a tiered escalation protocol:

- Field to Project Management: Issues identified in the field are documented and elevated to the PM within a defined timeframe

- Project Management to Executive: Issues exceeding authority, cost thresholds, or schedule impact are escalated to executive leadership

- Executive to Legal: When contractual rights, formal notices, or dispute risk are implicated, legal is engaged early to guide strategy

4. Meeting Language Protocol

Encourage objective, fact-based language:

- "You never answer RFIs."

- Instead of utilizing "you" – responses should be fact based.

- "RFI #203 has been open for 19 days with no response."

5. Shared Transparency Metrics

Use shared dashboards to create an everyday reality:

- Open RFIs

- CO approval time

- Daily report compliance

- Schedule float erosion

Chapter Conclusion

From Behavior to Execution

Construction does not run on documents; it runs on people. Behind every claim is a story of miscommunication, missed expectations, or misunderstood roles.

The solution is not softer contracts; it is smarter alignment.

- Understand your counterparts' pressure points.

- Design workflows to prevent friction.

- Address emotions before they metastasize into legal positions.

Chapter 9 examined how human behavior, incentives, fear, and cognitive bias influence when construction claims are asserted, escalated, or resolved. These forces shape decisions long before disputes appear, often determining outcomes as much as the contract itself.

Understanding this psychology is essential, but insight alone does not prevent claims.

Behavior explains *why* teams act as they do under pressure. The chapters that follow focus on *where* those behaviors intersect with risk in the real work of delivering projects. From planning and design through procurement, construction, and closeout, risk presents itself differently at each phase of the project lifecycle.

Chapters 10 through 25 translate behavioral insight into execution discipline. Each chapter isolates a specific phase, identifies the risks most likely to emerge in that window, and shows how claims form when assumptions go unchallenged, responsibilities blur, or documentation lags behind decisions.

Psychology reveals the trigger.
Lifecycle discipline determines the outcome.

What follows is a phase-by-phase framework for managing construction risk where it actually lives, inside the daily decisions that shape cost, schedule, and defensibility long before a claim is ever filed.

"We do not see things as they are. We see them as we are." – **Anaïs Nin**

PART III – IDENTIFYING RISK DURING PRE-BID AND PROPOSAL PHASE

CHAPTER 10

PRE-BID AND PROPOSAL RISKS

Chapter Foreword

Every construction project begins with a pursuit phase, whether responding to a public RFP, engaging with private clients, or exploring unsolicited opportunities. It is precisely at this early stage that risk initially emerges, yet it often goes unnoticed or intentionally ignored due to competitive pressures and the desire to secure new work.

Estimators, business developers, and executives frequently overlook or downplay risk to keep bids attractive, inadvertently laying the groundwork for significant financial and operational issues down the line. Effective risk management starts not with groundbreaking, but with disciplined decision making during the proposal phase. This chapter outlines a structured approach to identifying, assessing, and managing proposal-phase risks and transforming risk awareness into a competitive advantage.

"Quality means doing it right when no one else is looking" – **Henry Ford**

Where Proposal Risk Emerges

Three key groups typically influence the proposal stage:

1. Business Development: Focuses on client relationships and capturing market share.

2. Estimating: Responsible for competitive pricing, accurate scheduling, and resource allocation.

3. Executive Leadership: Manages critical Go/No-Go decisions based on risk assessment and strategic alignment.

Despite tight deadlines and competitive pressures, bypassing structured risk evaluation at this stage can lead directly to margin erosion, operational setbacks, and ultimately project failure.

Common Risks in the Proposal Stage Include

- Ambiguous or incomplete scope definitions.

- Underdeveloped design documentation (less than 80% complete).

- Unrealistically compressed schedules.

- Aggressive liquidated damages clauses.

- Unclear or unfavorable contract terms.

- Hidden or undisclosed site conditions.

- Material price volatility and availability issues.

Common Mistakes in Proposal Development

Proposal teams frequently fall victim to misconceptions that inadvertently heighten project risk:

- "We will handle it during buyout." Once awarded, contractual commitments are locked in, making post-award adjustments difficult and costly.

- "We have done similar projects before." Assuming past project experience covers new risks neglects site-specific and client-specific complexities.

- "Our numbers look competitive." Pricing without comprehensive risk analysis leaves profitability dependent on assumptions rather than accurate forecasting.

Proposal Phase Risk Assessment Checklist

A structured pre-bid risk assessment ensures key risks are identified and addressed proactively:

- Contract Terms: Are indemnity, delay, and payment terms balanced and clearly defined?

- Design Completeness: Are design documents sufficiently developed (>80%) with clearly outlined assumptions?

- Client History: Has the client historically demonstrated prompt payment and fair dispute resolution?

- Schedule Realism: Is the proposed schedule practical and achievable, given the critical path analysis?

- Permits and Approvals: Are required permits and approvals clearly identified, along with the associated risks of delay?

- Site Conditions: Have geotechnical reports been thoroughly reviewed, and utility conditions confirmed?

- Team Capabilities: Do internal resources align effectively with project requirements?

- Subcontractor Reliability: Are dependable subcontractors available and aligned with the project scope and timeline?

- Dispute Resolution: Are dispute forums, escalation steps, and attorney fee provisions aligned with the project risk profile?

- Insurance and Bonds: Have additional insurance or bonding requirements been factored into project costs?

Each risk factor should be clearly scored (e.g., Low/Medium/High), facilitating objective and informed Go/No-Go decisions.

Case Study: The "Free Parking" Project

A contractor pursuing a municipal parking garage assumed minimal risks, opting to skip detailed site investigations and design coordination. Mid-construction, unanticipated utility conflicts and incomplete design documents emerged, resulting in $1.2 million in non-reimbursable change orders due to contractual restrictions on owner-directed changes.

This costly oversight highlights the critical importance of rigorous risk assessment and documentation during the proposal phase.

The Go/No-Go Decision Framework

A disciplined Go/No-Go process provides a structured means of objectively evaluating potential projects. Criteria and scoring metrics typically include:

1 = Low Risk

5 = High Risk

- Contract Risk (1–5)

- Design Risk (1-5)

- Scope Clarity (1–5)

- Client Relationship/History (1–5)

- Schedule Feasibility (1–5)

- Margin Opportunity (1–5)

- Strategic Alignment (1–5)

- Resource Availability (1–5)

Threshold guidelines:

Scores will range between 8 (Very Low Risk) and 40 (Very High Risk)

- Scores >32: Do Not Pursue

- Scores 25–31: Pursue with Caution

- Scores <24: Proceed with close monitoring

A more advanced Pre-Bid Risk Analysis Template.

If you have ever heard of a Benjamin list, where you make two columns and evaluate the pros and cons of an idea. This is the Construction Mastermind, Turbo-Charged Benjamin List for Pre-Bid Risk Analysis. Walking away from a project can be more important than accepting a risky one.

	RISK	GO / NO GO ANALYSIS							CRITERIA
		POINTS							
		+ 5	+ 3	+ 1	0	- 1	- 3	- 5	
A	Owner / Client Relationship		X						Based on Private or Public Agency and good relationships or disputes in the past. Private clients get more positive points than a State or Federal Agency. (+ 5 to – 5)
B	Designer Relationship					X			Based on Relationship and Designers Reputation. (+ 3 to – 3)
C	Profit %				X				5% would be considered = 0 Points. Over 15% = + 5 Points.
D	Contract Terms				X				Favorable versus unfavorable contracts that have very strict notice provisions and no damage for delay clauses.
E	Payment Terms				X				Net 30 days would be considered = 0 Points.
F	Retention Terms				X				5% Retention would be considered = 0 Points
G	Liquidated Damages					X			If Daily LD's are $500 per million in contract value = 0 Points. +3 Points for no LD's.
H	Site and Working Conditions				X				Generally normal site conditions = 0 Points
I	Workforce Limitations				X				Limitations on workforce availability or the lack of a skilled local workforce result in negative values.
J	Bond Requirements				X				100% Payment and Performance Bond = 0 Points. No bond requirements are + 3 Points.
K	Insurance Requirements				X				Standard Insurance Requirements = 0 Points.
L	Contract Amount				X				Contract amounts that are considered average for your company and no more than 10% of the company's total capacity = 0 Points.
M	Constructability Issues				X				If the Construction Plans and Specifications are industry standard quality = 0 Points. Vague or unusual specifications that shift responsibility to the contractor receive negative values.
N	Schedule Issues				X				A feasible schedule that allows float and weather calendars, as well as normal 40–hour work weeks = 0 Points. Schedules with generous float = + 3 Points.
O	Access to Site Limitations				X				Standard road access to the site and adequate laydown areas = 0 Points.
P	Scope Clarity						X		Standard well defined scope of work = 0 Points.
Q	Familiarity with Type of Work			X					Work your company performs on a regular basis is = 0 Points.
R	Familiarity with Location of Work			X					Location of work that your company typically works in = 0 Points.
S	Familiarity with Subcontractors			X					Subcontractors that you have good relationships with = 0 Points. If multiple ongoing projects are with the same Subcontractor = + 1 Point. New Subcontractors or Subcontractors with prior disputes receive negative Points.
	TOTAL RISK SCORE	+ 2							

Advanced Go / No Go Analysis

This systematic approach ensures consistent, informed risk assessment across all pursuits. Adding in larger contingencies or profit margins can reduce the risk score further to account for specific assumptions.

Historical Note

The Origin of the Benjamin Franklin Pro-and-Con List

1. Created by Benjamin Franklin (circa 1772). In a letter to his friend Joseph Priestley in 1772. Franklin described a structured method he used for making difficult decisions. He called it "my way of resolving doubts," and later referred to it as "moral algebra."

2. The Method
Franklin would take a sheet of paper, draw a line down the middle, and label the two sides:

"Pro" on one side and
"Con" on the other

He would then spend several days listing items under each side as they occurred to him, updating the list over time.

3. Weighted Reasoning

Franklin's method wasn't just a simple list; he also assigned weights to each reason:
Some reasons counted more heavily than others.
If a strong "pro" outweighed several more minor "cons," he would cross them out to "balance the ledger."
This is why he compared it to algebra, where values can cancel each other out.

4. Why It Became Famous
The idea became widely popular because:
It provided a formal structure for rational decision-making.
It was associated with Franklin's reputation for logic, practicality, and common-sense wisdom.
It was simple, teachable, and universally used in business, daily life, politics, and personal decisions.

Today, when people say, **"the Benjamin list,"** they're referring to this exact method.

Estimating as a Strategic Risk Tool

Estimators play a vital role in identifying and managing project risks. Effective estimating practices include:

- Clearly documenting scope exclusions and assumptions.

- Incorporating alternate pricing and contingency for high-risk elements.

- Conducting historical productivity analysis to validate pricing assumptions.

- Highlighting potential RFIs or scope gaps prior to award.

- Creating a preliminary schedule to assess sequencing logic and realistic time requirements to build.

- Understanding current market conditions for workforce and material procurement.

Empowering estimators to act as strategic risk advisors strengthens project accuracy and reduces future risk exposure.

Managing Owner-Driven Risks

Owners frequently impose aggressive schedules, incomplete designs, or unrealistic budget constraints. Mitigating these risks involves proactively documenting and communicating concerns through a "Risk Clarification Memo" included in bid submissions. This memo details:

- Design conflicts and assumptions.

- Unknown site conditions.

- Schedule feasibility concerns.

- Explicit scope exclusions.

- Recommended contingency allocations.

Clear, proactive communication safeguards your contractual position, demonstrating transparency and diligence.

Chapter Conclusion

Most Project Risk Is Accepted Before the First Price Is Submitted

Winning contracts is essential, but only when the project remains profitable and manageable from start to finish. Firms that systematically evaluate and document risks during the proposal phase consistently avoid financial pitfalls, operational disruptions, and contractual disputes.

By instilling disciplined risk assessment processes early, you protect project margins, strengthen client relationships, and establish a culture of accountability. Risk management truly begins with pursuit, setting the foundation for sustained success.

"The bitterness of poor quality remains long after the sweetness of low price is forgotten." – **Benjamin Franklin**

Part IV – Identifying Risk at the Owner Contracting Phase

CHAPTER 11

OWNER CONTRACT RISK: KEY LANGUAGE EVERY CONTRACTOR SHOULD KNOW

Chapter Foreword

In construction, the contract is not just a legal formality; it is your first and most critical line of defense against project risk. Each clause assigns responsibility, allocates uncertainty, and outlines how disputes will be handled. Poorly written or vague contracts are among the leading causes of costly construction claims.

This chapter demystifies the core contract clauses that either prevent or provoke claims. By identifying high-risk language and offering practical revisions, we arm contractors, subcontractors, and legal teams with the tools to negotiate smarter and protect their interests before the project even begins.

"The law is reason, free from passion" – **Aristotle**

Contracting as Risk Management: Well Written Construction Contracts:

- Establish procedures for changes and notices

- Allocate risks related to time, cost, and unforeseen events

- Control dispute resolution mechanisms

Why Contractors Sign Risky Contracts:

- Time pressure to mobilize

- Lack of legal review

- Inexperience with hidden risk terms

The consequence is expensive disputes that could have been avoided with a single sentence.

Ten Essential Contract Clauses for Claim Prevention

1. Notice of Claim

- Purpose: Sets the timeline and format for notifying the other party of delays or claims.

- Why It Matters: Missed notice deadlines are a leading reason claims get dismissed.

- Key Language Tip: Use "potential claim" language that preserves rights before full impacts are known.

2. Change Order Procedure

- Purpose: Defines how changes are authorized and priced.

- Why It Matters: Unclear change protocols are the #1 cause of contract disputes.

- Key Practice: Allow interim T&M tracking with later pricing.

3. No Damages for Delay (ND4D)

- Purpose: Limits delay compensation.

- Why It Matters: Many courts enforce these clauses unless you negotiate exceptions.

- Key Tip: Add carve-outs for active owner interference and permitting failures.

4. Float Ownership

- Purpose: Clarifies who controls schedule float.

- Why It Matters: Undefined float leads to scheduling and cost disputes.

- Key Language: Define float as a shared project resource.

5. Differing Site Conditions

- Purpose: Allows equitable adjustment for unexpected physical conditions.

- Why It Matters: Without it, the contractor eats all unknowns.

- Key Tip: Include both Type I (different from documents) and Type II (unusual) conditions.

6. Dispute Resolution

- Purpose: Dictates how and where disputes are handled.

- Why It Matters: Venue and process determine cost and time to resolve.

- Best Practice: Use tiered clauses: field → exec review → mediation → arbitration.

7. Indemnification

- Purpose: Assigns liability for damages and third-party claims.

- Why It Matters: Broad indemnity can make you liable for others' mistakes.

- Key Tip: Limit indemnity to your own negligence or misconduct.

8. Termination for Convenience

- Purpose: Allows the owner to cancel the contract at will.

- Why It Matters: It can erase expected profits and leave you unreimbursed.

- Protective Language: Include demobilization costs and unearned profit in recovery.

9. Force Majeure

- Purpose: Provides relief for uncontrollable events.

- Why It Matters: COVID-19 exposed how vague clauses fail.

- Key Tip: Define events clearly and allow both time and cost relief.

10. Flow-Down Clauses

- Purpose: Binds subcontractors to the terms in your prime contract.

- Why It Matters: Without them, you carry upstream risk without downstream control.

- Best Practice: Attach or reference key prime clauses in subcontracts explicitly.

Negotiating Better Contract Terms

If the contract is non-negotiable, negotiate the execution

- Ask for Examples: "How has this clause been applied previously?"

- Focus on Fairness: Recast one-sided clauses into mutual obligations.

- Offer Language: Propose alternatives instead of just objecting.

- Use Pre-Bid RFIs: Flag red-flag clauses in writing early.

- Escalate Wisely: Involve legal or executive voices when needed.

Contract Review Tools and Templates

Innovative companies use standard tools to spot and revise risky clauses

- Contract Clause Tracker: For redlines and revisions

- Risk Review Checklist: Pre-signing due diligence

- Contract Summary Sheet: Plain-language guide for PM teams

- Subcontract Flow-Down Matrix: Ensures pass-through language

Chapter Conclusion

Owner Contracts Define Risk Before Construction Starts

If it is not in writing, it is not real. Memories fade, staff rotate, but the contract endures. Every construction claim is ultimately a contract interpretation. Make yours unambiguous, equitable, and tailored to your scope and risk appetite. Do not just accept the boilerplate. Rewrite the rules.

in Chapter 12 we will discuss specific contract language and suggested modifications to reduce risk.

***"Hard cases make bad law."* – Oliver Wendell Holmes Jr.**

CHAPTER 12

CONTRACT LANGUAGE AND RISK ALLOCATION

Chapter Foreword

In construction, the contract is not merely paperwork; it is the blueprint that governs your project's success or failure. It defines the responsibilities of each party, outlines risk allocation, and determines your profitability. However, many professionals overlook critical clauses, assuming standard language is harmless. This oversight can lead directly to significant financial and operational risks.

This chapter explains how contract language can create, shift, or mitigate risk. We will examine essential clauses, evaluate their implications, and illustrate through real-world scenarios how seemingly minor terms can substantially impact a project's outcome.

"We shape our buildings; thereafter they shape us." – **Winston Churchill**

Why Contract Language Matters

The contract determines:

- Liability distribution

- Responses to schedule changes

- Change order pricing

- Delay claim entitlements

- Dispute resolution methods

- Preservation or waiver of contractual rights through notice and documentation

Risk management is as much legal and financial as it is operational. Skipping detailed reviews during negotiation means you are navigating mindlessly.

Critical Clauses that Commonly Influence Risk

Below are key problematic clauses, reasons they are risky, and recommended alternative language that aligns with industry best practices to make the terms more reasonable for the Contractor or Subcontractor.

1. "No Damages for Delay" Clause

Current Risky Clause:

- Contractor receives time extensions as the sole remedy for delays, without additional compensation.

Recommended Revised Language:

"Contractor shall be entitled to an equitable adjustment, including reasonable costs for delays caused by the Owner, or other parties not attributable to Contractor."

2. Pay-If-Paid When Paid Clause

Current Risky Clause:

- Payments to Subcontractor depend entirely on Contractor's receipt of payments from the Owner, shifting all non-payment risk to the subcontractor.

Recommended Revised Language:

"Contractor shall pay Subcontractor within thirty (30) days of Subcontractor's approved payment application. In the event Contractor has not received payment from Owner through no fault of Subcontractor, payment shall be made to Subcontractor within sixty (60) days from the Subcontractor's invoice submission, unless the non-payment by Owner is directly related to Subcontractor's work."

3. Indemnification Clause

Current Risky Clause:

- Broad indemnification, holding Contractor responsible for claims even partially caused by the Owner or third parties.

Recommended Revised Language:

"Contractor shall indemnify Owner only to the extent caused by Contractor's negligent acts or omissions. This indemnity obligation shall not extend to liabilities arising from Owner's or other third parties' negligence."

4. Termination for Convenience

Current Risky Clause:

- Limits what a Contractor can recover to "reasonable direct close-out costs" without overhead or anticipatory profits.

Recommended Revised Language:

"Contractor shall be compensated for all Work performed prior to termination plus reasonable overhead, demobilization costs, and a percentage of anticipated profit based on Work completed."

5. Change Orders

Current Risky Clause:

- Change orders initiated by Contractor (not Owner-driven) are performed at cost without overhead or profit markup.

Recommended Revised Language:

"Changes ordered by Contractor, regardless of Owner initiation, shall be compensated at cost plus a reasonable overhead and profit markup not to exceed 15%."

6. Final Payment

Current Risky Clause:

- Final payment conditioned on Contractor receiving final payment from Owner, regardless of reason.

Recommended Revised Language:

"Final payment shall be due to Subcontractor upon completion and acceptance of Subcontractor's Work, independent of Owner's final payment to Contractor, provided the delay in Owner's payment is not attributable to Subcontractor."

7. Bonds

Current Risky Clause:

- Contractor requires bonds at subcontractor's expense without considering subcontract size or risk profile.

Recommended Revised Language:

"Performance and payment bonds shall be required for subcontracts exceeding a specified monetary threshold. Costs for such bonds shall be reimbursable to the Subcontractor as a separate line item."

8. Schedule and Time Management

Current Risky Clause:

- Contractor may unilaterally change schedules without notice or consideration of subcontractors' impacts and costs.

Recommended Revised Language:

"Contractor shall provide reasonable notice of any schedule amendments. If such amendments materially impact Subcontractor's costs or timing, Subcontractor shall be entitled to submit a request for equitable adjustment."

9. Documentation and Notice Requirements

Current Risky Clause:

- The Contractor is required to provide notice within three (3) days and detailed claims within twenty (20) days or forfeit claims entirely.

Recommended Revised Language:

"Contractor shall provide written notice of claims within seven (7) calendar days of discovery. Detailed supporting documentation shall be submitted within thirty (30) calendar days thereafter. Late notice shall not waive claims unless the Owner can demonstrate material prejudice specifically from such delay."

10. Backcharges

Current Risky Clause:

- Allows Contractor unilateral rights to complete punch lists and clean-up with significant markup without adequate notice or remedy period.

Recommended Revised Language:

"Contractor shall notify Subcontractor of deficiencies in writing, providing a minimum of five (5) working days to rectify issues before proceeding with self-performance or subcontracting to others. Any backcharges shall include reasonable costs plus a maximum markup of 5% for overhead."

11. Dispute Resolution

Current Risky Clause:

- Owner holds unilateral right to choose arbitration or litigation and control dispute processes entirely.

Recommended Revised Language:

"Disputes shall first undergo mediation. If unresolved, parties mutually agree to arbitration or litigation. The venue shall be mutually agreed upon and conducted in the jurisdiction where the Project is located."

12. Waiver of Mechanic's Lien

Current Risky Clause:

- Blanket waiver of subcontractor's mechanic's lien rights.

Recommended Revised Language:

"Subcontractor waives lien rights only upon receipt of full payment for its completed work. Any lien waivers provided before full payment shall be conditional."

Contracts that contain clauses that shift excessive risk to the Contractor or Subcontractor, particularly regarding payment terms, delay damages, indemnification, and unilateral decision-making powers, should be carefully reviewed and the risks understood prior to entering into any such agreement.

Implementing revised language will help create a balanced risk profile, ensuring Contractors and Subcontractors are protected and able to manage their risks effectively.

Careful negotiation of these clauses will improve overall project execution, reduce disputes, and promote healthy and collaborative relationships between all parties involved.

Risk Allocation: Clearly Define Ownership

Contracts allocate risk across owners, designers, general contractors, subcontractors, and suppliers. Excessive downstream risk transfer leads to increased pricing and potential project failures. Use a Risk Allocation Matrix to clarify and negotiate acceptable risk levels.

Negotiation Best Practices

- Start reviewing contracts early.

- Document assumptions explicitly.

- Negotiate professionally and factually.

- Seek early legal consultation.

Case Study: Poorly Negotiated Clauses

A California CM signed a GMP contract with:

- ND4D clauses

- Full indemnity for third-party design claims

- 30-day unilateral termination

Mid-project impacts:

- Permits delayed by 5 months

- Design flaws caused rework

- Termination executed with minimal notice

Result: $1.6M loss in unrecoverable expenses.

Lesson Learned: The CM failed to mitigate contract risk effectively during negotiation, resulting in severe financial damage.

Contract Review Checklist

Before signing, confirm:

- Indemnity and LD clauses reviewed legally

- Delay damages are clearly defined and capped

- Payment and retainage terms are explicit

- Insurance and bonding coverage aligned

- Dispute resolution clearly outlined

- Proposal assumptions documented

Chapter Conclusion

Your Contract Defines Your Project Risk

Project success depends heavily on contract management. Carefully negotiated contracts yield fewer claims, better relationships, and healthier margins. Effective risk management begins with precise, intentional contract language. Make sure your contracts protect you rather than harm you.

"Between stimulus and response there is a space. In that space is our power to choose our response." – **Viktor E. Frankl**

PART V – IDENTIFYING RISK DURING THE DESIGN AND PRECONSTRUCTION PHASE

CHAPTER 13

RISK MANAGEMENT IN DESIGN AND PRECONSTRUCTION

Chapter Foreword

If the proposal phase risks plant the seeds, the design and preconstruction phases determine whether those risks flourish or are effectively controlled. During this critical period, project vision transitions into actionable plans, budgets solidify, and construction professionals begin addressing how to build the designed structures. However, design-phase risks are often neglected or underestimated and treated as solely the architect's responsibility, an oversight that frequently proves costly.

Design gaps do not announce themselves. They appear later as change orders, delays, and claims, when they are most expensive to fix.

In reality, most downstream risks, such as schedule delays, change orders, and coordination failures, originate here. Effective risk management during design and preconstruction requires early engagement, proactive questioning, and rigorous collaboration to establish strong safeguards before construction begins.

"You don't lead by pointing and telling people some place to go. You lead by going to that place and making a case." – Ken Kesey

Understanding the Dangers of Design-Phase Risk

Design-phase risk is particularly challenging because it:

- Emerges early but impacts projects significantly later.

- Frequently hides within assumptions or ambiguous details.

- Becomes exponentially more expensive to fix once construction begins.

Unaddressed flaws in specifications or details can cost millions during construction, underscoring the importance of meticulous documentation and cross-disciplinary collaboration early on.

Critical Risk Categories and Mitigation Strategies

1. Incomplete or Ambiguous Drawings

- Missing dimensions, unclear elevations, or inconsistent references.

  - Mitigation:

    - Structured drawing reviews and "Red Flag" logs.

    - RFI forecasting.

    - Regular coordination meetings at key design milestones.

2. Scope Gaps

- Undefined work scopes between general contractors (GC) and trades.

- Items overlooked during design (e.g., fire-stopping, anchors).

  - Mitigation:

    - Develop and maintain a comprehensive scope gap matrix.

    - Conduct scope alignment meetings before finalizing pricing.

    - Use responsibility matrices across all disciplines.

3. Unvetted Value Engineering (VE)

- Hasty VE solutions that overlook quality and coordination.

- Changing facade elements without analyzing structural implications.

  - Mitigation:

    - Implement design review committees with both CM and architect input.

    - Monitor VE changes through risk-adjusted pricing and constructability assessments.

    - Require thorough cost-impact analyses for proposed VE items.

4. Permit and Regulatory Risks

- Delays from permit approvals due to design noncompliance.

- Overlooked fire safety, ADA, or environmental compliance issues.

  - Mitigation:

    - Early engagement and pre-application meetings with Authorities Having Jurisdiction (AHJ).

    - Independent third-party code consultant reviews.

    - Maintain a detailed permit tracking log integrated with project schedules.

5. Constructability Risks

- Designs challenging or unsafe to build as planned.

- Field sequencing, safety issues, or logistical constraints were overlooked.

  - Mitigation:

    - Conduct constructability reviews by experienced field personnel.

    - Perform clash detection with BIM and Navisworks.

    - Use mock-ups for critical or innovative construction methods.

6. Design Coordination Failures

- MEP and structural conflicts.

- Scope overlaps between consultants.

- Uncoordinated spatial planning (ceilings, shafts, etc.).

  - Mitigation:

    - Regular BIM coordination cycles and milestone reviews.

    - Comprehensive Navisworks model walk-throughs with all stakeholders.

    - Establish discipline-specific "freeze dates" to lock in geometry.

7. Basis of Design and Performance Criteria Gaps

- Equipment performance requirements not defined.

- Redundancy criteria unclear.

- Commissioning requirements vague.

  - Mitigation:

    - Require formal owner sign-off on performance criteria, redundancy levels, and acceptance thresholds prior to procurement or delegated design release.

    - Tie submittal approval, factory testing, and commissioning acceptance directly to documented performance criteria rather than drawings alone.

    - Develop basis of design narrative, performance specification matrix, and commissioning plan alignment at 60 percent design.

SCOPE GAP RISK POINTS IN THE PROJECT LIFE CYCLE

SCOPE GAP RISK HOTSPOTS (INTERFACES)

1. PLANNING ↔ PRECON

- Unverified assumptions (capacities, code, program intent)
- Conceptual elemerts treated as fixed without validation
- Lack of documented basis-of-design requirem

2. PRECON ↔ DESIGN

- Ambiguous performance vs prescriptive specifications
- Designers providing 'example models' mistaken as required equipment

3. DESIGN ↔ PROCUREMENT

- Delivery sequence vs installaliation sequence misalignment
- Supplier assumptions on unloading times and site access
- Inadequate labelling, staging, or storage planning

4. PROCUREMENT ↔ CONSTRUCTION

- Interfaces between trades (e.g., steel ↔ concrete ↔ façade anchors
- Design responsibilities not clearly assigned
- Missing detailling or connection geometry during shop drawing phase

Scope Gap Analysis: Legal and Practical Exposure

This section is intentionally more technical and is included as a reference for claims planning and responsibility mapping

Major capital projects progress through multiple phases: planning, design, procurement, construction, and commissioning. Although each phase is often assigned to different professionals or contracting entities, the law does not treat these stages as isolated. The industry standard of care requires continuity, coordination, and reasonable efforts to integrate work across disciplines. Where that integration fails, "scope gaps" arise, exposing owners, designers, contractors, and suppliers to significant risk, including design defects, delays, cost growth, and disputes regarding responsibility. The examples below illustrate how such gaps are created and why they routinely become the subject of claims.

1. Planning vs. Design

A common source of disputes arises when the planning consultant and the architect proceed under differing assumptions regarding code compliance, design criteria, or owner expectations.

For example, a planning consultant may prepare a conceptual program for a civic building and include illustrative sketches of a prominent architectural element, such as a grand staircase. If the planner assumes that the architect will verify code compliance during design development, while the architect assumes the planner's work already incorporates such compliance, a latent error is created.

Undocumented assumptions concerning room capacities, egress requirements, or other code-driven variables can materially alter downstream design obligations. Likewise, when early conceptual elements are treated as fixed "artistic" components, an architect may be reluctant to modify them even when required by applicable codes. These misunderstandings create classic planning-to-design scope gaps that can expose both parties to allegations of professional negligence.

2. Design vs. Construction

Scope gaps also arise in the handoff between design professionals and trade contractors. It is common for mechanical, electrical, plumbing, and fire protection systems to be shown only diagrammatically, with the expectation that specialty contractors will produce detailed shop drawings and final equipment selections.

However, when an architect includes illustrative information, such as a specific model of a water heater intended only to convey a desired capacity, contractors may interpret this information as a mandatory, prescriptive requirement. Suppose a contractor installs such equipment without independent analysis or evaluation of alternatives. In that case, the owner may later claim that the design professional exceeded its intended role or that the contractor failed to exercise appropriate professional judgment. This blurring of responsibility is a textbook design-to-construction scope gap.

3. Contractor vs. Contractor

Multiple contractors working concurrently creates another frequent point of contention. Consider a structure where:

- A structural steel contractor details the frame

- A concrete contractor places floor slab

- A façade contractor designs and installs a window wall

Between these scopes exists a critical interface: the structural anchors required to attach the façade system to the frame through the slab. If no party is expressly assigned responsibility for coordinating or detailing this interface, the project may experience delays, redesign, or claims for extra compensation.

Trade Scope & Responsibility Gaps

(The most common claim origin)

☐ Final equipment connections clearly assigned (MEP vs vendor vs GC)
☐ Miscellaneous metals scope defined (supports, frames, embeds, access)
☐ Fire protection design responsibility identified (design vs delegated)
☐ Firestopping and fire caulking explicitly assigned by trade
☐ Vibration isolation, housekeeping pads, and equipment bases assigned
☐ Sleeves, embeds, and penetrations clearly allocated
☐ Controls and integration responsibility defined

Common Failure:
Everyone assumes someone else is doing it.

Cross-Discipline Coordination Gaps

(Where drawings "line up" but scopes don't)

☐ MEP clearances verified above ceilings and in shafts
☐ Structural openings coordinated and detailed
☐ Architectural finishes aligned with MEP requirements
☐ Drainage, slopes, and access coordinated
☐ Conflicts resolved in design, not deferred to construction
☐ BIM coordination milestones completed and documented

Common Failure:
Drawings coordinate geometry, not responsibility.

Materials & Specification Gaps

(Compliance vs availability)

☐ Material specifications coordinated across disciplines
☐ Conflicting material standards resolved
☐ Long-lead items identified and aligned with schedule
☐ Approved equals process clearly defined
☐ Substitution approval authority and timing defined

Common Failure:

Materials meet one spec and violate another.

A well-known example occurred on the Seattle Central Library project, where the exterior's diamond-grid façade required highly sophisticated geometric coordination. Neither the design team nor the steel detailer presumed responsibility for reconciling the pattern across the building's irregular geometry. When construction commenced, it became evident that no party had addressed this issue, resulting in significant confusion, delay, and the need for specialized computational modeling. Such situations often lead to disputes regarding who bore contractual responsibility for design coordination.

4. Contractor vs. Supplier

Procurement introduces its own set of legal risks. Contractors rely on suppliers to fabricate, package, sequence, and deliver materials in a manner consistent with the construction schedule and site constraints. Even when commercial terms such as ICC Incoterms allocate shipping risk, they do not resolve issues such as:

- Required unloading times

- Staging space

- Delivery sequencing

- Inspection protocols

- Responsibility for packaging or labeling

Delivery Term	Delivery Point	Risk Transfers When	Responsible Party After Transfer	Key Construction Risk Note
EXW (Ex Works)	Supplier factory or warehouse	Equipment made available for pickup	Buyer / Contractor / Owner	Highest buyer risk; common source of damage and delay claims
FCA (Free Carrier)	Named carrier location	Equipment handed to buyer-designated carrier	Buyer	Cleaner than EXW, but buyer assumes early transit risk
FOB (Free On Board)	Loaded on vessel at export port	Loaded onto vessel	Buyer	Frequently misused domestically; port must be defined
CFR (Cost and Freight)	Export port (risk), destination port (cost)	Loaded at export port	Buyer	Seller pays freight, buyer still carries transit risk
CIF (Cost, Insurance, Freight)	Export port (risk), destination port (cost + insurance)	Loaded at export port	Buyer	Insurance often minimal unless contractually increased
DAP (Delivered at Place)	Named site, yard, or warehouse	Arrival at location, before unloading	Supplier until delivery	Unloading responsibility must be clearly assigned
DPU (Delivered at Place Unloaded)	Named location, unloaded	After unloading	Supplier	Best clarity for owners; minimal logistics ambiguity
DDP (Delivered Duty Paid)	Final destination, fully cleared	Final delivery	Supplier	Customs and tax exposure often underestimated

Delivery Point, Risk Transfer, and Responsibility

Definition: ICC Incoterms® are standardized international trade rules published by the International Chamber of Commerce that define the responsibilities of buyers and sellers for the delivery of goods, including the allocation of cost, risk of loss, insurance, customs clearance, and transfer of title at specific points in the supply chain.

Suppose a supplier expects immediate unloading upon arrival, while a contractor assumes flexible delivery windows. In that case, conflicting expectations may lead to delay claims, standby charges, or disputes regarding who caused the disruption. These gaps in procurement logistics commonly evolve into contractor-supplier disagreements over entitlement and compensation.

Pro Tip: Add this sentence after any delivery definition:

Delivery terms govern logistics and risk of loss only and do not transfer responsibility for performance, specification compliance, warranties, or schedule obligations unless expressly stated.

5. Construction vs. Commissioning

Commissioning activities present additional exposure if not coordinated with ongoing construction. Many systems, such as HVAC, security controls, audiovisual components, and specialized industrial equipment, cannot be adequately tested until the building is substantially complete and permanent power is available.

- These systems often require staged commissioning, such as:

- Factory or pre-installation inspection

- Stand-alone functional testing

- Integrated systems testing

If commissioning activities are not sequenced with interior finishes, power availability, or other ongoing work, they can result in damage, rework, or delays. Projects involving proprietary or highly specialized equipment face heightened risk because the supplier may need to mobilize multiple times. Failure to clearly assign responsibility for coordinating these activities routinely results in claims related to schedule impacts and scope misalignment.

6. Managing and Mitigating Scope Gaps

While scope gaps pose significant legal and practical risks, they are manageable with proactive measures. Effective mitigation generally requires:

Comprehensive Interface Planning

Each phase of the project design development, procurement, fabrication, installation, and commissioning must be analyzed to identify interfaces where responsibilities could overlap or fall between parties.

Documented Communication and Alignment

Frequent, documented exchanges of information among project participants reduce ambiguity. Contractual provisions may require such coordination, but they do not substitute for genuine, continuous communication.

Clear Assignment of Responsibility

Contracts should explicitly identify which party is responsible for each interface, approval, submittal, or design element. Ambiguous scopes are a primary driver of claims.

Collaborative Problem Resolution

No single entity can prevent all gaps in isolation. Owners, designers, contractors, and suppliers share an obligation to coordinate their work and resolve issues promptly to avoid impacts that later become claims.

Design GAP Analysis Checklist

Identifying Risk Before It Becomes a Claim

Purpose:

To identify scope, performance, and interface gaps during design that routinely result in change orders, delays, rework, and disputes.

1. Existing Conditions & Capacity Gaps

(Assumptions vs reality)

☐ Existing utility capacities verified against new demand (power, water, gas, sewer, cooling)

☐ Available electrical service confirmed (voltage, amperage, short-circuit rating)

☐ Cooling capacity validated for new loads (chilled water, condenser water, airside)

☐ Fire water supply tested for pressure and flow (not assumed)

☐ Structural capacity confirmed for new equipment loads

☐ Existing systems compatibility reviewed (controls, BMS, SCADA, communications)

☐ Field verification performed – not desk-based record drawings only

Common Failure:

Design assumes capacity exists. Construction discovers it does not.

2. Basis of Design & Performance Gaps

(What the system must actually do)

☐ Basis of Design (BOD) narrative issued and aligned across all disciplines

☐ Performance criteria defined for all major systems (not just equipment cut sheets)

☐ Redundancy requirements clearly stated (N, N+1, 2N)

☐ Operating conditions defined (ambient, part-load, future expansion)

☐ Commissioning and acceptance criteria explicitly defined

☐ Testing responsibility and success thresholds documented

Common Failure:

Systems meet drawings but fail performance expectations.

3. Utility & Infrastructure Interface Gaps

(Who provides what, and to where)

☐ Utility point of connection clearly defined and shown

☐ Responsibility for off-site vs on-site utility work assigned

☐ Temporary utilities addressed (power, water, heat, cooling)

☐ Booster pumps, pressure regulating valves, or transformers identified if required

☐ Metering and utility company requirements incorporated

☐ Shutdowns, tie-ins, and outages coordinated and approved

Common Failure:

No one owns the gap between the utility and the building.

Constructability Review Basics

Tool Insert:

Constructability Review Checklist (Reference Use)

Use this checklist during 30%, 60%, and 90% design reviews to catch coordination, specification, and interface gaps before they become field changes.

PROJECT MANUAL

- Is the strategy for submittal processing, quality control, testing, inspections, and mock-ups suitable and adapted to the subject project?

Standards

- Are appropriate standards of performance, quality, and testing cited?

- Do they correspond to what is specified and drawn?

- Are they current?

- Examples: UL standards, FM standards, ASTM standards?

Products

- Do all of the specified products match what is drawn or specified?

- Examples: catalog numbers, model numbers, and processes.

- New Systems, Assemblies, Products unfamiliar to the local market or designer.

- Will unwanted procurement delays result?

- Are the submittal requirements reasonable?

- Are the specifications formatted according to accepted standards of practice, such as CSI's Manual of Practice, Master Format, Section Format, and Page Format?

- Are the warranty strategies coordinated, transparent, and reasonable? When exposed to the intended uses and environments, such as traffic, solar radiation, thermal cycles, and moisture, will the completed construction achieve the life expected by the Owner?

- Is there boilerplate content that has not been tailored to the subject project?

- Are there Sole source and/or proprietary specifications?

- Will substitutes to proprietary specifications be accepted?

- Has the relevant knowledge gained from problems recently experienced on previous projects been carried forward to the subject project?

DRAWINGS

General

- Are all of the views needed to construct provided, such as plans, elevations, sections, schedules, riser diagrams, and details?

- Are all the necessary supplementary documents provided to define the relevant existing conditions, for example, land surveys, geotechnical, and environmental?

- Do all extensive scale plan views match the smaller scaled views?

- Is the layout and content of each sheet clear, concise, and makes sense?

- Is there adequate cross-referencing?

- Is all the built-in equipment scheduled? Are all of the necessary rough ins indicated?

- Have the subconsultant disciplines been combed for unsightly issues? For example, what exposed work should an architectural finish conceal?

Title Blocks, Scales, Symbols, Abbreviations, Sheet

- Are all symbols and abbreviations provided in the appropriate legends?

- Are all scales correctly shown?

- Are the title blocks complete and current?

- Is the drawing-layering, sequencing, and numbering in conformance with CSI's Uniform Drawing System [UDS]?

- Have all of the *drawings by* and *checked by* blocks been initialed? Have the drawings that are initialed been carefully checked?

Geometry [Dimensions, Angles, Radii, Fixed Positions & Benchmarks, etc.]

- Have all of the dimensions, angles, radii, and fixed benchmarks been established?

- Does the above geometric information translate to all of the subconsultant's sheets, where relevant?

- Will all of the construction systems and assemblies fit within the available spaces, leaving all of the necessary clearances and tolerances for operational, maintenance, and replacement access?

- Are the site grade elevations, finish floor elevations, and building location footprints coordinated with the other disciplines?

- Are the dimensional strings as simple as possible? Do they all *close,* or can they be easily *parity* checked against overall dimensions? Are the start points and end points of every dimension unmistakably clear?

- Have all drawings that show a graphic scale been drawn at that scale?

- Will alternate or approved substitutes also fit when the details provided have been developed around a specific manufacturer?

Civil

- Are all relevant controlling datum/benchmarks, property lines, setbacks, easements, rights of way, legal incumbrances, relevant existing conditions, existing and proposed contours, existing and proposed inverts, and limits of construction been indicated?

- Has the electrical engineer's electrical site plan been coordinated with the civil engineering site plans, landscape plans, and profiles?

- Are all of the primary utilities shown, connected, and coordinated on the MEP documents?

- Do all pipes and structures appear reasonably sized?

- Are all profiles coordinated with the plan views? Are all relevant utilities shown on profile sheets where they run close or cross each other?

- Do all exposed surfaces have positive drainage to move water away from potential incursion zones and towards catchments or drain locations?

Structural

- Are all the relevant *primary* structural elements shown, sized, scheduled, detailed, and coordinated to the extent necessary to construct, for example:

Substructure

- Underpinning?

- Sheeting and shoring?

- Footings, piers?

- Below-grade walls?

On-Grade

- Slabs on grade, slab thickenings, grade beams, depressed slabs, troughs, pads?

Superstructure

- Columns?

- Girders?

- Beams?

- Decks?

Secondary structural elements

- Bearing plates?

- Lintels?

- Bracing?

- Bridging?

- Joints, clips, connections, etc.?

Surface Treatments

- Fireproofing?

- Waterproofing, coatings, sealers?

Other Structural

- Do all of the structural perimeter overhangs match the architectural, for example, roof overhangs and projections?

- Are all primary utility assemblies coordinated with all below-grade structural foundation and wall conditions?

- Have all of the relevant equipment loads and supports been structurally accommodated and detailed?

- Will the expansion and control joint designs and locations handle the differential movements? Are they coordinated with all the other affected disciplines?

- Shaft and chase penetrations through floors can affect many other design disciplines. Are all penetrations coordinated with all the other affected disciplines?

- Are all structural elements, such as footings and columns, correctly designated and scheduled?

Architectural

General

- Do the interior and exterior functions, massing, spatial organizations, circulation, future expansions, appearance, and quality levels address the programmatic requirements?

Exterior Enclosure

- Primary Enclosure Systems and Assemblies: identified and coordinated?

- Examples: Masonry, Precast Concrete, EIFS, Glass & Glazing

- Secondary Enclosure Elements: identified and coordinated?

- Examples: Precast concrete trim, lintels, spandrel beams, knee braces, etc.?

Exterior Enclosure Moisture Control Systems and Assemblies

- Identified and coordinated?

- Above Grade Examples: Roofing, waterproofing, damproofing, condensation controls, architectural sheet metals and flashings, weeps, caulking, glazing, drainage to daylight?

- Below Grade Examples: drainage board or gravel, foundation drains, sump pits, French drains?

Exterior Enclosure Thermal Control Systems and Assemblies

- Identified and coordinated?

- Examples: Insulation, caulking, and glazing?

Exterior Enclosure Connections and Details

- Interior ceiling and wall locations coordinated with window wall framing?

- Sill and head flashing?

- Coatings, priming, galvanizing?

- Joining of dissimilar materials?

- Finish hardware?

- Tolerances and clearances?

Shafts and Chases

Will the shafts and chases accommodate all the intended assemblies?

Finishes

- Scope, limits [horizontal and vertical], bulkheads, transitions, and room numbers indicated and coordinated on the Finish Schedules, Reflected Ceiling Plans, Interior and Exterior Elevations?

- Are all finishes, special coatings, surface treatments, and colors identified and scheduled?

Casework, Built-in Equipment & Specialties

- Is the scope fully indicated?

- Will it fit as drawn?

- Is all of the necessary information provided, for example, the interior/exterior surfaces, hardware, details, specifications, and schedules?

Doors, Frames & Hardware

- Is all of the finish HW indicated, specified, and coordinated?

- Are doors, frames, and HW assemblies coordinated with required undercuts [to permit air flow], electrified hardware, door security requirements, and code requirements?

Coordinated Imbeds, Anchors, Supports, Blocking

- Are all concrete embedded items fully identified and specified?

- Are all the necessary connection details, anchors, hardware, supports, backing, and blocking coordinated, detailed, and specified?

Conveyance

- Are all the necessary dimensional and rough-in requirements indicated and coordinated?

- Is there a disconnect required at the elevator machine room?

- Is there a shunt trip required at the elevator shaft?

- Are the pit requirements fully detailed, for example, rough-in requirements, waterproofing, drains, sump pumps, and lights?

- Is the door circuitry coordinated with the life safety systems?

Mechanical

General

- Is the design a complete system, from supply connection to terminus?

- Are all sizes provided?

- Do all sizes appear reasonable?

- Do they match all the riser diagrams provided?

- Does each component fit with everything else occupying the same volume? Have the necessary thicknesses of insulation, jackets, and housings been considered?

- Have repeating problems of the past been debugged, such as coordination of the starters, disconnects, interlock wiring, smoke detectors, color-coding, and stenciling responsibilities?

- Do all mechanical and architectural reflected ceiling plans match? For example, are the registers, grills, and equipment located in the same place mechanically and architecturally?

- Are all sleeve locations coordinated with concrete?

- Are the composite coordination drawings specified?

- Has the composite coordination drawing - lead trade - been specified?

HVAC

- Are the quantities and sizes provided of all equipment, fixtures, piping, ductwork, controls, special accessories, etc.?

- Is the duct outside sizes, including insulation, also indicated to ensure the insulation will fit?

- Are all the required fire dampers indicated in the correct locations?

- If there are any large duct runs over bathrooms with ceiling-mounted toilet partitions. Have these conflicts been coordinated?

- Are the control sequences, such as those pertaining to the kitchen exhaust fans, coordinated with the fire alarm system and the local authority? Have the necessary diagrams been provided?

- Have the necessary riser diagrams been provided?

- All equipment & fixtures scheduled?

- Does the Site Plan indicate the relevant location, sizes & connections of, for ex., cooling towers, fuel oil storage system, etc.?

- Interior exhaust fans and roof fans.

Plumbing

- Are the quantities and sizes provided of all equipment, fixtures, piping, special accessories, etc.?

- Are floor and roof drains located and dimensioned?

- Are waste line clean-outs spaced per code?

- Has the roof overflow system been correctly indicated?

- Has a backflow preventer at the incoming water service been correctly indicated?

- Has floor drain trap priming been clearly specified?

- Are all valves sized and shown?

- Have the necessary riser diagrams been provided?

- Does the Site Plan indicate the relevant location, sizes & connections of, for ex., fuel oil storage system, etc.?

Sprinkler

- Are the quantities and sizes provided of all equipment, fixtures, piping, special accessories, etc.?

- Do sprinkler drops and heads conflict with any other construction?

- Have fire and jockey pump assemblies been shown and coordinated?

- Have the necessary riser diagrams been provided?

- Does the Site Plan indicate relevant location, sizes & connections?

Electrical

- Has a layout of all the relevant electric panels and equipment rooms been provided?

- Are the voltage and phasing requirements shown and coordinated with those required by the manufacturers / suppliers / contractors of the mechanical systems, electrical systems, fire alarm system, security systems, and other special systems?

- Do the fixture quantities differ between architectural and electrical engineering drawings?

- Has the missing device circuitry been checked for?

- Is the required rating of the fire alarm strobe provided?

- Are all of the floor boxes indicated and accurately specified?

- Are the panels and electrical switch gear reflected in both the plan views and riser diagrams and coordinated with the other disciplines?

- Have the necessary contacts with the power and communications primary service utilities been made? Is the relevant information reflected on the contract documents? Example: power company, telephone company, plus any specialized communications firms such as Cable TV, wireless, satellite?

- Have all of the special electrical requirements been adequately shown, for example, electrified door hardware assemblies?

- Have all of the necessary empty conduits been indicated, such as the conduit required for the elevator fire alarm and controls?

- Have any electrical panels been recessed into rated walls without the necessary rated protection?

- Are controls, starters, and EMS protocols coordinated?

Life Safety

General

- Is the design compliant with all relevant codes, standards, and regulations? For example, most projects must simultaneously conform to numerous layers of Federal, state, and local codes and regulations, plus other standards that may be included by incorporation.

- Is there adequate coordination between the owner, design professionals, contractors, and the relevant governing code officials, including the officials responsible for enforcing zoning, site, building, transportation, utilities, health, etc.?

- Have all the necessary research and coordination with governing authorities, such as historic, architectural, and community review boards, been completed?

- Do all of the cited standards match what is shown on the drawings or specified? For example, UL standards, FM standards, ASTM standards?

- Have all of the contractor-provided jurisdictional permit fees and labor to process been indicated?

Fire Separations, Protections, and Retardancies

Are all of the following identified where applicable and in conformance with the applicable codes?

- Wall, floor, ceiling, and roof ratings?

- Vertical egress, shaft, and chase ratings?

- Horizontal egress ratings?

- Spray-on fireproofing and other fireproofing protections of specific elements?

- Door ratings [labels], closers, wire glass, or listed fire-rated glass?

- Smoke controls, such as smoke hatches, compartments?

- Correlated MEP ratings and enclosures, such as at flues and exhaust stacks?

- Carpet, wallcovering, and drape retardancies?

Discharge and paths of egress

Are all of the following vertical and horizontal discharge paths of egress efficient and clear?

- Egress loading units?

- Egress identification signs, etc.?

- Egress lighting?

- Stair and railing designs?

- Number of exits?

- Exit widths?

- Lighting?

- Dead-end corridor lengths?

- Travel distances?

ADA

Are all of the following in conformance with the applicable codes?

- Building Entrance?

- Parking?

- Ramps?

- Vision-impaired items?

- Signs?

- Toilet room clearances, stall door widths, door swing, and five-foot radii, plumbing fixtures?

Primary Utilities

- Have all jurisdictionally adopted codes and standards of practice pertaining to primary utilities been adequately reflected?

- Have all of the contractor-provided primary utility fees, connection fees, availability fees, and labor to process been indicated?

Interdisciplinary Coordination

- Are the design disciplines coordinated as necessary to complete the project?

- Refer to *Geometry [dimensions, angles, radii, etc.]* above, regarding systems and assemblies fitting within the available spaces.

- Have equipment weights, noise, vibration, heat, and fumes been managed to the degree the Owner anticipates?

- Do all the drawing backgrounds of the various disciplines match?

- Do all details on the drawings correspond with what has been specified and vice versa?

- Do the documents reflect all of the necessary trade interfaces? For example, does the electrical design provide the proper voltage and phase to the correct location of every mechanical device? Has all the necessary concealed blocking been provided for subsequent trades requiring it to complete their work?

- Have all interstitial spaces, ceiling spaces, shafts, wet stacks, chases, and furred spaces been appropriately sized to accommodate all current and future systems? Has adequate access been provided?

- Are all of the necessary MEP hangers and supports provided?

- Are all concealed, cast-in, and embedded items indicated and coordinated?

- Has there been a review to verify that there is no incomplete, incorrect, or circular intra or interdisciplinary referencing?

Best Practices for Managing Design Phase Risks

Design Stage Gates: Formal checkpoints at design milestones (30%, 60%, 90%, IFC) to review:

- Document completeness.

- Pending design decisions.

- Risk scores and outstanding RFIs.

- Alignment with budget and schedule.

Each gate should produce a documented release decision, open issues log, and assigned closures.

Lessons Learned Check List

(Ask these questions explicitly)

☐ Where did similar projects experience change orders?
☐ What scope items were disputed last time and why?
☐ What was assumed "by others" on prior jobs?

☐ What was approved but later rejected?
☐ Where did commissioning fail previously?

Pro Tip:
If it caused a claim before, assume it will again unless addressed.

Guidelines for a Design Checklist

A Design Checklist is created to align the client expectation with the GC and the designer on the outcome of each package and or deliverables. In addition, the purpose is to eliminate any confusion regardless of the selected designer.

The Construction Manager may wish to consider including this checklist as part of the RFP (Request for Proposal) so the design bidder is aware of the expectations for each design milestone so that they price their effort accordingly.

These checklists will provide the customer with an understanding of what the 30% and 60% Design Deliverables should include. The 60% design deliverables should be close to a completed package. The last portion of design (60% to 90%) will require minimal revision changes, which can include working out some routing, and or implementing comments from the 60% design review.

Each design package is unique, and no two projects are the same. The idea behind this checklist is that is to remain a live document and will require tailoring for each project.

An example of a typical 30% Schematic design checklist.

Disc	Level of Completeness, Schematic Design	Applicable? (Y,N)	Done? (Y,N)	Notes and Comments
CSA	**ARCHITECTURAL**			
CSA	Title Sheet 90% Complete with All Drawings identified in an Index, Code Data, Sign Off Block; etc.	Y		
CSA	Code Information Sheets covering Project Scope Of Work. 50% Complete.	Y		
CSA	Building Elevations necessary to show principle elements, general arrangement identified.	Y		
CSA	Sections necessary to show principle elements, general arrangement identified.	Y		
CSA	Preliminary Door Hardware and Door Schedule (Identify standard schedule items. Identify any non-standard items that require hardware consultants)	Y		
CSA	Building Footprint & Ext Walls	Y		
CSA	Exterior Materials Selection	Y		
CSA	Floor & Roof Elevations	Y		
CSA	Prelim Code Analysis & AM&M list complete	Y		
CSA	Layout of building trenches & sumps	Y		
CSA	Location of Interior Hardwalls	Y		
CSA	Specification TOC with all specifications required for pkg scope	Y		
CSA	Dwgs, data sheets, etc. match POR criteria and CMD.	Y		
CSA	Summary of Work (Spec Section 01010) substantially complete for pkg scope content	Y		
CSA	Floor Plans - For each floor, show complete field verified, principal elements and areas, such as equipment and clearances, entrances, exits, stairs, cores, and equipment areas, structural bays, interior walls and partitions, fire rated walls, and doors, fire stairs, exits and exit-ways, mechanical and electrical equipment rooms, shafts, closets, etc. that are respective to the project. Show enough surrounding floor plan area for evaluation of adjacencies and impacts. Separate Drawings for Demolition and Installation Scope. 30% Complete Overall.	Y		
CSA	Composite equipment layouts for floor plans and roof plans with all discipline proposed equipment locations and proposed access. (compilation of the other discipline equipment dwgs/locations in one).	Y		
CSA	Equipment and Tool move in / move out paths shall be specified from point of origin to final destination. The design shall note any possible obstructions.	Y		
CSA	**CIVIL**			
CSA	Specification TOC with all specifications required for pkg scope	Y		
CSA	Site Plans - The site plans shall show all buildings, auxiliary structures and pertinent existing utilities (above- and underground) as well as preliminary layouts	Y		
CSA	Plan locators of all support elements, critical details and sections, specification list, critical details & sections, loading dock ramps, critical spot elevations, critical storm water system inverts	Y		
CSA	**STRUCTURAL**			
CSA	Specification TOC with all specifications required for pkg scope	Y		
CSA	Grid lines, column locations, wall locations, bracing/shearwall locations established.	Y		
CSA	Geotechnical report complete	Y		
CSA	Foundation plan(s) indicating preliminary foundation sizes	Y		
CSA	Floor plan(s) indicate extent of gravity framing. Depth of framing indicated on plans. Preliminary trench locations identified	Y		
CSA	Roof plan(s) indicate extent of gravity framing. Depth of framing indicated on plans.	Y		
CSA	Live load and vibration plans established	Y		
CSA	Preliminary analysis of new gravity and lateral framing complete, including input from vibration consultant as necessary. Calcs submitted to Intel. (Preliminary could be based on documented assumed weights of equipment)	Y		

Disc	Level of Completeness, Schematic Design	Applicable? (Y,N)	Done? (Y,N)	Notes and Comments
CSA	Preliminary analysis of existing gravity and lateral framing complete, including input from vibration consultant as necessary. Calcs submitted to Intel.	Y		
CSA	Where required by IMDS, provide preliminary lateral calculations to seismic peer reviewer.	Y		
CSA	Site structures (pads, pipe racks, etc.) shown on plans, along with preliminary foundation sizes.	Y		
M	**MECHANICAL**			
M	Specifications required for package identified in a Table of Contents.	Y		
M	Preliminary project P&IDs based on POR created, with initial markups included.	Y		
M	Preliminary projectprocess flow diagrams based on POR created, with initial markups included.	Y		
M	Preliminary equipment / floor plans for all sectors included, showing major equipment	Y		
M	Preliminary piping plans for all sectors included, showing major equipment Piping partial plans and section details in progress.	Y		
M	Preliminary fire protection plans for all sectors included. Isometric drawings and details not required at this stage.	Y		
M	Preliminary detail drawings included, many will be works in progress.	Y		
M	Calculations (heat load, chilled water, etc.) complete.	Y		
M	Preliminary Pipeflo modeling complete for major equipment only.	Y		
M	Utility Capacity Tracker in progress, major systems information included.	Y		
M	Preliminary Master Equipment List with limited information included.	Y		
P	**PROCESS MECHANICAL**			
P	Specifications required for package identified in a Table of Contents.	Y		
P	Preliminary project P&IDs based on POR created, with initial markups included.	Y		
P	Preliminary projectprocess flow diagrams based on POR created, with initial markups included.	Y		
P	Preliminary equipment / floor plans for all sectors included, showing major equipment	Y		
P	Preliminary piping plans for all sectors included, showing major equipment Piping partial plans and section details in progress.	Y		
P	Preliminary fire protection plans for all sectors included. Isometric drawings and details not required at this stage.	Y		
P	Preliminary detail drawings included, many will be works in progress.	Y		
P	Calculations (heat load, chilled water, etc.) complete.	Y		
P	Preliminary Pipeflo modeling complete for major equipment only.	Y		
P	Utility Capacity Tracker in progress, major systems information included.	Y		
P	Preliminary Master Equipment List with limited information included.	Y		
P	**PROCESS (Water & Waste)**			
P	Specifications required for package identified in a Table of Contents.	Y		
P	Preliminary project P&IDs based on POR created, with initial markups included.	Y		
P	Preliminary equipment / floor plans for all sectors included, showing major equipment. Containment areas and associated traffic plans for area. Identify equipment access zone in layouts. Ensure adequate Move In Move Out paths for all locations on plans	Y		
P	Preliminary piping plans for all sectors included, showing major equipment Piping partial plans and section details in progress. For all gravity lines identify all routing paths needed to meet slope requirements	Y		
P	Preliminary detail drawings included, many will be works in progress.	Y		
P	Preliminary Pipeflo modeling complete for major equipment only.	Y		
P	Utility Capacity Tracker in progress, major systems information included.	Y		
P	Preliminary Master Equipment List with limited information included.	Y		
P	Calculations and utility requirements identified for all supporting disciplines including Electrical, HVAC, I&C, LSS etc..)	Y		
P	Summary of Work (Spec Section 01010) substantially complete for pkg scope content	Y		

P	**PROCESS (Bulk Gas)**			
P	Specifications required for package identified in a Table of Contents.	Y		
P	Preliminary project P&IDs based on POR created, with initial markups included.	Y		
P	Preliminary equipment / floor plans for all sectors included, showing major equipment. Containment areas and associated traffic plans for area. Identify equipment access zone in layouts. Ensure adequate Move In Move Out paths for all locations on plans	Y		
P	Preliminary piping plans for all sectors included, showing major equipment Piping partial plans and section details in progress. For all gravity lines identify all routing paths needed to meet slope requirements	Y		
P	Preliminary detail drawings included, many will be works in progress.	Y		
P	Preliminary Pipeflo modeling complete for major equipment only.	Y		
P	Utility Capacity Tracker in progress, major systems information included.	Y		
P	Preliminary Master Equipment List with limited information included.	Y		
P	Calculations and utility requirements identified for all supporting disciplines including Electrical, HVAC, I&C, LSS etc..)	Y		
P	Summary of Work (Spec Section 01010) substantially complete for pkg scope content	Y		
E	**ELECTRICAL**			
E	Specifications required for package identified in a Table of Contents.	Y		
E	Preliminary one-line diagrams with major equipment shown. No panel schedules.	Y		
E	Preliminary lightning protection plan drawings included.	Y		
E	Preliminary cable tray plan drawings included.	Y		
E	Preliminary underground plans, with main ductbank conduits only included.	Y		
E	Preliminary power plan drawings for all sectors included. Equipment identified by other disciplines shown with circuiting.	Y		
E	Preliminary equipment plan drawings for all sectors. Major equipment located with move in aisles identified.	Y		
E	Preliminary grounding plan drawings for all sectors, showing underground grid, connections to building steel.	Y		
E	Preliminary lighting plan drawings for all sectors, with 80% of fixtures shown. Switching locations shown. Circuiting not shown.	Y		
E	Preliminary luminaire schedule based on POR.	Y		
E	Preliminary short circuit, load flow, voltage drop studies included for equipment on one-lines.	Y		
E	Preliminary device coordination study included for equipment on one-lines. Protective device types identified, preliminary settings provided.	Y		
E	Preliminary Master Equipment List with limited information included.	Y		
E	Heat tracing identified on P&ID drawings. Plan drawings not expected at this phase.	Y		
E	POR installation details, schematic/wiring diagrams, power monitoring network drawings pulled into project set. Preliminary project specific details included.	Y		
I&C	**I&C**			
I&C	Specifications required for package identified in a Table of Contents	Y		
I&C	Preliminary Master Equipment List with limited information included.	Y		
I&C	Preliminary P&ID's based on POR included, new P&IDs identified.	Y		
I&C	Preliminary network block diagrams included.	Y		
I&C	Instrument Index created. List of non-POR instruments identified.	Y		
I&C	Preliminary Network Cable Schedules (inter-building, inter-panel, intra-panel) with limited information included.	Y		
I&C	Point Management Database (PMD) created for the project.	Y		
I&C	Preliminary control panel drawings (Wiring/Schematic, Dimensions, Component Layout, BOM) for 50% of PLC and Remote I/O panels included.	Y		
I&C	Preliminary equipment and device sector plans for all sectors included. Equipment identified by other disciplines shown.	Y		
I&C	POR or existing site SOOs pulled into project set. Drafts of project SOOs included.	Y		
I&C	POR or existing site SOOs pulled into project set. Drafts of project SOOs included.	Y		
LSS	**LSS**			
LSS	Specifications required for package identified in a Table of Contents	Y		
LSS	Fire Alarm Functional Matrix (MDP) including Legend	Y		
LSS	Preliminary LSS Partial Plans for fire, evacuation, VESDA	Y		
LSS	Format for Fire Alarm device level Action/Reaction Matrices developed.	Y		
LSS		Y		
LSS	Final Equipment Locations proposed/shown for Approval. Supporting discipline driven equipment to be at DD.	Y		
LSS	Preliminary Life Safety System Drawings	Y		
LSS	Preliminary scope of work required electrical, I&C, LSS and IT services	Y		
LSS	Preliminary Underground ductbank routing and manhole locations. Ductbank sections should be included to indicate duct quantity and arrangement.	Y		
LSS	All FCL line items defined and identified on plans to same degree as base line items above.	Y		
LSS	HPM LSS and TAS Tool requirements defined and analyzed against existing capacity.	Y		
LSS	HPM LSS Matrix/SOOs baseline identified	Y		
LSS	Preliminary riser diagrams indicating system configuration and connections to existing site systems shall be provided for each of the following: Public Address System, Fire/Life Safety System, Eyewash and Emergency Shower.	Y		
LSS	Necessary Details to show principle elements, general arrangement.	Y		
LSS	**SECURITY**			
LSS	Specification TOC with all specifications required for pkg scope	Y		
LSS	Dwgs, data sheets, etc. match POR criteria and CMD.	Y		
LSS	Summary of Work (Spec Section 01010) substantially complete for pkg scope content	Y		
LSS	Final Equipment locations proposed for approval by Intel.	Y		
LSS	Preliminary Security and Life Safety System Drawings	Y		
LSS	Preliminary riser diagrams indicating system configuration and connections to existing site systems shall be provided for each of the following:	Y		
LSS	(i) Preliminary controlled access system.	Y		
LSS	Preliminary scope of work required electrical, I&C, LSS and IT services	Y		
LSS	Preliminary Underground ductbank routing and manhole locations. Ductbank sections should be included to indicate duct quantity and arrangement.	Y		
TELE	**TELECOM**			
TELE	Determine Port availability	Y		
TELE	Determine TO saturation	Y		
TELE	Determine cable path - Preliminary, Large bore/cable trays. Not less than 2" dia.	Y		
TELE	Determine Long Lead for primary equipment. Not supporting discipline.	Y		
TELE	Specification TOC with all specifications required for pkg scope	Y		
TELE	Dwgs, data sheets, etc. match POR criteria and matching matrix.	Y		
TELE	Summary of Work (Spec Section 01010) substantially complete for pkg scope content	Y		
TELE	Preliminary Equipment list substantially complete with commissioning document requirement noted. N/A except for new building. Equipment applicable for CR,BCR,SCR, etc...	Y		
TELE	Proposed Equipment locations to be finalized. Not including WAPs	Y		

TELE	Preliminary one-line diagrams indicating system configuration and connections to existing site systems shall be provided for each of the following *four line items* :	Y		
TELE	*(i) Preliminary separate "IT plan drawings indication the location of system components. Also show existing equipment/room to be connected to*	Y		
TELE	*(ii) Preliminary IT and data systems changes, show existing IT/data connections as applicable.*	Y		
TELE	*(iii) Preliminary plan drawings (1/4) = 1' - 0" minimum) showing enlarged detail of the communication rooms and cabinets.*	Y		
TELE	*(iv) Preliminary Telecom plan drawing indicating wireway cable tray, and conduit 2" dia. And larger. .*	Y		
TELE	Preliminary Plan View drawings of building layout and footprints of existing equipment and furniture	Y		
TELE	All FCL line items defined and identified on plans to same degree as base line items above.	Y		
TELE	Preliminary Clear designation of all IT specific rooms and cabinets on Plan view drawings. Including as needed 　CCR – Campus Communications Room 　BCR – Building Communications Room 　SCR – Satellite Communications Room 　SCC – Satellite Communications Closets 　Data Centers 　Conference Rooms – For A/V and Network 　Training Rooms – For A/V and Network	Y		
TELE	Placeholders for Elevation and Detail drawings	Y		
TELE	Non-Detailed One-Line Diagrams	Y		
TELE	*(i) Campus Distribution*	Y		
TELE	*(ii) Vertical Distribution*	Y		
TELE	Necessary Details to show principle elements, general arrangement.	Y		
PSSS	**PSSS**			
PSSS	Specification TOC with all specifications required for pkg scope	Y		
PSSS	Documents (MDPs, Dwgs, data sheets, etc.) match POR criteria and CMD.	Y		
PSSS	Calculations substantially complete except distribution calcs on SG, BSGS, and PCD. BCD distribution calcs are required to be complete based on best known pipe routing.	Y		
PSSS	Summary of Work (Spec Section 01010) substantially complete for pkg scope content	Y		
PSSS	Final Equipment locations proposed for approval by Intel. Submit documentation of Intel approval of locations with review documents.	Y		
PSSS	**Preliminary piping and instrumentation diagrams (P&ID's) using MDPs shall cover the equipment and systems (including any interfaces with existing equipment, heat trace, and systems)** *(the following two lines include additional detail)*	Y		
PSSS	*Preliminary main PSSS systems on a total system basis.*	Y		
PSSS	*PSSS related dampers, valves, piping, and accessories defined.*	Y		
PSSS	Preliminary plan views of all areas of the project with the background views.	Y		
PSSS	The equipment spaces must be laid out with the actual equipment sizes from the base manufacturer for all major pieces of mechanical equipment.	Y		
PSSS	All major maintenance access space, code required clearances, should be provided for and shown at this time. Areas such as maintenance/access spaces should be delineated with dashed lines. All information, which is required for use by other disciplines, shall be shown.	Y		
PSSS	Move in path has been Identified and evaluated. Construction drawings show any demo/relo scope required for move in. If no scope, move in path can be demonstrated other than on the drawings.	Y		

PSSS	Preliminary toxic gas monitoring systems. System analysis completed for both tool and PSSS equipment requirements. System scope direction identified (new, expansion, re-use, demo)	Y		
PSSS	Preliminary BCDS system capacity calculation completed for both tool and PSSS equipment requirements.. Preliminary FIOP/RIO calcs completed. System scope direction defined (expansion of existing, new, reuse, demo)	Y		
PSSS	Preliminary leak detection systems. System analysis completed for both tool under RMF and PSSS room requirements. System scope direction identified (new, expansion, re-use, demo)	Y		
PSSS	Preliminary equipment selections and data cut sheets.	Y		
PSSS	All FCL line items defined and identified on plans to same degree as base line items above.	Y		
PSSS	Panels defined and requirement from other disciplines defined and noted in a table. Drawings indicating type fluid and gases being heat traced with preliminary estimates of total length and wattage.	Y		
PSSS	Any additional items, which have been developed in rough sketch form but have not yet been drafted, shall be submitted in sketch form	Y		
PSSS	Necessary Details to show principle elements, general arrangement.	Y		
BIM	**BIM**			
BIM	Composite Navisworks Model will all applicable Design Models submitted (with Saved ViewPoints for clashes).	Y		
BIM	SD Clash report summary submitted (risk level indicator)	Y		
BIM	CAD Compliance QA check sign-off submitted.	Y		
GEN	**GENERAL**			
GEN	General arrangment plan drawings, section views, etc. showing space planning, future routing zones, etc. 40% complete.	Y		
GEN	Designs from third-party designers and suppliers for vibration analysis, cleanroom ceilings, door hardware, waste skids, and other systems as necessary are sufficiently progressed to support the Project.	Y		

Example of a 30% Design Review Score Card

At the 60% design the drawings and specifications should be sufficiently detailed so that long lead materials can be procured.

At the 90% design the drawings should have the following level of detail.

Disc	Level of completeness, Construction Document Review	Disc	Level of completeness, Construction Document Review
CSA	**ARCHITECTURAL**	E	**ELECTRICAL**
CSA	Code AM &M approved by AHJ	E	Specifications complete and finalized.
CSA	All comments from previous milestone dispositioned	E	One-line diagrams and panel schedules complete and finalized. Circuit requests approved.
CSA	All Documents (Drawings, Specifications and Calculations) 100% Complete	E	Lightning protection plan drawings and details complete and finalized.
CSA	Room ready checklists complete	E	Cable tray plan drawings, details, cable tray "database" complete and finalized.
CSA	**CIVIL**	E	Underground/Ductbank plans complete and finalized, including ductbank section details.
CSA	Foundation Drain Complete with sump details	E	Power plans complete and finalized.
CSA	Rough Grading and Finish Grading Complete with sections at pads.	E	Equipment plans complete and finalized.
CSA	Utility Corridor Systems complete with profiles, details, and sections	E	Grounding plans complete and finalized.
CSA	Final plans, revised final specifications, final details and sections	E	Lighting plans complete and finalized.
CSA	All comments from previous milestone dispositioned	E	Luminaire schedule complete and finalized.
CSA	All Documents (Drawings, Specifications and Calculations) 100% Complete	E	Lighting calculations complete and finalized.
CSA	**STRUCTURAL**	E	Lighting controls complete and finalized.
CSA	Previous design review comments addressed.	E	Short circuit, load flow, voltage drop studies complete and finalized.
CSA	Specifications complete.	E	Device coordination study complete and finalized.
CSA	Foundation plan(s) complete indicating all foundation sizes, schedules, and details.	E	Master Equipment List complete and finalized.
CSA	SOG complete including thickness, reinforcement, edges, depressions, and embeds shown.	E	Heat trace plans/isometric drawings and details complete and finalized.
CSA	Floor plan(s) complete.	E	Heat trace summary table complete and finalized.
CSA	Roof plan(s) complete.	E	Installation details, schematic/wiring diagrams, power monitoring network drawings complete and finalized.
CSA	Elevations and sections complete.	E	Power restart/load shedding plans, electrical SOOs complete and finalized.
CSA	Typical and common details indicated on drawings.	I&C	**I&C**
CSA	Details complete.	I&C	Specifications complete and finalized.
CSA	Analysis of new gravity and lateral framing complete, including final input from vibration consultant as necessary. Cales submitted to Intel.	I&C	Master Equipment List complete and finalized.
CSA	Analysis of existing gravity and lateral framing complete, including final input from vibration consultant as necessary. Cales submitted to Intel.	I&C	P&ID's complete and finalized.
CSA	Site structures (jungle gyms, pipe rack, etc.) complete.	I&C	Network block diagrams complete and finalized.
CSA	Pipe stress reaction steel complete, including any modification in the existing structure(s). Gravity framing complete for piping.	I&C	Instrument index complete and finalized.
CSA	Gravity and seismic design capacity shown on drawings for all structural systems, including pipe racks, trenches, jungle gyms, platforms, catwalks, etc.	I&C	Instrument data sheets complete and finalized.
CSA	Seismic/wind anchorage of nonstructural items complete, or an indication on the plans of the deferred submittals	I&C	Network cable schedules (inter-building, inter-panel, intra-panel) complete and finalized.
CSA	Framing complete for AHUs and other major mechanical/electrical units.	I&C	Point Management Database (PMD) complete and finalized.
CSA	Cleanroom ceiling framing and support system (gravity and lateral) indicated in final form along with essentially complete detailing.	I&C	Instrument power schedules complete and finalized.
P	**PROCESS (Water & Waste)**	I&C	Control panel schedules complete and finalized.

P	All comments from DD reviewdispositioned.	I&C	Control panel drawings and datasheets complete and finalized.
P	Specifications complete and finalized.	I&C	Equipment and device plan drawings complete and finalized.
P	P&IDs complete and finalized.	I&C	Instrument installation details complete and finalized.
P	Process flow diagrams complete and finalized.	I&C	Sequence of Operations (SOO) complete and finalized.
P	Equipment / floor plans complete and finalized.	LSS	**LSS**
P	Pipeflo modeling complete for all systems.	LSS	Final specification Table of Contents (TOC) Full set of POR Specifications Final non-POR Specifications
P	Utility Capacity Tracker completed	LSS	Final equipment location backgrounds Final LSS/FIRE/HPM equipment location plan diagrams Final LSS/FIRE/HPM device location plan diagrams
P	Master Equipment List complete and finalized.	LSS	Final LSS/FIRE/HPM Partial Plans and Elevations
P	Piping plans, piping partial plans, and section details complete and finalized.	LSS	Final Fire Alarm Functional Matrix
P	Piping support plans and pipe stress analysis complete and finalized.	LSS	Final Fire Alarm Data and Audio Block Diagrams
P	Detail drawings complete and finalized.	LSS	Final fire smoke zone diagrams
P	Calculations complete and finalized.	LSS	Final fire alarm FDU Layout
P	POC/Point management database requests approved, ready for IFC bulk loading files for database (i.e. FaSTr load file)	LSS	Final EWSD block/4VDC diagram
P	**PROCESS (Bulk Gas)**	LSS	Final fire alarm panel module configuration diagrams
P	All comments from DD reviewdispositioned.	LSS	POR Panel Drawings Final non-POR panel drawings
P	Specifications complete and finalized.	LSS	Final LSS rack elevations
P	P&IDs complete and finalized.	LSS	POR LSS/FIRE/HPM installation details Final non-POR LSS/FIRE/HPM installation details
P	Process flow diagrams complete and finalized.	LSS	**SECURITY**
P	Equipment / floor plans complete and finalized.	LSS	Final specification Table of Contents (TOC) Full set of POR security specifications Final non-POR security specifications
P	Pipeflo modeling complete for all systems.	LSS	Final equipment location backgrounds Final Security Equipment locations plan diagrams Final Security device locations plan diagrams
P	Utility Capacity Tracker completed	LSS	Final block diagram for Access control/CCTV/Two-Way radio
P	Master Equipment List complete and finalized.	LSS	Final FDU layout for Accesss control/CCTV/Two-Way radio
P	Piping plans, piping partial plans, and section details complete and finalized.	LSS	Final riser diagrams for access control/CCTV/Two-Way Radio
P	Piping support plans and pipe stress analysis complete and finalized.	LSS	POR Secuity installation details Final non-POR Secuity installation details
P	Detail drawings complete and finalized.	LSS	Final rack elevations
P	Calculations complete and finalized.	TELE	**TELECOM**
P	POC/Point management database requests approved, ready for IFC bulk loading files for database (i.e. FaSTr load file)	TELE	Supporting discipline scope - final. - Separate "IT plan drawings indication the location of system components.

P	**PROCESS MECHANICAL**	TELE	Design criteria for final IP address assignments (by Intel) for supporting disciplines complete.
P	Specifications complete and finalized.	TELE	Provide cable schedule (will include all voice and data ports), pop-out schedule, CP schedule (including port #s for PMO/CAPMS), and fiber schedule.
P	P&IDs complete and finalized.	TELE	All comments from previous milestone dispositioned
P	Process flow diagrams complete and finalized.	TELE	All Documents (Drawings, Specifications and Calculations) 100% Complete
P	Equipment / floor plans complete and finalized.	TELE	Necessary Details to show principle elements, general arrangement.
P	Piping plans, piping partial plans, and section details complete and finalized.	PSSS	**PSSS**
P	Piping support plans complete and finalized.	PSSS	Specifications complete and finalized.
P	Fire protection plans, isometric drawings, details complete and finalized.	PSSS	P&IDs complete and finalized.
P	Detail drawings complete and finalized.	PSSS	Process flow diagrams complete and finalized.
P	Calculations (heat load, chilled water, etc.) complete and finalized.	PSSS	Equipment / floor plans complete and finalized.
P	Piping support calculations complete and finalized.	PSSS	Piping plans, piping partial plans, and section details complete and finalized.
P	Pipeflo modeling complete for all systems.	PSSS	Piping support plans and pipe stress analysis complete and finalized.
P	Utility Capacity Tracker completed	PSSS	Detail drawings complete and finalized.
P	Master Equipment List complete and finalized.	PSSS	Calculations complete and finalized.
P	POC database requests approved and updated in Database.	PSSS	POC/Point management database requests approved, ready for IFC bulk loading files for database (i.e. FaSTr load file)
P	Plumbing schedules complete and finalized.	BIM	**BIM**
M	**MECHANICAL**	BIM	Composite Navisworks Model will all applicable Design Models submitted (with Saved Viewpoints for clashes).
M	Specifications complete and finalized.	BIM	CD Clash report summary submitted (risk level indicator)
M	P&IDs complete and finalized.	BIM	CAD Compliance QA check sign-off submitted.
M	Process flow diagrams complete and finalized.	GEN	**GENERAL**
M	Equipment / floor plans complete and finalized.	GEN	General arrangement plan drawings, section views, etc. showing space planning, future routing zones, etc. complete.
M	Piping plans, piping partial plans, and section details complete and finalized.		
M	Piping support plans complete and finalized.		
M	Fire protection plans, isometric drawings, details complete and finalized.		
M	Detail drawings complete and finalized.		
M	Calculations (heat load, chilled water, etc.) complete and finalized.		
M	Piping support calculations complete and finalized.		
M	Pipeflo modeling complete for all systems.		
M	Utility Capacity Tracker completed		
M	Master Equipment List complete and finalized.		
M	POC database requests approved and updated in Database.		
M	Plumbing schedules complete and finalized.		

Example of 90% Design Review Score Card

Design Risk Register

Maintain a dynamic log capturing design risks, including risk ownership, likelihood, impact, and mitigation status. This register should serve as a clear communication tool bridging design, preconstruction, and construction teams.

Early Trade Involvement (Design Assist): Integrate key trades (MEP, structural steel, facade) early in the design process to:

- Enhance schedule certainty.

- Minimize rework and redesign costs.

- Align design more closely with budget constraints.

Case Study:

When Design Coordination is Neglected

A Southwest hospital expansion project faced severe coordination failures within the operating room ceilings. The initial design failed to consider HVAC, fire suppression, and medical gas coordination, resulting in substantial rework, significant schedule delays, and over $1 million in additional costs. Root cause analysis indicated the absence of effective BIM coordination and constructability reviews during design phases.

Field Insight: Bridging the Design-Build Gap

Proactive construction teams do not merely review drawings—they simulate construction scenarios early by asking:

- Where will material staging occur?

- How will equipment access be maintained?

- What trade sequencing prevents overlaps?

- Does the design accommodate clear and safe means of egress?

Unresolved questions at 90% completion signify high latent risk.

Clear Roles and Responsibilities in Design Management

- Document quality control: Architect of Record (AOR)

- Design schedule oversight: Owner's Project Manager or Design Manager

- BIM integration: Construction Manager or Virtual Design and Construction Manager

- Constructability reviews: Preconstruction Team and Superintendent

- Risk management: Construction Manager, Risk Manager, or Project Manager

Defined roles significantly reduce unnoticed risks.

Preconstruction Risk Readiness Checklist

Before finalizing the design, confirm

- Constructability and scope gap reviews are complete.

- The design risk register is current and reviewed regularly.

- Long-lead materials and items are identified and coordinated with procurement.

- Permit requirements and regulatory compliance issues are resolved.

- Budgets reconcile accurately with design and approved VE items.

"No" responses to these checks indicate potential latent construction risk.

Chapter Conclusion

Owning Design Risk Means Managing Future Success

Design risk extends beyond architects' responsibilities. Construction managers and contractors share equally in its management. Effective project leaders engage deeply during preconstruction, advocating clarity, facilitating coordination, and rigorously documenting decisions. This proactive management approach prevents minor design oversights from becoming costly construction issues.

Successful design risk management is foundational to overall project success, directly influencing cost, quality, and schedule outcomes. Early intervention, detailed reviews, and consistent cross-team communication ensure that risks are identified and addressed, setting the stage for efficient, profitable construction.

"The difference between the right word and almost the right word is the difference between lightning and a lightning bug" – **Mark Twain**

Part VI – Identification of Risk During the Bidding, Procurement and Subcontracting Phase

CHAPTER 14

BIDDING, PROCUREMENT AND SUBCONTRACTOR RISK

Chapter Foreword

In construction, your project's success hinges significantly on the quality of your estimating, bidding, and procurement decisions. Accurate estimating is the first, and often the most consequential, risk decision made on any project. A flawed estimate guarantees downstream failures, including budget overruns, scope disputes, unrealistic schedules, and desperate procurement decisions made under pressure. Procurement extends far beyond purchasing. It is a cornerstone of risk management and is capable of either preventing or precipitating project failure.

Selecting unreliable subcontractors, working with undependable vendors, accepting unbalanced bids, or using inadequately defined scopes frequently leads to cost overruns, delays, and contentious claims. Yet estimating and procurement often suffer from rushed deadlines, incomplete information, insufficient staffing, and an overemphasis on the lowest price rather than the lowest total risk.

This chapter presents estimating, bidding, and procurement as integrated pillars of risk management. It covers bid day risk assessments, scope gaps, subcontractor prequalification, comprehensive contract buyouts, escalation mitigation, and meticulous long lead tracking. By creating accurate estimates, verifying scopes, and mastering procurement, you will secure accountability, ensure clarity, and significantly reduce project risk.

"Every act of creation begins with an act of destruction" – **Pablo Picasso**

Strategic Importance of Estimating and Procurement

Estimating and procurement decisions drive scope clarity, risk allocation, and the accuracy of budgets and contingencies. They also determine third party commitments, material availability, locked in pricing, schedule realism, and exposure tied to escalation and quantities.

Most claims trace back to early estimating and procurement assumptions that were inaccurate, unverified, or never carried into buyout.

Approach estimating and procurement strategically, with clear accountability and structured oversight. A robust procurement foundation provides clarity, control, and the foresight necessary for project success. When executed correctly, it becomes a powerful asset in managing construction risk and securing project profitability.

Estimating and Bidding Risk: Where Mistakes Begin

Estimating is risk forecasting: every quantity, productivity factor, and assumption is a risk decision.

Poor estimating failures usually fall into five buckets:

- Productivity assumptions that do not match field reality.

- Scope gaps and missed quantities.

- Design intent errors and reliance on incomplete documents.

- Subcontractor bids with exclusions that contradict the documents.

- Missing escalation, manpower peaks, general conditions, and indirects.

Many estimates are also distorted by bidding to win rather than bidding to deliver.

To avoid these failures, a best-in-class estimating process includes several key steps.

Bid Document Clarity Check

Confirm drawing completeness. Identify design gaps requiring RFIs. Verify alignment between specifications and drawings. Confirm which specification sections govern when conflicts exist.

Risk-Based Estimate Review

Conduct internal peer reviews that focus on productivity assumptions, high-risk scopes such as MEP, earthwork, structural steel, and finishes, escalation forecasts, general conditions budgets, schedule feasibility, subcontractor exclusions, and contingency logic.

Bid Day Controls

Track last-minute subcontractor clarifications. Analyze unusually low bids. Review alternates, allowances, and bid forms for omissions. Confirm that all prime contract obligations have been passed through to subcontractors.

A strong estimate is the first line of defense against risk. A weak estimate becomes a permanent liability that cannot be repaired during construction.

Pricing Review Requirements

Scheduling Pricing Reviews

Pricing Reviews should be conducted on the final proposal prior to submission to the Owner. In limited cases, a draft proposal may be reviewed to accommodate reviewer availability and submission deadlines. All proposals must be reviewed and approved by the Manager before the Pricing Review.

Submit the following to the attendees prior to the meeting:

Project Risk Assessment

Tool Insert: Bid Day Pricing Review Agenda

Use this agenda for final proposal review before submission. It forces scope, schedule, pricing, and risk alignment before bid day decisions become contractual promises.

1. Scope Overview

   - Present an overview of the scope of the project

   - Identify document control of scope

2. Schedule Review

   - Critical Milestones

   - What are the commitments to the Owner

   - Are critical milestones in subcontracts and Material Vendors

3. Pricing Review

   - Subcontractors and Material Suppliers

   - Scope of Work Review per Package

   - Bid Coverage

   - Clarifications and Assumptions

   - Pricing Review

   - Bid Comparison Sheets

   - Sole Source Justifications

- Gap Analysis

4. Corporate Management, Labor and General Conditions

    - Review Staffing Plan

    - Taxes

    - Insurance Requirements

    - Bond Requirements

5. Allowances

6. Risk Log & Contingency

7. Proposal Language Review

8. Risk Process Conditions

9. Other

Prequalification: Identifying Risk Before It Materializes

Poor subcontractor selection can result in project abandonment, default, substandard workmanship, safety violations, payment disputes, and expensive litigation.

A robust prequalification process verifies:

- Financial stability, audited statements, and bonding capacity

- Relevant experience and safety history

- Legal exposure and OSHA record

- Staffing depth and supervision strength

- References from recent comparable work

Warning signs include limited financial transparency, excessive litigation history, unusually low bids compared to the market, high staff turnover, and inadequate staff depth.

Subcontractor and Vendor RFP Discipline

One of the most common sources of procurement-related claims is not pricing error, it is **scope ambiguity at the RFP stage**. When subcontractors and vendors are asked to price incomplete, undefined, or loosely framed requests for proposals, the result is predictable: assumptions replace clarity, gaps are buried in lump sums, and disputes surface later as change orders.

A well-structured RFP is a risk management tool. It does not exist simply to solicit a number. It exists to force scope definition, align assumptions, and confirm that pricing reflects the actual project requirements, not the subcontractor's interpretation of them.

To obtain a full and defensible price, every subcontractor and vendor RFP should clearly define the scope of work, pricing structure, schedule expectations, and contractual framework under which the work will be performed.

Required Elements of a Disciplined RFP

Defined Scope of Work
The RFP must clearly describe the subcontractor's scope, including specific systems, limits of work, and interfaces. Ambiguous phrases such as "by others" or "as required" invite assumption-driven pricing.

Includes, Excludes, and Assumptions
Each proposer should be required to explicitly state what is included, excluded, and assumed. Silence should not be interpreted as inclusion.

Pricing Breakdown Requirements
RFPs should dictate how pricing is presented—labor, material, equipment, allowances, unit rates, alternates, and contingencies—rather than accepting a single lump sum that conceals gaps.

Schedule and Milestones
The RFP must identify required start dates, durations, interim milestones, and constraints. Pricing without schedule context is incomplete pricing.

Plans and Specifications Reference
The RFP must clearly identify the drawings and specifications that govern the scope, including addenda and clarifications. Outdated or partial document references create immediate risk.

Contractual Flow-Down
Subcontractors must be informed of owner contract requirements that flow down to their work, including insurance, indemnity, schedule obligations, notice provisions, and performance standards.

Draft Subcontract Agreement

The RFP should include the form of subcontract agreement and required exhibits so pricing reflects the actual commercial terms—not assumptions about future negotiations.

When these elements are missing, bid comparisons become meaningless, low bids become expensive, and procurement disputes become inevitable. When they are present, pricing becomes transparent, scopes align, and claims risk is materially reduced.

Procurement discipline does not increase bid cost. It reduces downstream exposure.

Example: Subcontractor / Vendor RFP (Condensed)

Project: [Project Name]
RFP No.: [Number]
Trade / Package: [e.g., Electrical, Chillers, Fire Protection]

1. Scope of Work

Provide all labor, materials, equipment, supervision, and coordination necessary to complete the scope described herein in accordance with the Contract Documents.

2. Documents for Pricing

Pricing shall be based on the following:

Drawings: [List numbers, dates]

Specifications: [Sections]

Addenda: [List]

Reference Standards: [If applicable]

3. Scope Includes

[List key inclusions]

[Example: Final connections, testing, startup]

[Example: Coordination with other trades]

4. Scope Excludes

[List exclusions explicitly]

[Example: Utility fees, permanent power beyond point of connection]

5. Assumptions

Proposer shall list all assumptions made in developing the proposal. Unstated assumptions will not be accepted.

6. Pricing Requirements

Provide pricing in the following format:

Base Scope Lump Sum

Labor Breakdown

Material Breakdown

Equipment

Allowances (if any)

Unit Rates (if requested)

Alternates (if applicable)

7. Schedule Requirements

Required start date: [Date]

Substantial completion: [Date]

Interim milestones: [List]

Work hour or access constraints: [If any]

8. Contractual Requirements

This scope is subject to owner contract flow-down provisions, including insurance, indemnity, schedule compliance, and notice requirements.

9. Subcontract Agreement

Pricing shall be based on the attached draft subcontract agreement, including exhibits and schedule.

10. Proposal Submission

Proposals shall be submitted by [Date/Time] and include all requested breakdowns and disclosures.

If the RFP is vague, the price will be incomplete, and the gap will surface later as a claim.

Pro Tip:

Price Protection before and on Bid Day.

- Clear bid instructions to subs

- Include written instructions to all subs stating that the subcontractors price:

  - Will be relied upon in preparing the GC's prime bid.

  - Is irrevocable for a stated period (e.g., 30–60 days) following bid day.

- Subcontractor's bid is an offer that:

  - If the GC is awarded the prime contract and timely tenders a subcontract consistent with the sub's bid, the sub agrees to execute and perform at that price.

  - Sub acknowledges that GC may recover damages (including cover costs) if sub refuses to honor its bid.

- This doesn't guarantee a win if litigated, but it:

  - Makes your reliance even more reasonable

  - Edges their offer closer to an option contract (less revocable)

What the law says in a nutshell

In many U.S. states, when a GC reasonably relies on a subcontractor's bid in submitting its own bid to the owner, the law may treat the subcontractor's bid as temporarily irrevocable under promissory estoppel.

Key case: **Drennan v. Star Paving Co., 51 Cal.2d 409 (1958)**

Facts: GC used a paving subcontractor's low bid to price and win the prime contract. After the GC was awarded the job, the sub tried to back out, saying its price was a mistake.

Holding: The court held that:

The sub's bid was an offer.

The GC reasonably relied on that bid in submitting its own bid.

Because the sub should reasonably have expected that reliance, the offer was binding under promissory estoppel, at least long enough for the GC to accept it once awarded the prime contract.

Takeaway: In "Drennan" jurisdictions, the subcontractor can be held liable for the difference between its bid and the cost of a replacement subcontractor if it refuses to honor its price, assuming your reliance was reasonable and foreseeable.

Some courts have been more formal and less protective of GCs.

Key case: James Baird Co. v. Gimbel Bros., 64 F.2d 344 (2d Cir. 1933)

The Court held that a sub's bid is a freely revocable offer until the GC formally accepts it.

Reliance alone does not make the bid irrevocable, unless there's a specific option contract or consideration to keep the offer open.

Takeaway: In "Baird" type jurisdictions, you may have a much harder time holding a sub to its number unless you created an option-type arrangement or had a clear written commitment.

Subcontract Buyout: Aligning Estimate Assumptions with Reality

- Buyout is where estimate assumptions either become contract language or become future claims. It is a critical step in eliminating risk.

- Effective buyout practices include the use of standardized subcontract scope checklists, cross-referencing bid scope with design documents, defining all inclusions, exclusions, allowances, and alternates in writing, eliminating scope gaps and double coverage, flowing down all prime contract requirements, and verifying bonding, insurance, and safety compliance.

- A common failure occurs when trade responsibilities are not clearly defined. An example is missing firestopping between floors that surfaced late and created an unbudgeted contractor liability due to unclear buyout responsibilities.

Integrating Procurement with the Project Schedule

- Misalignment between procurement and scheduling is one of the leading causes of delay claims.

- A proper procurement schedule identifies long lead items, vendor and engineering submittal durations, fabrication timelines, required on-site delivery dates, and permit-driven procurement tasks.

- A procurement log that is tied to the project schedule, whether in Primavera P6 or Microsoft Project, ensures visibility and accountability throughout the project.

Material and Equipment Risks: Escalation and Availability

- Material and equipment risks must be actively managed.

- Escalation risk is mitigated through escalation clauses, early price locking, using letters of intent, early purchase orders, thoughtful contingency planning, and the use of alternate materials when approved.

- Long lead risks are reduced by early identification, proactive specification verification through RFIs, dedicated procurement tracking schedules, and clearly assigned procurement responsibilities.

Case Study: Consequences of Poor Estimating and Unvetted Subcontractors

A drywall subcontractor won with a significantly low bid that relied on a general contractor estimate, which missed several scope items and failed to include labor escalation. The subcontractor later filed for bankruptcy after missing multiple scheduled milestones. The resulting delays, rework, and legal fees exceeded seven hundred fifty thousand dollars. The initial savings vanished entirely due to inaccurate estimating assumptions and the absence of a disciplined prequalification process.

Best Practices in Estimating and Procurement Control

Top-performing organizations consistently apply strong estimating and procurement controls.

AACE Estimate Classification Matrix

AACE Estimate Class	LEVEL OF PROJECT DEFINITION Expressed as % of Complete Project Definition	END USAGE Typical Purpose of Estimate	METHODOLOGY Typical Estimating Techniques	EXPECTED ACCURACY RANGE At 90% Confidence Level	TYPICAL CONTINGENCY To Achieve 50% Probability of Overrun/Underrun
5	<=5%	Preliminary Project Screening Estimate, Capital Budget OOM Estimate, Alternate Schemes Evaluation, Strategic Analysis	Capacity Factored, Parametric Models, Judgment, Analogy, Historical Project Comparison, Cost Unit Cost	Low: -20% to -50% High: +30% to +100%	15% to 40%
4	1% to 15%	Preliminary Project Estimate, Reality Check Estimate, Alternate Schemes Evaluation, Feasibility Study	Equipment Factored Parametric Models, Historical Relationship Factors, Broad Unit Cost Data	Low: -15% to -30% High: +20% to +50%	10% to 25%
3	10% to 40%	Project Funding Estimate, Fair Price Check Estimate, Alternate Schemes Evaluation	Semi-Detailed Unit Costs with Assembly Level Line Items by Trade, Historical Relationship Factors	Low: -10% to -20% High: +10% to +30%	5% to 15%
2	30% to 99%	Project Funding Estimate, Control Estimate, Bid Estimate	Detailed Estimating Data by Trade, with Detailed Takeoff Quantities	Low: -5% to -15% High: +5% to +20%	5% to 15% of unexpected funds
1	50% to 100%	Firm Bid Estimate	Detailed Estimating Data by Trade with Detailed Firm Takeoff Quantities	Low: -3% to -10% High: +3% to +15%	3% to 10% Of unexpected funds

DESIGN COMPLETION VS. ESTIMATE CLASS			AACE Estimating Class				
Division	Title	Class 5 Initiation	Class 4 Planning	Class 3 30% Design	Class 2 60% Design	Class 1 90% to IFC Design
00	Procurement & Contracting Requirements					
01	General Requirements					
02	Existing Conditions					
03	Concrete					
04	Masonry					
05	Metals					
06	Wood, Plastics & Composites					
07	Thermal & Moisture Protection					
08	Openings (Doors, Windows, Glazing)					
09	Finishes					
10	Specialties					
11	Equipment					
12	Furnishings					
13	Special Construction					
14	Conveying Equipment					
20	Reserved					
21	Fire Suppression					
22	Plumbing					
23	HVAC					
25	Integrated Automation					
26	Electrical					
27	Communications					
28	Electronic Safety & Security					
29	Reserved					
31	Earthwork					
32	Exterior Improvements					
33	Utilities					
34	Transportation					
35	Waterway & Marine Construction					
40	Process Integration					
41	Material Processing & Handling					
42	Process Heating, Cooling, Drying					
43	Process Gas & Liquid Handling					
44	Pollution & Waste Control Equipment					
45	Industry-Specific Manufacturing					
46	Water & Wastewater Equipment					
48	Electrical Power Generation					

- **Estimating Controls**

  Peer review sessions.

  Quantitative risk assessments on major scopes.

  Independent schedule validation before bid submission.

  Use of historical cost databases for benchmarking.

  Scenario-based contingency planning.

- **Procurement Controls**

  Procurement kickoff checklists.

  Weekly buyout meetings.

  Vendor and subcontractor risk scorecards.

  Escalation and required on-site forecasting.

  Early trade partner engagement during design.

Before finalizing a bid or procurement decision, confirm the following items.

- **Estimating Readiness**

  Quantities verified.

  Scope fully captured with all assumptions validated.

  Productivity factors benchmarked against real-world data.

  Escalation included for high-risk trades.

  Contingency is structured logically and proportionate to the scope risk.

  Subcontractor bids reviewed for exclusions and irregularities.

- **Procurement Readiness**

  Subcontractors and vendors fully prequalified.

  Prime contract obligations flowed down correctly.

  Long lead materials identified and tracked.

  The procurement schedule aligned with the project schedule.

  The procurement log is updated and reviewed weekly.

Best Practices: Policies, Procedures, and Checklist Templates for Estimating Turnover Meetings

Purpose of the Turnover Meeting

The purpose of a formal project handover after the contracts have been signed and before the building project starts is to ensure that the project manager gets the best possible conditions for an effective project start-up. The project manager must get familiar with the bid, associated contracts, and other agreements. The estimating turnover meeting bridges the gap between the estimating and project management teams, ensuring a seamless transition from planning to execution. This process facilitates clear communication, minimizes risks, and establishes a shared understanding of the project scope, schedule, risks, opportunities, and expectations.

The initial planning, organization, and communication of the goals and associated objectives for any project is crucial to its ultimate success. When new contracts are secured, it is vitally important that those assumptions, parameters, and methodologies utilized are understood by those required to prosecute the work. To achieve a successful outcome in terms of meeting our expectations regarding quality, safety, and financial performance, the following best practices and procedures shall be followed in preparation for beginning the work of a new contract:

Best Practices

- Structured Agenda:

Create a detailed meeting agenda shared in advance to keep discussions focused and comprehensive.

- Complete Documentation:

Ensure all relevant documents (e.g., estimates, schedules, contracts, and risk assessments) are prepared and organized.

- Cross-Functional Participation:

Include representatives from estimating, project management, safety, procurement, scheduling, risk, and quality control.

- Clarity of Responsibilities:

Clearly define roles and responsibilities for all parties involved to prevent gaps or overlaps.

- Focus on Risks and Mitigation:

Highlight potential challenges and strategies for addressing them during project execution.

- Post-Meeting Follow-Up:

Document action items, assign responsibilities, and set deadlines to ensure accountability.

Policies and Procedures

Turnover Meeting Policy

- The turnover meeting is mandatory for all projects exceeding a defined value threshold.

- The estimating team must finalize all deliverables and documentation at least five working days before the meeting.

- The project manager (PM) must review turnover documents and prepare specific questions or concerns before the meeting.

- Follow-up meetings are required for unresolved issues or updates.

Procedure for Conducting the Meeting

- Preparation Stage:

- Schedule the meeting for at least two weeks in advance.

- Distribute the agenda and turnover package, including estimates, schedules, contracts, and risk assessments.

- Set up a Teams Folder containing all documents utilized during the pursuit, bidding, and contract award of the project pursuant to company standards.

- During the Meeting:
  Follow the agenda rigorously.
  Discuss each component (e.g., schedule, contracts, risks) in detail.
  Document key decisions, changes, and action items in real-time.

- Post-Meeting Actions:
  Distribute meeting minutes within two business days.
  Assign unresolved items to appropriate team members with deadlines.

Estimating Turnover Agenda

1. General Project Information

- Project name and number

- Location, address, and site access details

- Key project stakeholders (client, architect, consultants, subcontractors)

- Project overview, description, and scope of work

- Procurement Method (Hard Bid, Design Build, Alternate Delivery)

- Award Status – Notice to Proceed

2. Estimate Overview

- Detailed estimate breakdown by trade/discipline

- Assumptions and exclusions used in the estimate

- Identification of any value engineering opportunities

- Discuss the Project approach that was developed during the preparation of the estimate

3. Project Schedule [Copy of bid estimated project schedule]

- Critical milestones and completion date

- Long lead items and procurement timelines

- Key dependencies and potential delays

- Identify any other work being performed outside the contract that could affect our work.

- Review Implementation Schedule

- Critical Path Analysis – where are the key critical elements

- Actions for managing the schedule

4. Contract Requirements

- Contract Terms - Review and identify critical contract provisions

- Special Notices and Reporting

- General conditions

- Special provisions

- Submittals/Shop Drawing Process

- Documentation of Issues

- Maintain/Monitor Construction Schedule

- Project Payment Processing

- Conduct Project Closeout Activities/Correction of Work

- Assist in Owner Activation

- Liquidated damages, incentives, retention

- Subcontractor agreements and scope delineations

- Permits and approvals status

- Notice Provisions

- Substantial and Final Completion

- Key Contract Terms and Requirements

- Warranties and Guarantee's

- Delay Clauses

- MBE/WBE Requirements

- Addenda and responses to Bid Questions

5. Risks and Mitigation Strategies

- Identified risks and their potential impact

- Subcontractor and supply chain risks

- Labor and workforce risk

- Site access, site conditions, and environmental risks

- Scope and design risks

- Proposed mitigation measures

- Contingency allowances

- Schedule risks

- Financial risks

6. Safety and Security Plan

- Project-specific safety concerns

- Required certifications and training for site personnel

- Emergency response procedures

- Badging Requirements

7. Staffing and Resource Plan

- Proposed staffing levels and organizational chart

- Owner Project Team and Personnel (Owner, Designers, Engineers, Consultants)

- Anticipated resource requirements (Subcontractor, Equipment, Labor, and Materials)

8. Cost and Budget Management

- Initial project budget with breakdown by category

- General conditions breakdown

- Self-perform versus subcontract work

- Buyout assumptions

- Distribute Bid Books

- Tax Exempt Status

- Review the Total Bid form submitted along with unit pricing and alternates

- Review of all proposed vendors, subcontractors, and scopes of work

- Discussion of potential scope gaps

- Procurement strategies

- Discuss the purchase of large equipment and bulk materials

- Review any schedule of values that have been submitted by estimating

- Review any major pricing deltas and or advantages with subcontractors and vendors

- Anticipated profit

- Cash flow projections

- Allowances and contingencies

9. Site Logistics and Access

- Site layout and constraints

- Material storage and staging areas

- Access restrictions and traffic management plans

10. Quality Control Plan

- Standards and Specifications

- Inspection Procedures

- Documentation

11. Communication

- Reporting Structure

- Meeting Schedules

- Documentation Protocols

12. Bonding and Insurance

- Owners OCIP (Owner Controlled Insurance Program) (if applicable)

- Payment and Performance Bonds

- Builders Risk

- General Liability

- Pollution Control

13. O&M and CSU

- O&M Requirements

- Startup and Commissioning Requirements

14. Lessons Learned

- Past Project Insights

- Best Practices

- Areas for Improvement

15. Follow-Up Actions

- Immediately following the meeting with the estimator, the project team will meet. The goal of this meeting will be the development of a Project Management Approach Plan.

- The project-specific management approach plan will outline the assignment of duties and responsibilities of the project team. The project-specific plan will support the requirements necessary to fulfill the scheduled delivery of information as outlined herein for review with the Executive Project Director.

Project Manager:

- Buy-out and Procurement Plan

- Contract Compliance Plan WBE/MBE/DBE

- Schedule of Values

- New Project Start-Up Form

- List of open issues requiring resolution

- Assigned team members and deadlines for each action item

- Schedule Project Team Management Administrative Plan Meeting Date and Time

Superintendent:

- Assemble Budget with PM

- Schedule Outline

- Finalize with PM to Incorporate Buys & Logic

- Manpower Staffing/Resource Plan/Equipment Utilization

- Job Mobilization Schedule (Trailers, Utilities, etc.)

- Specialized Equipment

- Picketing Activity Action Plan and Procedures

- Site-specific safety plan and new JSAs

Project Engineer:

- Submittal Schedule

- Contact List

- Coordinate with Subs for Schedule information

Chapter Conclusion

In procurement, numbers win bids, but disciplined process and reliable partners win projects.

Bidding, procurement, and subcontractor selection sit at the heart of a contractor's risk profile. The numbers you carry on bid day are not just estimates; they are commitments that can define your profitability, your relationships, and, in some cases, your survival on a project.

By treating subcontractor pricing as a potential point of failure rather than a mere input, you move from reacting to problems to actively managing them. Clear bid instructions, documented reliance, disciplined vetting of "too good to be true" prices, and consistent follow-through from award to subcontract execution form the backbone of a defensible strategy. In the end, the goal is not to eliminate risk, because that is impossible, but to understand it, allocate it deliberately, and build structures that keep one bad number from sinking a good project.

Construction projects unravel most often due to early estimating and procurement missteps. Unrealistic budgets, overlooked scope, risky subcontractor choices, and delayed materials all originate from weak front-end controls. When estimating and procurement are treated as disciplined risk management functions, profitability becomes predictable instead of hopeful.

"Without data, you are just another person with an opinion." – **W. Edwards Deming**

CHAPTER 15

SUBCONTRACTOR CLAIMS AND PASS-THROUGH RISKS

Chapter Foreword

Subcontractors perform the majority of the physical work on a construction project, but they also represent one of the most significant sources of claims. From change orders to payment disputes, from defective work to acceleration demands, subcontractor-related issues frequently escalate into formal legal claims against general contractors, construction managers, or even project owners.

Whether you are the prime contractor or the owner, you are at risk of becoming the **pass-through recipient** of subcontractor claims. Many of these disputes are rooted in unclear contract scopes, inconsistent documentation, and misalignment between prime and sub agreements.

This chapter explores how subcontractor claims arise, how to prevent them, and how to manage them when they escalate. It also covers the unique legal and contractual risks associated with **pass-through claims, flow-down clauses**, and **prime-sub coordination failures**.

"Success is the sum of small efforts, repeated day in day out" – **Robert Collier**

Why Subcontractor Claims Happen

Subcontractor claims typically arise from three recurring conditions. The sample clauses below illustrate key subcontract provisions that govern these risks, which are rarely created in the field and almost always originate in the subcontract language itself.

1. Out-of-Scope Work

- Sub believes it performed extra work without a formal change order

- Often based on RFIs, field directives, or site conditions

- Subcontract clause to mitigate General Contractor's risk:

  - It is the intent of this contract to provide a "complete" and "operational" system as shown or inferred by the contract specifications and drawings. Completeness shall mean not only that all material and equipment has been installed properly, but that all material and equipment is operating as intended by the contract. The descriptions of the work included in this contract are clarifications of specific items and are not intended to limit the overall scope of work required, or reasonably inferred, for a complete system per the contract documents.

  - Without restricting the generality of work which shall be performed within the Subcontract Price, including any work not explicitly called for, but reasonably implied, it is clearly understood and agreed that the Subcontractor shall provide all the labor, materials, equipment, scaffolding, tools, supervision, layout, surveying, and appurtenances of every kind and nature required and incidental for the whole and complete performance of all work in accordance with the Contract Documents including, but not limited to the following:

2. Delay or Disruption

These clauses fail most often not because they are invalid, but because project teams do not enforce them consistently.

- Subcontractor experiences inefficiency due to stacked trades, resequencing, or late access

- Asserts loss of productivity and seeks compensation

- Subcontract clause to mitigate General Contractor's risk:

  - Should Subcontractor's performance of the Work be directly delayed, hindered, accelerated or disrupted by Contractor, other subcontractors or Contractor's suppliers, or by any acts or causes of the Owner for which the Owner grants Contractor an extension of time, and Subcontractor notifies Contractor in writing within three (3) days after commencement of such delay, inefficiency, loss of productivity, hindrance or, disruption as provided in this Article, Subcontractor will receive an extension of time for the performance of Subcontractor's obligations under this Agreement. Such extension of time will not exceed the lesser of the number of days of such delay, hindrance or disruption affecting the Project's critical path or the duration of any time extension granted by the Owner to Contractor and shall be Subcontractor's sole and exclusive remedy. In the case of any delay, hindrance, or disruption, caused by Contractor, other subcontractors, or Contractor's suppliers, Subcontractor shall not be entitled to any additional compensation for any costs or damages relating to delay, suspension, inefficiency, loss of productivity, acceleration, disruption, etc. of the Work. Nothing in this Article shall be construed as entitlement by the Subcontractor to any increase in the Subcontract Sum or to direct or indirect damages or additional compensation of any kind as a consequence of such delays, hindrances, inefficiency, loss of productivity, accelerations, disruptions, etc. unless the Owner pays Contractor in full for all such costs in which case Contractor will pay Subcontractor the amount paid by the Owner on behalf of Subcontractor for the delay, hindrance or disruption that directly affected Subcontractor.

- The three (3) day written notice set forth above shall state the full details of the cause of such delay. This notice will be considered in evaluating the extension of time, but in no way will it be construed as entitlement by Subcontractor to any additional compensation. In addition to the three (3) day written notice, within twenty (20) days after delivering such notice, Subcontractor must make and deliver to Contractor a written itemized breakdown of the nature and amounts of such damages, duly verified by Subcontractor and notarized.   Subcontractor's failure to comply with the notice requirements shall constitute an absolute waiver by Subcontractor of such claim. Compliance with the notice requirements shall be a condition precedent to any entitlement for relief.

3. Nonpayment

Enforceability varies significantly by state and delivery method; consult counsel.

- Progress payment or retention is withheld, often due to upstream owner disputes or defective work allegations

- Subcontract clause to mitigate General Contractor's risk:

  - Prior to the submission of its first invoice for payment, Subcontractor shall furnish a detailed schedule of values acceptable to Contractor to be used for progress payment purposes. Subcontractor shall not be entitled to submit its invoice prior to Contractor's approval of the schedule of values. All invoices to Contractor shall be submitted in accordance with Attachment XX – Invoice Requirements.

  - Subcontractor shall invoice in at least as much detail as the schedule of values furnished by Subcontractor and approved by Contractor. The terms of the Prime Contract, insofar as they apply to progress payments, final settlements, and measurements of the Work will apply as between Contractor and Subcontractor, except as herein modified.

  - In consideration of Subcontractor's satisfactory performance of the Work in accordance with the terms of this Agreement, Contractor shall pay to Subcontractor, from the funds actually received from the Owner and attributable to the Work performed by Subcontractor, the amounts computed on the basis of the prices set forth in Article XX of this Agreement, as amended by change orders as herein provided, less previous payments to Subcontractor. Subcontractor agrees that Contractor's receipt of any payment from the Owner (including final payment and retention) is a condition precedent to the corresponding payment by Contractor to Subcontractor, and Subcontractor agrees to accept the risk of late or non-payment by the Owner. Subcontractor agrees that it will not be paid by Contractor for work or materials in place until seven (7) days after Contractor's receipt of payment from the Owner for said work or materials. Contractor shall withhold retention from Subcontractor's payments in accordance with the terms of the Prime Contract or ten percent (10%), whichever is greater. If the Owner should reduce the retained percentage withheld from Contractor, Contractor may, at its sole discretion, reduce the retained percentage withheld from Subcontractor. No payment will be deemed as an approval or acceptance of the Work or as an acknowledgment that Subcontractor has completed the Work or any portion thereof. Prior to final payment, a proper adjustment and settlement of progress payments and other accounts will be made. No payment will be required to be made which will reduce the balance to be paid under this Agreement below a sum which will be adequate to fully cover the cost of completion of the Work and possible corrective work.

○ Should Contractor perform any work or incur any cost that is Subcontractor's responsibility under this Agreement, Contractor will be entitled to recover from Subcontractor such expense and cost plus ten percent (10%) overhead and other sums, and ten percent (10%) profit. Should any such charges remain unpaid thirty (30) days after notice is given to Subcontractor, such change will be deemed accepted by Subcontractor and may be deducted by Contractor from any amounts due Subcontractor.

○ Subcontractor's acceptance of the final payment pursuant to the terms of this Agreement shall constitute a complete and unconditional release by Subcontractor of Contractor from any and all existing or future claims or demands, whether known or unknown, by Subcontractor against Contractor arising under this Agreement or relating to the Project.

○ Subcontractor understands and agrees that the following are conditions precedent to any and all payments to Subcontractor:

- Contractor's receipt of payment from the Owner (including final payment and retention);

- Contractor's receipt from Subcontractor of satisfactory evidence that all entities supplying labor, materials, services or equipment in connection with the Work have been paid in full and have provided full and final releases of all liens and claims;

- Contractor's receipt of a full and final release and waiver of all liens and claims by Subcontractor through the date of payment, in the form to be provided by Contractor;

- Contractor's receipt of signed Change Orders from Subcontractor;

- Contractor's receipt of current certificates for all insurance coverage provided by Subcontractor as required under this Agreement or the Prime Contract; and

- Contractor's receipt of the signed Agreement from Subcontractor.

○ In the case of final payment, final payment shall not be due until after the last of the following occurs:

- Subcontractor's Work has been completed and approved by Contractor and the Owner;

- Completion of the entire Project;

- All requirements for final payment under this Agreement have been satisfied;

- Contractor has been paid in full for the entire Project;

- Subcontractor has delivered to Contractor a full and final release of all liens and claims arising from the Work from Subcontractor and all sub-subcontractors, materialmen, suppliers, and others, claiming by and through Subcontractor, in the form to be provided by Contractor; or

- Subcontractor has delivered to Contractor all applicable guarantees, warranties, bonds, manuals, as-built drawings, charts, tags, and similar items required with respect to Subcontractor's Work, and said items have been approved by the Owner.

- If at any time all monies due Contractor from the Owner are not paid, Contractor shall, at its sole discretion, apportion the non-payment equitably and reduce the payments otherwise due Subcontractor accordingly.

- Contractor is authorized to deduct and offset from any payments due under this Agreement an amount equal to any and all sums, obligations, liabilities, backcharges, claims (liquidated or unliquidated) owed by Subcontractor to Contractor under this Agreement or any other contract or agreement between Subcontractor and Contractor.

Understanding Pass-Through Claims

A **pass-through claim** occurs when a subcontractor asserts a claim against the **owner** but must do so **through the general contractor**. In many cases, the prime contractor becomes both the **advocate and the filter**.

Legal Context

- U.S. courts allow pass-through claims under the **Severin Doctrine**, but only when:

  - The prime is liable to the sub

  - The prime is not fully released from obligation

  - The prime pursues the claim "on behalf" of the sub

Practical Risk:

- GC may be **caught between the owner and the sub**, bearing risk but lacking resolution authority

- GC's position can be weakened if documentation, notice, or flow-down obligations are inconsistent

Flow-Down Clauses and Risk Transfer

The key to managing subcontractor claims is to ensure that **your subcontract matches your prime contract**. That is where **flow-down clauses** come in.

What is a Flow-Down Clause?

A provision in the subcontract that binds the sub to the **same terms and conditions** the GC agreed to in the prime contract.

Standard Language:

"Subcontractor agrees to be bound to the Contractor by the terms of the Prime Contract, and to assume toward the Contractor all the obligations and responsibilities the Contractor assumes toward the Owner."

Clauses to Flow Down Explicitly

Flow-Down Best Practices

- Include the **entire prime contract** as an exhibit or reference

- Require subs to review and sign a **prime contract acknowledgment**

- Customize flow-down language for design-build or CMAR delivery

Pro Tip:

Use a **Subcontract Risk Checklist** for every award.

Have legal verify flow-down clauses on projects >$5M or with complex scopes.

Have a Standard Subcontract Agreement for Large Contracts, Small Contracts, and Material Purchases. Any changes to the corporate standard contract format must be approved by legal.

Subcontract Claim Prevention Strategies

Many subcontractor claims can be **avoided entirely** with better documentation, clearer scopes, and stronger field coordination.

Strategy 1: Create Detailed Subcontract Scopes of Work

Vague scopes = finger-pointing

Action Steps:

- Use CSI or Uniformat breakdowns

- Stipulate that the work must be whole and complete in accordance with the contract documents

- Attach drawings and specifications explicitly

- Define exclusions and overlaps with related trades

Strategy 2: Require Baseline Schedules from Key Subs

Delay claims often stem from vague expectations

Action Steps:

- Require logic-linked schedules from subs >$500K

- Review and incorporate into master CPM

- Update monthly and review float usage

Strategy 3: Control Field Change Documentation

Most "unapproved work" claims come from poor field discipline

Action Steps:

- Enforce Field Change Authorization (FCA) forms

- Require T&M tickets to be signed daily by GC rep

- Link all out-of-scope work to the PCO log

Strategy 4: Use a Submittal/RFI Impact Tracker

Subs often claim delay without evidence

Action Steps:

- Maintain a log of delayed submittals by trade

- Connect RFIs to impacted activities

- Escalate aging items in owner meetings

Strategy 5: Weekly Coordination + Conflict Meetings

Many claims come from trade interference or resequencing

Action Steps:

- Hold foreman-level coordination meetings

- Use digital drawings to resolve spatial conflicts

- Document all interference for future defense

What to Do When a Subcontractor Threatens a Claim

When a subcontractor signals intent to file a claim or threatens legal action, take immediate steps to control the narrative.

Step-by-Step Response Protocol

1. **Acknowledge Receipt in Writing**

   - Confirm you have received the notice (do not admit fault)

2. **Review Notice Timeliness**

   - Was the claim submitted within the contract window?

3. **Evaluate Documentation**

   - Request T&M backup, delay logs, and relevant RFIs

4. **Isolate Upstream Impact**

   - Will this be a pass-through to the owner?

5. **Consult Legal & Insurance**

   - Determine potential exposure, indemnity triggers, and coverage

6. **Offer Interim Mitigation Options**

   - Could partial payment, resequencing, or joint escalation resolve the issue?

Proactive Communication Template (Internal)

Subject: Subcontractor Claim – [Trade Name] – Preliminary Assessment

1. Subcontractor:

2. Nature of Claim:

3. Claim Amount (Preliminary):

4. Notice Timeliness:

5. Supporting Documentation:

6. GC Exposure Estimate:

7. Prime Contract Flow-Down Status:

8. Legal Consultation: Y/N

9. Owner Pass-Through Intent: Y/N

10. Recommended Next Steps:

Subcontractor Bond Claims vs. GC Default Claims

Performance Bonds (Sub Level)

- Required by GCs from subs to ensure performance

- If the sub defaults, GC may **file against the bond**

- Must follow proper notice and documentation protocols

GC Obligations

- GC must not impair the surety's defenses

- Failure to provide written notice, opportunity to cure, or proper documentation may invalidate the bond

- Default is a legal weapon, not a management tool.

Pro Tip: Maintain a **Default Checklist** and involve legal before terminating a subcontractor.

- Cure letters

- Nonperformance evidence

- Field logs and QA issues

- Subcontract clause to mitigate General Contractor's risk:

  - If, in the sole opinion of Contractor, Subcontractor shall at any time (1) refuse or fail to provide sufficient properly skilled workers, adequate supervision or material of the proper quality, (2) fail in any material respect to prosecute the Work according to the current Project Schedule, as amended, (3) cause, by any action or omission, the stoppage or delay of or interference with the work of Contractor or any other contractor or subcontractor, (4) fail to comply with any provision of this Agreement or the Contract Documents, (5) make a general assignment for the benefit of Subcontractor's creditors, (6) fail to pay for labor and material, payroll taxes, contributions or insurance premiums, (7) have a majority interest in the Subcontractor sold to any third party, (8) become physically disabled, (9) have a receiver appointed, (10) become insolvent, or (11) any other breach of this Agreement, then after serving written notice, unless the condition specified in such notice shall have been eliminated by Subcontractor within forty-eight (48) hours, Contractor, at its option without voiding the other provisions of this Agreement or prejudicing any other right or remedy that Contractor may have and without notice to the sureties, may (i) take such steps as necessary to overcome the condition, in which case Subcontractor shall be liable to Contractor for the cost thereof, or (ii) terminate for default Subcontractor's performance of all or a part of Subcontractor's Work. Should Contractor believe in good faith that the Work, the current Project Schedule, as amended, or project safety is being endangered by Subcontractor's failure to prosecute the Work or to take action, such written notice may be omitted and Subcontractor's performance in whole or in part may be immediately terminated. In the event of termination for default, Contractor may, at its option, (a) enter onto the premises and take possession, for the purpose of completing the Work, of all materials and equipment of Subcontractor, (b) take assignment of any or all of Subcontractor's subcontracts, and/or (c) either itself or through others complete the Work by whatever method Contractor may deem expedient. In the case of termination for default, Subcontractor shall continue to be liable for all costs to complete and any damages and expenses to Contractor, including but not limited to reasonable attorney fees, liquidated damages assessed by the Owner and other liabilities which may result from the default or breach, without waiver of any other rights or remedies available to Contractor, including right of set off and collection of any funds which may be due Subcontractor under other subcontracts with Contractor. Subcontractor shall not be entitled to receive any further payment until the Work is fully completed and accepted by the Owner and payment in full is made by the Owner. At such time, if the unpaid balance of the price to be paid exceeds the expense incurred by Contractor, including overhead and profit, Contractor shall pay such excess to Subcontractor. If the expense incurred by Contractor exceeds the unpaid balance, Subcontractor shall pay Contractor the difference on demand.

- If Contractor wrongfully exercises its options under this Article, that action shall be treated as a Termination for Convenience and Subcontractor shall be entitled to the applicable compensation provided in the Termination for Convenience Article. Subcontractor's remedies under this Article shall be exclusive. Nothing herein shall bar withholdings by Contractor permitted by other provisions of this Agreement.

- Subcontractor agrees to reimburse Contractor for any and all damages, including any liquidated damages, that may be assessed against Contractor which are related to, arise out of, or are caused by, Subcontractor's failure to perform the Work within the time fixed or in the manner provided for herein, and in addition thereto, Subcontractor agrees to pay to Contractor such other or additional damages as Contractor may sustain by reason of such failure by Subcontractor, including but not limited to, extended field and home office overhead costs and any attorney fees incurred by Contractor, including attorney fees incurred in enforcing this Agreement. Any payment pursuant to the terms of this paragraph shall not act as a release of Subcontractor from any of its obligations under this Agreement.

- Should Subcontractor fail to comply for any reason with the provisions hereof as to the character or time of performance of the Work, which, in the sole opinion of Contractor, are necessary to the immediate continuation of the Project, then, and in such event, and notwithstanding the notice requirements as otherwise provided for herein, Contractor may at its sole option, perform such portions of Subcontractor's Work with its own forces or others, and Subcontractor will be liable for the costs thereof.

- In addition to Subcontractor's liability for Contractor's costs as set forth above, Subcontractor shall also be liable to Contractor for an additional ten percent (10%) overhead and ten percent (10%) profit.

- In the event Contractor incurs costs due to Subcontractor's failure to perform, Contractor shall prepare a deductive change order, which must be signed by Subcontractor as a condition precedent to payment of the currently due progress payment or final payment. If the balance due to the Subcontractor is insufficient to cover the costs, the Subcontractor shall remain liable to the Contractor for the difference.

Chapter Conclusion

Subs Can Build Your Job, or Blow It Up

Subcontractor claims are not an unfortunate side effect of construction; they are a predictable consequence of unclear scopes, weak contracts, and inconsistent field control. The construction site is only as strong as its weakest subcontractor, and when subs fall short, the risk does not disappear, it moves upstream into your contract, your schedule, and your bottom line. Every unresolved issue in the field is a future change order, a delay claim, or a pass-through demand waiting to surface.

Strong contractors do not merely react to subcontractor claims; they design their projects to withstand them. They build precise scopes, enforceable flow-downs, and unambiguous notice requirements into every subcontract. They back those contracts with written directives, contemporaneous field documentation, and disciplined issue tracking that turns "he said, she said" into a clear evidentiary record. They treat change management as a daily discipline, not a year-end negotiation.

Pass-through risk is ultimately a test of your systems and your resolve. When owner-driven changes or design defects trigger downstream impacts, you either have the documentation, contract language, and notice to flow those impacts up, or you absorb them. When you preserve rights, align your positions with your subs, and control the narrative with timely, factual communication, you turn chaotic claims into managed disputes and, often, negotiated resolutions.

In the end, every claim you prevent with clarity and documentation, and every risk you properly pass through with enforceable contracts and timely notice, is profit you keep. Because every claim you stop at the subcontractor level is a claim you never have to fight at the top, and a cost you never have to pay.

"The palest ink is better than the best memory." – Chinese proverb

PART VII – IDENTIFICATION OF RISK DURING THE CONSTRUCTION PHASE

CHAPTER 16

CONSTRUCTION PHASE RISK

Chapter Foreword

Planning, estimating, and procurement lay the groundwork for success, but the construction phase is where theoretical risks become tangible challenges. Each coordination oversight, scheduling misstep, labor inefficiency, or safety incident can swiftly escalate into financial losses, delays, and reputational harm.

This chapter equips construction professionals with proven strategies for managing on-site execution risks proactively. The best-managed projects deploy structured controls, disciplined leadership, and timely responsiveness to mitigate potential crises before they materialize.

"Trust but verify" – **Ronald Reagan**

Understanding Construction Phase Risks

Once construction starts, contractors must manage:

- Complex coordination of subcontractors and vendors.

- Delivery and installation of diverse materials and equipment.

- Compliance with multiple inspection requirements and regulatory milestones.

- Active safety management and environmental compliance.

- Pressure from tight schedules, liquidated damages, and fixed budgets.

- Unpredictable factors like weather, utility coordination, and site conditions.

The dynamic and complex nature of construction sites demands robust controls, clear communication, and strong leadership to prevent minor issues from becoming major disruptions.

Core Risks and Mitigation Strategies

1. Coordination and Sequencing Failures

- Risks: Trade conflicts, incomplete layouts, and out-of-sequence work causing rework.

- Mitigation:

  - Conduct weekly trade coordination meetings.

  - Maintain detailed 6-week lookahead schedules integrated with procurement.

  - Utilize visual management tools and BIM clash detection on-site.

2. Labor Productivity Losses

- Risks: Material delays, poor weather planning, unnecessary downtime, and inefficient workflows.

- Mitigation:

  - Implement daily productivity tracking (time-on-tools).

  - Schedule regular performance reviews with foremen.

  - Leverage productivity management software like SmartPM or Rhumbix.

3. Documentation and Communication Gaps

- Risks: Unrecorded verbal instructions, missing daily logs, and delayed RFIs causing disputes.

- Mitigation:

  - Employ cloud-based field management platforms (Procore, Fieldwire).

  - Track RFIs actively and set auto-alerts for response delays.

  - Enforce strict documentation protocols for field directives.

4. Safety and Environmental Risks

- Risks: OSHA violations, workplace injuries, public hazards, and environmental noncompliance.

- Mitigation:

  - Conduct pre-task safety planning and regular job hazard analyses.

   ○ Schedule routine third-party safety audits.

   ○ Maintain rigorous environmental compliance logs (e.g., SWPPP inspections).

5. Unforeseen Site Conditions

- Risks: Hidden utilities, soil issues, and archaeological finds causing delays and additional costs.

- Mitigation:

   ○ Establish a formal Differing Site Conditions protocol.

   ○ Document conditions immediately with photographs and RFIs.

   ○ Notify clients promptly to preserve rights for cost and time adjustments.

6. Material and Equipment Delays

- Risks: Late deliveries, incompatible equipment dimensions, storage, or handling damage.

- Mitigation:

   ○ Maintain rigorous material tracking with required-on-site (ROS) dates.

   ○ Implement daily logistics management plans.

   ○ Use detailed quality control checklists tied to deliveries and installations.

7. Change Management Failures

- Risks: Unauthorized work, undocumented changes, delays in submitting change orders.

- Mitigation:

   ○ Adopt strict field change authorization procedures.

   ○ Train teams in immediate documentation and submission of change events.

   ○ Ensure all changes are promptly captured in the schedule and budget tracking systems.

On-Site Leadership and Accountability

Effective construction management depends heavily on visible, proactive leadership and clearly defined responsibilities. Recommended accountability structure:

- Daily work planning: Superintendent

- Safety monitoring: Safety Officer/Foreman

- RFI management: Project Engineer

- Submittal reviews: Assistant PM/Design Manager

- Change documentation: Project Manager/Cost Engineer

- Short-term scheduling (3-week lookahead): Superintendent and Project Engineer

Leadership accountability ensures rapid issue identification and timely resolution, minimizing potential disruptions.

Case Study: Consequences of Poor Coordination

On a California wastewater treatment project, inadequate scaffold verification and delayed shoring led to missed milestones. Mechanical trades were rescheduled without notification, causing significant delays and additional overhead costs totaling $380,000. Primary failures included:

- Absence of daily coordination and communication tools.

- Missing master trade lookahead schedules.

Lesson: Robust coordination and proactive scheduling practices are essential to prevent cascading project delays.

Risk Tracking During Construction

Effective risk management includes maintaining a real-time risk log documenting:

- Risk identification

- Assigned ownership

- Trigger events

- Proposed mitigations

- Current status

Project ID:			Project Name:									Risk (and Opportunities) Register		
#	Creation Date	Event	Cause	Effect	Risk or Opportunity	Probability	Schedule (WD)	Cost	Total Net Schedule Impact	Total Net Cost Impact	Response Strategy	Response Actions	R/O Owner	Last Update
	1/1/2020	What is the Risk or Opportunity	What is the Root Cause	What effect on the Cost, Schedule, Quality, Safety or Client will this have.	Risk	10%	5.0	$ -	0.5	$ -	Accept	Contractor shall hold the schedule reserve and cost contingency.	Client	1-Jan-21
1								$ -	0.0	$ -				
2								$ -	0.0	$ -				
3								$ -	0.0	$ -				
								TOTAL	0.5	$ -				

A **Project Risk and Opportunity Log** in construction is a structured document or tool that tracks potential risks and opportunities associated with a project. It is an essential part of project management, especially in industries like construction, where projects are often large, complex, and subject to many variables.

Purpose of the Project Risk and Opportunity Log

1. Identify Potential Risks and Opportunities: By documenting possible risks (like delays, cost overruns, or safety issues) and opportunities (like cost savings or efficiency gains), project teams can plan proactively.

2. Decision-Making Guide: The log serves as a central point of reference to guide decisions based on the potential impacts of risks and benefits of opportunities.

3. Align Team on Priorities: All team members are made aware of areas of concern and areas for improvement, encouraging proactive collaboration.

Key Components of a Project Risk and Opportunity Log

1. Risk and Opportunity Description: Detailed descriptions of each risk and opportunity, including what might trigger them and their possible impacts.

2. Risk/Opportunity Owner: The individual responsible for monitoring and managing each risk or opportunity.

3. Probability: An assessment of the likelihood of each risk or opportunity occurring.

4. Impact: The potential impact (usually quantified in terms of cost, time, or quality) if the risk or opportunity materializes.

5. Risk Response: The plan to mitigate, avoid, or transfer risks or to capitalize on opportunities.

6. Status: The current status, such as "Open," "In Progress," or "Closed."

7. Target Resolution Date: The date by which each risk or opportunity is expected to be addressed.

8. Progress Updates: Regular updates on each item's status, including any changes in probability, impact, or responses.

Why It is Important to Set Up Early and Review Monthly

1. Early Detection: Identifying risks and opportunities at the outset allows for timely planning and minimizes the chance of surprises down the line.

2. Proactive Management: Regular reviews ensure that emerging risks are addressed and potential opportunities are leveraged, enhancing overall project control.

3. Tracking Performance Against Baseline: Monthly updates allow teams to measure actual performance against initial expectations, offering insights that can lead to adjustments and better outcomes.

4. Continuous Improvement: By managing and updating the log monthly, teams learn from each risk or opportunity, building a knowledge base for future projects.

Establishing and maintaining a Project Risk and Opportunity Log is crucial for minimizing unexpected issues and maximizing value, both for current and future construction projects.

This log provides transparency, facilitates communication, and ensures swift action.

Construction Phase Risk Readiness Checklist

Regularly verify:

- Fully updated short-term schedules.

- Weekly safety audits.

- Complete documentation and pricing of field directives.

- Active logistics planning aligned with current work.

- Consistent trade attendance at coordination meetings.

- Timely reporting and documentation of unforeseen conditions.

- Ongoing engagement of foremen in productivity tracking.

Project Management Administrative Plans (PMAP)

1. Purpose

A Project Management Administrative Plan (PMAP) is a document that defines how a project is executed, monitored, and controlled. The Project manager creates the PMAP following inputs from the project team and the key stakeholders. The PMAP is a formal, approved document that defines the approach the project team takes to deliver the intended scope of the project, safely, on time and, on budget. As the work proceeds, the performance of the project is measured against the scope, schedule and, cost baselines included in the project management plan.

2. Importance

Effective project planning is a cornerstone of any successful project. A comprehensive Project Management Approach Plan serves as a roadmap, outlining how resources and time will be allocated and identifying potential risks and opportunities that could impact the schedule or budget. Below are ten key reasons that highlight the importance of the PMAP.

Serves as a Starting Point for The Project

Establishing the project baseline, outlining the scope, time frame, and budget, will allow you to compare the actual progress of your project against what was initially anticipated. This allows you to assess whether the project is progressing according to plan rapidly and, if it isn't, what needs to be done to correct or mitigate any issues.

The Project Is More Organized

There are no surprises when your project is written out in a clear project plan. To avoid any miscommunication, the project plan will lay out all the deadlines and deliverables in detail so that everyone involved is aware of their expectations.

Defines the Project's Scope in Detail

The project plan will prevent issues related to the scope of work. The project plan will clearly define the stakeholders' expectations and all agreed-upon deliverables.

Provides for More Efficient Project Management

Breaking down the project's work into digestible parts like deliverables, goals, or tasks makes it simpler to figure out what resources are needed to perform the work successfully.

Instills Confidence in the Success of the Project

When you have a project plan document, everyone can understand how your expertise as a project manager is advancing the project's and the organization's objectives in unambiguous terms.

Provides Alignment of Objectives

Ensures that all stakeholders have a unified understanding of project goals and deliverables.

Identifies Risk and Risk Management Strategies

Identifies potential risks early and outlines mitigation strategies to prevent project delays or cost overruns.

Allocates Resources

Provides a clear plan for resource deployment, including labor, materials, and equipment, optimizing efficiency.

Establishes Quality Assurance

Establishes standards and procedures to maintain quality throughout the project.

Defines the Communication Framework

Defines communication protocols to facilitate adequate information flow among stakeholders.

3. Best Practices

Structured Agenda:

Create a detailed meeting agenda shared in advance to keep discussions focused and comprehensive.

Complete Documentation:

Ensure all relevant documents (e.g., estimates, schedules, contracts, and risk assessments) are prepared and organized.

Clarity of Responsibilities:

Clearly define roles and responsibilities for all parties involved to prevent gaps or overlaps.

Focus on Risks and Mitigation:

Highlight potential challenges and strategies for addressing them during project execution.

Post-Meeting Follow-Up:

Document action items, assign responsibilities, and set deadlines to ensure accountability.

The PMAP should break down and specifically address the following key elements

1. Executive Summary.

2. Project Approach.

As-Bid / As-Sold Strategy

- Self-Perform Strategy.

- Owned Equipment vs. Rental Equipment

- Project Schedule / Sequencing of the Work.

- Means and Methods.

- General Conditions Estimate.

Risks and Mitigations.

Opportunities / Value Engineering.

Project Goals and Success Factors.

3. Safety.

- Safety Concerns and Mitigations.

- Environmental Concerns and Mitigations.

- Approach to Safety.

4. Quality.

- Quality Goals and Measurements for Success.

- Approach to Quality.

- Work Plans.

5. Project Team.

6. Prime Contract

- Key Contract Provisions.

- Liquidated Damages.

- Consequential Damages.

- Notification Requirements.

- Change Management

- Differing Site Conditions.

- Claims and Dispute Resolution.

- Bonds.

- Insurance.

- Retainage.

- Tax Considerations.

- Warranty.

- Annual Contract Review.

- Legal Review of Prime Contract

7. Procurement, Subcontracts, and Purchase Agreements.

- Procurement Plan.

- Procurement Plan Roles and Responsibilities.

- GAP Analysis.

- Plan Updates.

- Buy-out Log.

- Subcontracts.

- Subcontractor Management

- Insurance/Bond Checklist and Tracking.

- Purchase Agreements.

- Purchase Agreements Management

- Equipment/Material Tracking.

- Equipment/Material Storage and Maintenance.

- Field Purchase Orders.

- Credit Card Usage.

- Capital Expenditures Policy.

8. Budget and Cost

- Budget Setup.

- Financial Reporting.

- Change Management

- Use of Contingency.

- Invoicing.

- Positive Cash Flow.

9. Schedule.

- Prime Contract Milestones.

- Prime Contract Provisions

- Baseline Schedule.

- Periodic Updates and Schedule Revisions.

- Short Interval Schedule

- Recovery Schedule.

10. Self-Performance.

- Self Perform Budget

- Self Perform Roles and Responsibilities.

11. Project Engineering.

- Centralized Project Engineering

12. Digital Delivery.

- Digital Delivery Scope and Budget

13. Commissioning & Start-Up.

- C&SU Scope and Budget

14. Close-Out

PMAP Policies and Procedures

Following the turnover meeting with estimating, the project team will develop a project-specific plan. The project-specific plan will outline the assignment of duties and responsibilities of the project team. The project-specific PMAP plan will support the requirements necessary to fulfill the scheduled delivery of information as outlined herein for review with the Project Executive. Below is a suggested division of responsibilities; however, every project is unique, and the final assignment and requirements will be determined by the project team and identified in the project-specific plan.

Project Manager:

- Buy-out and Procurement Plan

- Contract Compliance Plan WBE/MBE/DBE

- Assemble Project Specific Templates

- Schedule Values

- New Project Start-Up Form

Superintendent:

- Assemble Budget with PM

- Schedule Outline

- Manpower Staffing/Resource Plan/Equipment Utilization

- Job Mobilization Schedule

- Specialized Equipment

- Assemble site-specific safety plan and new JSAs with Safety Lead

Project Engineer:

- Submittal Schedule

- Contact List

Scheduler:

- Coordinate with Subs for Schedule information

QA/QC:

- QA/QC Plan

CSU:

- CSU Plan

Timeline

The outline below is a guide and timeline for the completion of various documents, with the goal of being fully complete and ready to start work prior to the PMAP meeting. This schedule may need to be accelerated depending on the specific contract, time of award, and schedule of the PMAP meeting. It is the project team's responsibility to determine the requirements and resources needed to complete the activities as outlined, in support of the PMAP meeting or project start. No work should take place without a complete plan.

Within 2 weeks after the estimating turnover meeting (see Chapter 14)

- Buyout and Procurement Plan

- Contract Compliance Plan WBE/MBE/DBE

- Initial Budget with a comprehensive review of the estimate

- Conforming Contract Documents

Within 3 weeks after the estimating turnover meeting

- Initial Project Schedule

- Final Project Budget

- Resource Plan

- Submittal Log

- Resource Planning, manpower

- Construction Equipment Utilization

- Finalize Project Schedule

- Safety Plan

- Schedule of Values

- Site-specific safety plan and new JSAs

The estimating department has the responsibility of completing the contract documents. However, the project manager should confirm that all documents are in place or that the appropriate action is being implemented to ensure all the requirements are being fulfilled.

- Owner Agreement shall be reviewed by the Chief Estimator & PM, then forwarded for execution

- The Chief Estimator shall procure the necessary bonds and insurance

- The Project Manager shall schedule an initial project team meeting to review the roles and requirements of each team member to prepare the PMAP within 1 week after estimating turnover.

- The formal PMAP meeting shall take place within 4 weeks after the Estimating Turnover Meeting and following the assignment of the project team, by the Executive Project Director. In preparation for this meeting, copies of the completed PMAP shall be prepared by the Project Manager and submitted for review and comment by all attendees no later than 1 week prior to the date of the meeting to allow sufficient time for the review of this documentation prior to the meeting.

- Any comments and questions for the project team related to the completed PMAP should be provided to the Project Manager at least 2 days prior to the meeting.

- Follow-up meetings are required for unresolved issues or updates.

Procedure

Preparation Stage:

- Schedule the meeting at least two weeks in advance.

- Distribute the agenda and PMAP package, including estimates, schedules, contracts, and risk assessments.

- Set up a Teams Folder containing all documents utilized to create the Project Management Approach Plan.

During the Meeting:

- Follow the agenda

- Discuss each component in detail.

- Document key decisions, changes, and action items in real-time.

Post-Meeting Actions:

- Distribute meeting minutes within two business days.

- Assign unresolved items to appropriate team members with deadlines.

RACI Chart

Responsible:

- Project Manager

- Superintendent

- Project Engineer

- Scheduling

- QA/QC

- Safety

- CSU

Accountable:

- Project Executive

- Director of Estimating

- Business Development Manager

Consulted:

- Risk Manager

Informed:

- Digital Delivery

- Project Controls

Chapter Conclusion

Construction risk is decided in the field each day, either by your systems or by your silence.

Construction phase risks are inevitable, but they need not be catastrophic. By embedding structured processes, disciplined leadership, clear communication protocols, and continuous accountability into daily operations, risks can be identified and addressed early, preserving project margins, schedules, quality, and safety.

In construction, risk management is not just about responding to issues; it is about building resilience into your execution strategy. Proactively managed projects do not merely survive; they thrive, delivering value to clients and sustaining profitability.

"The greatest danger in times of turbulence is not the turbulence; it is to act with yesterday's logic." – **Peter Drucker**

CHAPTER 17

MONITORING KEY PERFORMANCE INDICATORS DURING CONSTRUCTION

Chapter Foreword

Construction is one of the most complex, fast-moving, and high-risk industries on the planet. Hundreds of activities unfold at once, thousands of decisions are made each day, and the most minor oversight can ripple into massive consequences. In this environment, intuition alone is not enough. Successful project teams rely on measurable, objective, and consistently monitored indicators to understand whether a project is truly on track.

These indicators known as Key Performance Indicators, or KPI's serve as the project's instrumentation panel. They reveal the health of a project in real time, translating field activity, financial data, coordination efforts, and schedule progression into clear signals of performance. When properly selected and rigorously monitored, KPI's give project leaders the ability to spot trends early, identify risks before they evolve into claims, and correct course long before a problem becomes an emergency.

KPI's bridge the gap between perception and reality. A project might "feel" busy, productive, or under control, but KPI's expose whether that feeling is backed by measurable progress. They highlight where the project is strong, where it is slipping, and where leadership needs to intervene. They establish a common language between owners, contractors, consultants, and field teams ensuring everyone is aligned on what success looks like and how it is measured.

This chapter presents a comprehensive system of KPI's explicitly designed for modern construction management. These indicators span cost, schedule, procurement, quality, safety, logistics, design coordination, and stakeholder engagement. Together, they form a complete performance framework that supports predictable outcomes, transparent communication, and disciplined risk management. In construction, KPI's are the tools that turn complexity into clarity, uncertainty into action, and good intentions into high-performance results.

"You cannot manage what you do not measure." – **Peter Drucker**

Construction Phase Key Performance Indicators

#	KPI Name	Category	Purpose / What It Indicates
1	Schedule Variance (SV)	Schedule	Tracks early schedule slippage or gains
2	Schedule Performance Index (SPI)	Schedule	Measures production rate vs plan
3	Cost Variance (CV)	Cost	Identifies cost overrun/underrun trends
4	Cost Performance Index (CPI)	Cost	Measures cost efficiency of labor & trades
5	Estimate at Completion (EAC)	Cost	Forecasts final cost outcome
6	Work-In-Progress (WIP)	Financial	Ensures accurate revenue recognition
7	Change Order Frequency	Risk	Measures design/scope stability
8	CO Cost Impact	Financial	Quantifies financial exposure from changes
9	CO Cycle Time	Process	Measures administrative efficiency
10	RFI Volume	Quality/Design	Indicates drawing completeness
11	RFI Aging	Design	Measures responsiveness and risk exposure
12	RFI-to-Contract Value	Quality	Normalizes drawing issues for scale
13	Submittal Review Cycle Time	Procurement	Measures design team responsiveness
14	Submittal Rejection Rate	Quality	Indicates spec clarity or subcontractor prep
15	Procurement Lead Time	Procurement	Predicts schedule impacts from equipment
16	Long-Lead Tracking Accuracy	Procurement	Prevents critical path blowouts
17	Labor Productivity Ratio	Cost	Measures field efficiency
18	Labor Overtime %	Cost/Safety	Identifies staffing shortages or schedule stress
19	Staffing Curve Accuracy	Schedule	Evaluates manpower planning effectiveness
20	Rework Rate	Quality	Indicates quality failures and cost risk
21	Inspection Fail Rate	Quality	Measures QC program health
22	Punch List Closure Rate	Turnover	Predicts substantial completion readiness
23	Safety Incident Rate	Safety	Measures field risk and project culture
24	Safety Observation Rate	Safety	Measures engagement & risk prevention
25	OSHA Audit Score	Safety/Compliance	Measures regulatory compliance
26	Subcontractor Performance Score	Management	Evaluates trade partner reliability
27	Subcontractor Financial Health	Risk	Prevents collapse or abandonment
28	Procurement Log Accuracy	Procurement	Measures reliability of supply chain data
29	Material Delivery Reliability	Logistics	Measures readiness & flow of materials
30	Workforce Readiness	Field Ops	Measures production continuity
31	Work Packaging Completion Rate	Schedule	Measures planning reliability
32	Temporary Works Readiness	Field Ops	Ensures safe and ready workfaces
33	Equipment Utilization	Logistics	Tracks efficiency of major equipment
34	Site Logistics Efficiency	Logistics	Measures material flow, congestion, access
35	Waste / Scrap Rate	Quality/Cost	Indicates planning & installation efficiency
36	Design Clarification Turnaround	Design	Measures A/E responsiveness
37	BIM Clash Resolution Rate	Coordination	Predicts rework risk
38	Coordination Drawing Completion	Design/MEP	Ensures installable design ahead of fieldwork
39	Precon Estimate Accuracy	Preconstruction	Measures forecasting discipline
40	Buyout Savings vs Budget	Procurement	Reflects precon assumption accuracy
41	Contingency Burn Rate	Cost	Measures design + construction stability
42	Allowance Drawdown Accuracy	Cost	Gauges precon quality of undefined scope
43	Issue Log Aging	Management	Measures decision-making responsiveness
44	Owner Decision Turnaround	Stakeholder	Measures alignment & schedule impact
45	PM/Engineer Response Time	Internal Ops	Measures operational responsiveness
46	Cost Forecast Accuracy	Cost	Measures discipline & predictability
47	Cash Flow Performance	Financial	Measures fiscal stability
48	Claims/Dispute Frequency	Risk	Measures relationship health
49	Closeout Readiness Index	Turnover	Predicts turnover risk & delay
50	Customer Satisfaction Score	Stakeholder	Measures trust, communication, expectations

Construction Key Performance Indicators Defined

1. Schedule Variance (SV)

What it measures:
Schedule Variance compares planned progress to actual progress by measuring the dollarized or quantified difference between Planned Value (PV) and Earned Value (EV).

Why it matters:
SV is one of the quickest and most objective indicators of whether a project is tracking on time. Because it reflects real work performed, it cannot be manipulated by optimistic schedules or inaccurate progress logs.

How it reflects project health:
A **positive SV** means the project is ahead of schedule, indicating strong coordination, steady field productivity, and effective sequencing. A **negative SV** signals delays and is often the earliest warning that the project is slipping.

What poor performance means:
Consistently negative SV suggests issues such as:

- Low trade productivity

- Out-of-sequence work

- Resource shortages

- Late submittals, RFIs, or approvals

- Delays in predecessor tasks

What leadership should do:
Conduct a root-cause analysis of late activities, review updated look-ahead schedules, and verify whether the critical path has changed. Leadership may need to resequence the work, add shifts, or introduce recovery actions.

Early warning threshold:
$SV < -5\%$ for more than two reporting periods typically indicates systemic schedule risk that requires escalation.

2. Schedule Performance Index (SPI)

What it measures:
SPI is a ratio ($EV \div PV$) that shows the rate at which the project is earning work compared to the plan.

Why it matters:
SPI provides a normalized productivity indicator and is more intuitive than raw variance when comparing periods, trades, or small vs large scopes.

How it reflects project health:

SPI = 1.0 → performing exactly as planned

SPI > 1.0 → performing ahead of plan

SPI < 1.0 → performing behind plan

Because it captures actual earned progress, it exposes optimism bias in schedules and reveals whether the plan is realistic.

What poor performance means:
SPI below 1.0 commonly points to:

- Incorrect crew sizing

- Field inefficiencies

- Logistical bottlenecks

- Missing materials

- Poor workforce planning

- Delayed inspections or hold points

What leadership should do:
Identify the worst-performing work packages and compare planned vs installed quantities. Ensure foremen use constraint-free look-ahead planning and confirm materials and information flow are supporting the field.

Early warning threshold:
SPI < **0.90** sustained across two updates is a high-risk indicator.

3. Cost Variance (CV)

What it measures:
CV (EV – AC) compares earned value to actual cost, revealing whether the project is spending more or less than planned for the work accomplished.

Why it matters:
It serves as the primary indicator of cost health. A favorable CV means crews are executing the work at or below the budgeted cost; an unfavorable CV means overruns exist.

How it reflects project health:

Positive CV → under budget, strong efficiency

Negative CV → over budget, deteriorating financial health

Because CV is tied directly to productivity, it helps identify which trades or scopes are burning labor faster than value is being created.

What poor performance means:
Chronic negative CV usually indicates:

- Low craft productivity

- Excessive rework

- Underestimated labor units

- Poor material utilization

- Extended general conditions or idle time

- Equipment inefficiency

What leadership should do:
Perform a productivity deep dive: compare planned vs actual crew hours per unit, analyze reasons for rework, verify quantities, and update trend logs. Consider implementing productivity trackers and measured-mile analyses.

Early warning threshold:
CV worse than **−5% of total labor budget** early in the project is a major red flag.

4. Cost Performance Index (CPI)

What it measures:
CPI (EV ÷ AC) indicates cost efficiency — how much value is earned for every dollar spent.

Why it matters:
CPI is powerful because it becomes a predictor of final cost at completion (Estimate at Completion, EAC).

How it reflects project health:

CPI = 1.0 → costs are exactly on plan

CPI > 1.0 → earning more than spending

CPI < 1.0 → spending more than earning

CPI below 1.0 early in the project often predicts major overruns unless corrective action is taken.

What poor performance means:
CPI deterioration signals issues such as:

- Low labor efficiencies

- Excessive change impacts

- Rework or defects

- Congested work areas

- Stacking of trades

- Poor supervision or planning

What leadership should do:
Verify accuracy of quantity tracking and cost coding. Review whether the productivity baseline was realistic. Leadership may need to apply targeted recovery plans or renegotiate subcontract scopes.

Early warning threshold:
CPI < **0.92** early in the job will almost always lead to a negative cost outcome.

5. Estimate at Completion (EAC)

What it measures:
EAC forecasts the total final cost of the project based on actual performance to date and predicted future productivity.

Why it matters:
EAC is the single most important forecasting KPI. It determines whether the project will finish within budget or experience a cost overrun.

How it reflects project health:

A rising EAC indicates deteriorating cost performance or changes in scope or labor efficiency. A steady or decreasing EAC suggests effective control and stable productivity.

What poor performance means:
An increasing EAC may reflect:

- Systemic productivity decline

- Incorrect original budget

- Excessive change orders

- Late design impacting labor

- Extended general conditions

- Material price escalation

What leadership should do:
Leadership should require explanation of all EAC shifts, verify forecasting logic, perform trend analysis, and require "bottom-up" EACs from subcontractors when thresholds are exceeded.

Early warning threshold:
EAC projected to exceed budget by **>3%** by mid-project indicates significant risk of final overrun.

6. Work-In-Progress (WIP) Analysis

What it measures:
WIP tracks whether the project is recognizing revenue and cost proportionate to actual progress. It identifies over-billings, under-billings, and the financial alignment between earned value and invoicing.

Why it matters:
Accurate WIP ensures the job's financial position is correctly represented. It prevents false profit recognition, cash-flow distortions, and surprise losses at the end of the job.

How it reflects project health:

Healthy WIP: billing closely matches earned progress and cost.

Over-billing: strong cash position, but risk of future productivity pressure.

Under-billing: indicates delays, unresolved change orders, or poor billing practices.

What poor performance means:
Common causes include:

- Delayed owner approvals

- Unpriced or unsubmitted change orders

- Inaccurate percent-complete reporting

- Incomplete cost coding

- Poor understanding of earned value

What leadership should do:
Perform reconciliation between revenue, cost, and earned progress monthly. Confirm subcontractor billings match actual work accomplished. Require PMs to align WIP values with schedule status and cost reports.

Early warning threshold:
Under-billing greater than **10% of earned value** is a severe indicator of cash-flow stress or incorrect forecasting.

7. Change Order Frequency

What it measures:
Tracks how often change orders are occurring and how frequently potential changes evolve into formal claims.

Why it matters:
High change frequency disrupts workflow, impacts schedule, increases soft costs, and is often tied to design issues or owner indecision.

How it reflects project health:

Low frequency: drawings are well-developed, scope is stable, and coordination is strong.

High or accelerating frequency: design gaps, unclear scope, or owner-driven changes are stressing the project.

What poor performance means:
Frequent changes often result from:

- Incomplete design at GMP or award

- Overlapping phases in fast-track projects

- Owner decision delays

- Late design clarifications

- Contractor discovery of scope gaps

What leadership should do:
Conduct root-cause trending: classify changes by discipline and origin (owner, design team, contractor). Enforce early design coordination, pre-award constructability reviews, and strict RFI closeout.

Early warning threshold:
More than **3 significant change events per month** on a mid-size project signals loss of scope control.

8. Change Order Impact on Cost

What it measures:
Quantifies the dollar impact of approved and pending changes compared to the original contract value or GMP.

Why it matters:
High CO cost impact erodes contingency, inflates the GMP, and exposes the project to claims or budget overruns.

How it reflects project health:

Low impact (<2–3%): well-defined scope, good planning, and effective stakeholder engagement.

High impact (>5–10%): systemic risk in design development, owner expectations, or field conditions.

What poor performance means:
Large CO impact often stems from:

- Design errors or omissions

- Unanticipated site conditions

- Revisions triggered by compliance or code

- Owner-requested enhancements

- Poor early procurement definition

What leadership should do:
Audit the top CO drivers, validate pricing, and ensure all pending changes are forecasted in the EAC. Require proactive trend logs before COs are formally priced.

Early warning threshold:

Changes exceeding **10% of original contract value** typically indicate severe scope instability.

9. Change Order Cycle Time

What it measures:
Tracks how long it takes to process a change from identification to approval, including pricing, negotiation, and execution.

Why it matters:
Slow cycle time delays revenue recognition increases subcontractor disputes and disrupts workflow by forcing work-at-risk.

How it reflects project health:

Healthy cycle (<30 days): strong communication and administrative discipline.

Slow cycle (>45–60 days): bottlenecks in pricing, owner review, or documentation.

What poor performance means:
Long cycle times are usually caused by:

- Owner indecision

- Designers slow to issue clarifications

- Incomplete pricing packages

- Poor documentation of merit and entitlement

- Excessive back-and-forth on T&M vs lump sum

What leadership should do:
Implement strict CO workflows with aging dashboards. Require detailed scope narratives, backup, and pricing templates. Consider weekly CO review calls with owner/design representatives.

Early warning threshold:
If more than **25% of open changes exceed 45 days**, administrative breakdown is occurring.

10. RFI Volume (Total RFIs Issued)

What it measures:
Counts how many RFIs have been submitted to the design team, acting as a proxy for drawing completeness, clarity, and constructability.

Why it matters:
High RFI volume often indicates incomplete design documents, coordination gaps, or insufficient detail for the contractor to proceed without clarification.

How it reflects project health:

Low/Normal RFI volume indicates good design quality and clear trade coordination.

High or accelerating volume: design gaps are creating productivity loss and schedule risk.

What poor performance means:
High RFI volume may be tied to:

- Poorly coordinated drawings

- Fast-track design development

- Late changes causing cascading clarifications

- Inexperienced design team

- Scope gaps between trades

What leadership should do:

Trend RFIs by discipline and root cause. Escalate unresolved RFIs older than 14 days. Require design team to issue RFI-response logs and weekly review cycles.

Early warning threshold:

100 RFIs per $10 million contract value indicates severe documentation deficiencies.

11. RFI Aging (Average Days Open)

What it measures:

RFI aging tracks how long RFIs remain unresolved from the date of submission, indicating the responsiveness of the design team and the effectiveness of project communication channels.

Why it matters:

RFIs are often information critical. A delayed response can stall field crews, disrupt sequencing, cause rework, and create cumulative delay impacts across multiple trades.

How it reflects project health:

Healthy projects: RFIs answered within 7–14 days.

At-risk projects: RFIs lingering 21–30+ days, especially if tied to critical path work.

What poor performance means:

Long aging durations typically indicate:

- Backlogged design consultants

- Incomplete design development

- Overloaded project teams

- Poor RFI quality (unclear question or inadequate detail)

- Bottlenecks in owner or AHJ decisions

What leadership should do:

Implement weekly RFI review meetings, aging dashboards, and priority flags for critical-path RFIs. Standardize RFI format, require supporting sketches, and escalate items older than 14 days.

Early warning threshold:

More than **20% of RFIs aged >21 days** is a serious risk signal and must be escalated.

12. RFI-to-Contract-Value Ratio

What it measures:
This KPI normalizes RFI volume against total contract value, making it possible to compare project documentation quality across different sizes and scopes.

Why it matters:
A high RFI-to-value ratio is a strong indicator of poor design completeness, poor coordination, or excessive ambiguity in contract documents.

How it reflects project health:

Low/expected ratio: design documents are stable, well-coordinated, and constructible.

High ratio: systemic design issues are draining project resources and labor productivity.

What poor performance means:
Ratios spike when:

- The project was rushed into procurement before designs were mature.

- There are many cross-trade interfaces (MEP-heavy facilities, hospitals, data centers).

- The owner changes scope frequently.

- The design team lacks experience with the building type.

What leadership should do:
Conduct a discipline-by-discipline trend analysis, perform a design quality audit, and escalate repeated RFI themes. Require the A/E to issue drawing supplements or bulletins where needed.

Early warning threshold:

10 RFIs per \$1M in contract value indicates documentation quality risk.

13. Submittal Review Cycle Time

What it measures:
Tracks the number of days required for the design team to review and return submittals, shop drawings, samples, and product data.

Why it matters:

Submittals drive procurement and installation. Slow review cycles disrupt material deliveries, delay fabrication, and stall critical-path work.

How it reflects project health:

Healthy: 10–14 day turnaround.

Concerning: 21–28 days.

Critical: 30+ days or repeated resubmittals due to unclear comments.

What poor performance means:
Slow submittal reviews often reveal:

- Overloaded designers

- Incomplete or incorrect submittals from subcontractors

- Poor front-end planning of procurement schedules

- Ambiguity in contract requirements

- High volume of RFIs delaying submittal evaluation

What leadership should do:
Establish a submittal priority log, implement weekly review coordination, pre-screen submittals before sending to designers, and escalate delayed reviews tied to long-lead items.

Early warning threshold:
Any long-lead submittal aged over **30 days** indicates risk of procurement delay.

14. Submittal Rejection/Resubmittal Rate

What it measures:
Tracks the percentage of submittals returned as "Revise and Resubmit," "Rejected," or "Returned for Correction."

Why it matters:
A high rejection rate signals misalignment between the subcontractor and design intent, poor document quality, or unclear specifications.

How it reflects project health:

Low rejection rate (<20%): Strong coordination and clear contract requirements.

Moderate (20–35%): Some specification gaps or subcontractor quality issues.

High (>35%): Major disconnects in design, scope interpretation, or trade coordination.

What poor performance means:
High rejection rates arise from:

- Inexperienced subcontractors

- Poor specification clarity

- Insufficient preconstruction coordination

- Lack of internal QA/QC before submittal

- Design detail missing in contract documents

What leadership should do:
Institute a strict submittal QA review process, provide subcontractors with samples of acceptable submittals, and ensure coordination drawings and BIM models are complete before formal submission.

Early warning threshold:

30% resubmittal rate across multiple trades indicates widespread document quality issues.

15. Procurement Lead Time Performance

What it measures:
Evaluates whether procurement activities (submittals, approvals, fabrication, and delivery) are occurring within the planned durations defined in the procurement schedule.

Why it matters:
Procurement timing directly affects the critical path. Delayed procurement is one of the top three causes of schedule overruns in major construction projects.

How it reflects project health:

Healthy: Most materials delivered on or before scheduled need dates.

At risk: Multiple long-lead items running late.

Critical: Materials or equipment arriving after installation dates, causing idle crews.

What poor performance means:
Late procurement usually indicates:

- Incorrect lead-times assumed in preconstruction

- Slow submittal turnaround

- Supplier capacity issues

- Incomplete engineering or late design changes

- Poor communication with vendors

What leadership should do:

Review procurement logs weekly; accelerate critical packages; conduct supplier readiness checks; and verify that procurement, submittals, and fabrication are fully tied to the CPM schedule.

Early warning threshold:

10% of procurement items "late to need date" is a major schedule threat.

16. Long-Lead Item Tracking Accuracy

What it measures:

This KPI evaluates how accurately the project team identifies, monitors, and forecasts long-lead materials and equipment—such as switchgear, custom HVAC units, structural steel, façade systems, and specialized process equipment.

Why it matters:

Long-lead items frequently drive the critical path. If procurement, fabrication, and delivery dates slip, no amount of field manpower can recover the schedule. Missing a long-lead item is one of the most common and most expensive schedule failures on large projects.

How it reflects project health:

High accuracy: The team is updating lead times, coordinating with vendors, and controlling procurement risk.

Low accuracy: Surprise delays appear late, forcing resequencing, temporary work, or idle crews.

What poor performance means:

Inaccurate long-lead tracking usually stems from:

- Incorrect or outdated lead-time assumptions

- Lack of vendor coordination

- Slow submittal approvals

- Designers issuing late revisions during fabrication

- Poorly maintained procurement logs

What leadership should do:
Require weekly coordination with suppliers, validate fabrication milestones, and integrate vendor schedules into the CPM schedule. Leadership must also ensure submittals are prioritized based on need dates, not simply by trade order.

Early warning threshold:
Long-lead items with **update variances >14 days** typically signal looming schedule impacts.

17. Labor Productivity Ratio (Planned vs. Actual Unit Rates)

What it measures:
Tracks whether field labor is installing work at, above, or below the planned productivity rate (e.g., labor hours per linear foot, per ton, per square foot, etc.).

Why it matters:
Labor is the most variable and most expensive component of construction cost. Productivity erosion directly drives cost overruns and schedule slippage.

How it reflects project health:

Meeting or beating unit rates: Healthy sequencing, well-planned workforces, and strong supervision.

Underperforming unit rates: Productivity problems that compound daily.

What poor performance means:
Productivity shortfalls may be caused by:

- Worker congestion or stacking of trades

- Excessive rework

- Insufficient prefabrication

- Poor workforce planning

- Bad logistics or material staging

- Inexperienced crews or supervision

What leadership should do:
Conduct root-cause analysis using measured-mile comparisons. Validate whether lost productivity is recoverable or must be converted into a change request. Ensure foremen create weekly work plans removing constraints.

Early warning threshold:
Actual productivity **10% below plan** for two consecutive updates is a high-risk indicator.

18. Field Labor Overtime Percentage

What it measures:

Tracks the percentage of total labor hours spent in overtime, which indicates whether staffing levels and schedule performance are being maintained without excessive premium labor.

Why it matters:

Overtime boosts short-term output but reduces long-term productivity and increases safety risk, burnout, and turnover. It also inflates labor cost significantly.

How it reflects project health:

Low controlled OT (<5%): The project is properly staffed and sequenced.

Moderate OT (5–10%): Indications of schedule pressure.

High OT (>10–15%): The project is in recovery mode and may be hemorrhaging cost.

What poor performance means:
High OT usage suggests:

- Inadequate staffing plans

- Late procurement or delayed predecessors

- Excessive rework

- Failed productivity in regular hours

- Unrealistic schedule durations

What leadership should do:
Analyze whether OT is corrective or compensatory. Evaluate whether hiring additional crews is more cost-effective. Ensure that critical workforces are fully ready before authorizing overtime.

Early warning threshold:
OT exceeding **10% of total labor hours** for more than two pay periods signals severe stress.

19. Crew Staffing Accuracy (Planned vs. Actual Staffing Levels)

What it measures:
Evaluates how closely on-site manpower aligns with the planned labor curve, identifying whether trades are appropriately staffed to support the schedule.

Why it matters:
Understaffing delays progress; overstaffing leads to congestion, reduced productivity, and increased safety risks. Accurate staffing is essential to stable workflow.

How it reflects project health:

Aligned staffing: Workforces are flowing smoothly, and supervisors are planning effectively.

Understaffed: Schedule threats, bottlenecks, missed milestones.

Overstaffed: Inefficient labor spend, coordination issues, and logistic strain.

What poor performance means:
Common root causes include:

- Inaccurate manpower planning during preconstruction

- Poor subcontractor performance

- Late design preventing work release

- Incomplete workforces

- Delayed predecessor activities

What leadership should do:
Demand updated manpower curves weekly, validate subcontractor hiring commitments, and ensure field planners are sequencing work realistically. Leadership should connect staffing trends with schedule variance and productivity indicators.

Early warning threshold:

15% deviation from the staffing curve for major trades indicates the labor plan is failing.

20. Percent of Work Requiring Rework (Quality Defect Rate)

What it measures:
Calculates the percentage of installed work that requires rework, repair, or replacement due to quality issues, design conflicts, or installation errors.

Why it matters:
Rework is one of the most expensive forms of waste, costing 5–15 times more than doing the work correctly the first time. It damages productivity, schedule, morale, and safety performance.

How it reflects project health:

Low rework (<2%): Strong quality control, supervision, and trade coordination.

Moderate rework (2–5%): Warning signs of systemic quality issues.

High (>5%): Severe quality breakdown affecting cost and schedule.

What poor performance means:
High rework rates often arise from:

- Incomplete design or late changes

- Poor coordination between trades

- Lack of formal QA/QC checks

- Inexperienced workforce

- Rushed work due to schedule pressure

- Misaligned installation tolerances

What leadership should do:
Increase inspections, implement hold-point checklists, enforce first-work-in-place reviews, and improve BIM/coordination workflows. Ensure foremen and installers understand tolerances and accepted installation standards.

Early warning threshold:
Rework exceeding **3% of total installed work** is already significant and requires aggressive mitigation.

21. Inspection Fail Rate (Failed vs. Passed Inspections)

What it measures:
Tracks the percentage of inspections, (internal, third-party, AHJ, or owner) that fail on the first attempt.

Why it matters:
Inspection failures are direct evidence of quality issues. They create rework, idle time, schedule delays, and friction with authorities or the owner. Persistent failures indicate systemic breakdowns in QA/QC.

How it reflects project health:

Low failure rate (<10%): Quality processes are working, and crews understand installation requirements.

Moderate failure (10–20%): Coordination or workforce skill issues emerging.

High failure (>20%): Serious quality control deficiencies affecting cost and schedule.

What poor performance means:
High failure rates typically reflect:

- Poor pre-inspection checks by foremen

- Incomplete or unclear drawings/specifications

- Crews not trained on project standards

- Productivity pressure pushing incomplete work into inspection

- Mistakes in layout or tolerances

What leadership should do:
Implement pre-inspection checklists, require QC signoffs, increase training, and hold field supervisors accountable for inspection readiness. Track failures by trade to identify which groups require intervention.

Early warning threshold:

15% repeat failures (same work failing more than once) indicate severe supervisory issues.

22. Punch List Closure Rate

What it measures:
Monitors how quickly punch list items are resolved compared to how fast they are being added, showing whether the project is on track for a clean and timely turnover.

Why it matters:
Punch list closure is often the last major hurdle before substantial completion. A slow closure rate leads directly to delayed turnover, liquidated damages exposure, and unhappy owners.

How it reflects project health:

Healthy: Items closed faster than they are created.

Unhealthy: Growing punch list backlog, especially nearing completion.

What poor performance means:
Slow closure typically comes from:

- Trades demobilizing too early

- Poor workmanship requiring multiple fixes

- Unclear acceptance criteria

- Late design decisions or owner changes

- Insufficient supervision or manpower

- Incomplete systems testing

What leadership should do:
Assign punch list captains, hold daily/weekly closure meetings, categorize items by trade/priority, and block demobilization until completion thresholds are met. Clarify acceptance criteria with owner and design team.

Early warning threshold:
If punch list items are **growing within 60 days of substantial completion**, turnover is in jeopardy.

23. Safety Incident Rate (TRIR / Recordables)

What it measures:
Tracks total recordable incident rate (TRIR), near misses, lost-time injuries, and safety observations relative to total man-hours.

Why it matters:
Safety performance is directly correlated with productivity and cost performance. Unsafe jobs slow down, lose morale, suffer staff turnover, incur financial exposure, and face regulatory penalties. Poor safety = poor production.

How it reflects project health:

Strong safety: consistent inspections, few incidents, high participation.

Weak safety: recordables, unsafe behaviors lack of reporting, or reactive measures.

What poor performance means:
High incident rates often arise from:

- Inadequate training

- Rushed work or excessive OT

- Poor housekeeping

- Congested work areas

- Lack of supervision

- Miscommunication between trades

What leadership should do:

Increase toolbox talks, enforce stop-work authority, perform root-cause investigations, retrain crews, and ensure that supervisors actively participate in safety programs.

Early warning threshold:

TRIR above **1.0** or any **lost-time incident** triggers immediate escalation on most major projects.

24. Safety Observation Rate (Positive or At-Risk Behaviors Identified)

What it measures:

Tracks the number of documented safety observations—positive or negative—submitted by field staff and supervisors.

Why it matters:

A high observation rate means the field is actively engaged in identifying risks before they lead to incidents. Low participation often indicates complacency, lack of buy-in, or insufficient supervision.

How it reflects project health:

High rate: strong safety culture, proactive hazard reduction.

Low rate: poor engagement, lack of inspections, or blind spots in the safety program.

What poor performance means:

Low observation counts usually reflect:

- Supervisors not walking the site enough

- Lack of empowerment to speak up

- Weak safety leadership

- Overstretched teams

- Fear of reporting issues

What leadership should do:

Set observation quotas, coach supervisors on what to look for, celebrate positive observations, and provide feedback loops so workers see real action from their reporting.

Early warning threshold:

Observation rate dropping **below 1 per worker per month** signals low engagement.

25. OSHA Compliance Score (Field Safety Audit Results)

What it measures:
Scores the project's adherence to OSHA standards based on inspections, audits, or third-party safety evaluations.

Why it matters:
OSHA compliance is the baseline legal requirement for any project. Violations expose the company to fines, shutdowns, insurance increases, and potential litigation.

How it reflects project health:

High score / few findings: strong safety program with active leadership.

Many findings: a reactive safety culture and significant exposure.

What poor performance means:
Low compliance often stems from:

- Poor supervision or lack of safety staffing

- Lack of training for high-risk tasks

- Inconsistent PPE use

- Equipment not maintained or improperly stored

- Lack of fall protection planning

What leadership should do:
Verify correction of deficiencies, conduct targeted training, ensure adequate safety staffing, and revisit hazard analyses. Leadership should walk the site frequently to reinforce expectations.

Early warning threshold:
More than **five repeat findings** in monthly audits signals systemic non-compliance.

26. Subcontractor Performance Score (Quality, Schedule, Documentation)

What it measures:
This KPI evaluates each subcontractor's overall performance based on quality of work, adherence to schedule, responsiveness, documentation quality, manpower reliability, and safety behavior.

Why it matters:
Subcontractors perform 80–95% of the physical work on most construction projects. Their performance directly determines whether the project finishes on time, within budget, and with acceptable quality.

How it reflects project health:

High-performing subs: deliver work on time, meet inspection standards, and maintain documentation discipline.

Low-performing subs: trigger rework, schedule slippage, safety incidents, and administrative chaos.

What poor performance means:
Low scores often stem from:

- Insufficient staffing levels

- Lack of supervision

- Poor financial health

- Inexperienced crews

- Weak shop drawing coordination

- Low-quality workmanship or repeated punch failures

What leadership should do:
Escalate performance issues early. Hold weekly coordination meetings, increase QC inspections, require updated manpower plans, and use corrective action notices if necessary. Reassign scopes or augment crews if the subcontractor cannot recover.

Early warning threshold:
Any key subcontractor scoring **below 75%** on quality or schedule metrics is a major project-wide risk.

27. Subcontractor Financial Health (Backlog, Bonding, Payment Timing)

What it measures:
Assesses subcontractor financial stability by tracking payment delays, lien notices, supplier complaints, bonding capacity, and overall cash-flow wellness.

Why it matters:
A financially distressed subcontractor is one of the biggest hidden risks on a project. Financial instability leads to insufficient manpower, material delays, inability to meet payroll, higher change order disputes, and potential abandonment.

How it reflects project health:

Financially stable subs: meet commitments, pay vendors on time, and maintain steady production.

Unstable subs: request early payments, slow down work, or file claims aggressively.

What poor performance means:

Warning signs typically include:

- Repeated requests for advance payments

- Slow payment to suppliers

- Missing manpower or skipped shifts

- Declining quality or morale

- Vendors refusing to release materials

What leadership should do:

Increase oversight, request proof of payroll and supplier payments, redirect material purchases through the GC/CM if needed, and involve bonding companies early. Avoid increasing scope to troubled subs.

Early warning threshold:

Any sub with **more than 60 days of unpaid supplier invoices** represents immediate project risk.

28. Procurement Log Accuracy & Aging

What it measures:

Evaluates the completeness and accuracy of the procurement log, as well as the aging of open items—submittals, approvals, fabrication, and deliveries.

Why it matters:

Procurement is the backbone of schedule reliability. An inaccurate or outdated procurement log creates blind spots that lead to missed long-lead dates, idle labor, and cascading schedule failures.

How it reflects project health:

Accurate log: up to date weekly, with clear need dates and verified statuses.

Inaccurate log: missing dates, old statuses, or mismatched information with vendor schedules.

What poor performance means:

Inaccuracy typically arises from:

- Poor administrative oversight

- Subcontractors not updating data

- Rapid design changes causing confusion

- Poor alignment between procurement and CPM schedule

- Lack of vendor communication

What leadership should do:
Require updates before weekly OAC meetings, cross-check with vendor schedules, and tie procurement status directly into WPIs (Work Plan Interfaces). Use color-coded statuses to highlight aging items.

Early warning threshold:
If > **15% of procurement items have outdated statuses**, the log is unreliable and the schedule is at risk.

29. Material Availability & Delivery Reliability

What it measures:
Tracks whether materials are arriving on time, in the correct sequence, in good condition, and in quantities required to support installation.

Why it matters:
Material delays are one of the fastest ways to lose labor productivity. Crews without materials become idle, project sequencing breaks down, and rework occurs from temporary workarounds.

How it reflects project health:

High reliability: Just-in-time deliveries, minimal shortages, predictable workflow.

Low reliability: frequent delays, missing components, or damaged goods.

What poor performance means:
Material availability issues usually stem from:

- Late submittals or long approval cycles

- Supplier manufacturing delays

- Inaccurate release dates

- Insufficient storage or staging areas

- Poor delivery coordination or traffic control issues

What leadership should do:
Establish material readiness meetings, perform weekly tracking of critical deliveries, use delivery windows, and confirm that materials are stored, tagged, and staged properly. Engage suppliers early when delays emerge.

Early warning threshold:
If > **10% of material deliveries miss scheduled delivery dates**, field productivity is in jeopardy.

30. Installation Sequencing & Workforce Readiness

What it measures:
Assesses whether workforces (areas where crews perform installations) are prepared, coordinated, and free of constraints—materials available, prior trades complete, inspections passed, and access unobstructed.

Why it matters:
Workforce readiness is one of the strongest leading indicators of labor productivity. Poorly prepared workforces create downtime, increase risk of stacking trades, and generate rework from incomplete predecessor tasks.

How it reflects project health:

High readiness: Crews arrive ready to work with all constraints cleared.

Low readiness: Crews arrive and wait, triggering lost hours, frustration, and reduced performance.

What poor performance means:
Workforces become unready due to:

- Late inspections

- Missing materials

- Incomplete layout or tolerances

- Predecessor trades behind schedule

- Delayed design clarifications

- Safety access restrictions

What leadership should do:
Implement a formal Workforce Planning process (WFP), require 2–3 week look-ahead constraint logs, and hold foremen accountable for clearing constraints before crews mobilize. Coordinate with BIM, QC, and safety teams to ensure area readiness.

Early warning threshold:
If more than **20% of workforces are not ready on planned start dates**, schedule reliability is collapsing.

31. Work Packaging Completion Rate (Weekly/Monthly)

What it measures:
Tracks the percentage of planned work packages (WPs), defined scopes of work tied to specific areas, crews, and durations, that are completed within the period they were originally planned.

Why it matters:
Work packaging is central to predictable production. If packages aren't being completed on time, the schedule becomes unreliable and productivity declines. Work packages also reflect the quality of planning and constraint removal.

How it reflects project health:

High completion rate (>80%): Coordinated work, predictable outputs, constraints cleared.

Low completion rate (<60%): Constant disruptions, unready workforces, and poor field planning.

What poor performance means:
Low completion often stems from:

- Materials arriving late

- Inspection failures

- Bottlenecks in predecessor tasks

- Missing or incomplete design details

- Poor weekly planning by field management

- Overly optimistic durations

What leadership should do:
Implement Last Planner® System principles: weekly planning meetings, constraint logs, and percent plan complete (PPC) analysis. Hold foremen accountable for planning and follow-through.

Early warning threshold:
PPC below **65% for two consecutive weeks** signals that the production system is breaking down.

32. Temporary Works Readiness (Scaffolding, Power, Access)

What it measures:
Evaluates whether temporary systems, such as scaffolding, temporary power, access platforms, hoists, crane access, and protection, are available and ready when needed.

Why it matters:
Temporary works enable production. If access or utilities are not ready, entire crews become idle. Late temporary works are a major hidden productivity killer and a significant safety concern.

How it reflects project health:

High readiness: Field teams have safe access and utilities on time.

Low readiness: Delays in scaffolding, lifts, or access routes directly impede installation.

What poor performance means:
Late or missing temporary works typically arise from:

- Inadequate preconstruction planning

- Poor coordination of scaffolding or access subcontractors

- Incomplete structural work preventing access routes

- Delays in power distribution or panel installations

- Insufficient safety or QC inspection of access systems

What leadership should do:
Tie temporary works into the CPM schedule, assign explicit responsibility, and pre-plan access routes during BIM coordination. Conduct daily readiness checks before releasing crews into a workforce.

Early warning threshold:

10% of planned workforces lacking required access or power indicates major readiness failure.

33. Equipment Utilization Rate (Cranes, Lifts, Tools)

What it measures:
Tracks how efficiently the project uses major equipment, cranes, hoists, manlifts, forklifts, generators, excavation equipment, and large tools, compared to available capacity.

Why it matters:
Equipment is expensive and often shared among multiple trades. Ineffective utilization increases rental cost, causes delays, creates site congestion, and limits productivity.

How it reflects project health:

Optimal utilization (70–85%): Equipment is neither idle nor overloaded.

Low utilization (<50%): Wasted rentals, lack of planning, idle equipment.

High utilization (>90%): Risk of bottlenecks and delays in high-demand periods.

What poor performance means:
Poor utilization reflects:

- Lack of coordinated lift plans

- Over-renting or under-renting

- Crew delays reducing equipment usage

- Misalignment between scheduled tasks and equipment availability

- Inefficient site logistics or access

What leadership should do:
Conduct weekly equipment planning, coordinate shared resources across trades, adjust rentals based on usage analytics, and tie equipment needs directly to the look-ahead schedule.

Early warning threshold:
If **crane utilization drops below 60%** or exceeds 90%, operational inefficiency or a future bottleneck is likely.

34. Site Logistics Efficiency (Material Flow, Access Routes, Staging)

What it measures:
Evaluates how well the project manages site logistics, material staging, delivery routes, laydown areas, waste removal, access points, hoist queues, and internal traffic.

Why it matters:
Logistics efficiency is a major driver of productivity. Poor logistics cause delays, congestion, waiting time, safety incidents, and rework. Highly efficient logistics enable predictable workflow and high crew performance.

How it reflects project health:

High efficiency: Materials arrive on time, routes are clear, staging areas are organized, and equipment moves easily.

Low efficiency: Materials pile up, access routes get blocked, and crews waste time walking or searching for materials.

What poor performance means:
Root causes include:

- Ineffective site logistics plan

- Insufficient laydown space

- Out-of-sequence deliveries

- Congested access routes

- Poor communication with suppliers

- Uncontrolled subcontractor staging behavior

What leadership should do:
Establish a strict logistics plan, enforce delivery windows, use visual controls (signage, maps, zone control), and assign a logistics superintendent. Monitor daily logistics readiness via walkdowns.

Early warning threshold:
Crews spending >**20% of time waiting for materials or access** is a critical logistics failure.

35. Material Waste & Scrap Rate

What it measures:
Tracks the percentage of materials discarded, scrapped, or wasted relative to total material usage. Applies to drywall, piping, wire, concrete, steel, lumber, and other construction materials.

Why it matters: High scrap rates indicate poor planning, inaccurate takeoffs, handling damage, or inefficient installation. Scrap also increases cost, clutter, safety risk, and project cleanup time.

How it reflects project health:

Low waste (<3%): Good planning, correct ordering, proper handling.

Moderate waste (3–7%): Handling or installation issues.

High waste (>7%): Severe material management breakdown.

What poor performance means:
Waste spikes due to:

- Incorrect quantity takeoffs

- Improper cutting or measuring

- Poor staging causing damage

- Water exposure or weather impacts

- Design changes after purchasing

- Inadequate material protection

What leadership should do:
Audit takeoff accuracy, enforce material protection standards, improve storage conditions, use prefabrication where possible, and track waste generation by trade.

Early warning threshold:
Scrap exceeding **5%** requires immediate corrective action.

36. Design Clarification Turnaround Time

What it measures:
Tracks the number of days it takes for architects, engineers, or consultants to respond to clarification requests, such as RFIs, sketch requests, design memos, or supplemental instructions.

Why it matters:
Design clarifications directly support field progress. Slow turnaround halts work creates out-of-sequence installation, triggers rework, and forces contractors into "work-at-risk" conditions that can generate claims.

How it reflects project health:

Fast turnaround (<14 days): Design team is aligned with the construction schedule.

Moderate (14–21 days): Some risk emerging; field may experience intermittent delays.

Slow (>21–30 days): Serious design bottleneck affecting critical-path activities.

What poor performance means:
Slow clarifications usually arise from:

- Overloaded design teams

- Incomplete design development

- Decision delays by the owner

- Insufficient detail in the contractor's request

- Complex coordination issues requiring multiple consultants

What leadership should do:
Improve submission quality, conduct weekly design review meetings, escalate aging clarifications, and prioritize critical-path items. Use formal logs with flags for urgent clarifications.

Early warning threshold:
If **25% of design clarifications exceed 21 days**, the project is at high risk of schedule impact.

37. BIM Coordination Clash Resolution Rate

What it measures:
Tracks how many BIM clashes are resolved each week compared to how many are newly identified. This includes structural, MEP, architectural, and specialty system conflicts.

Why it matters:
Coordination clashes are the leading cause of rework in complex buildings (hospitals, data centers, labs, industrial facilities). If clashes are not resolved quickly, field crews face installation conflicts and expensive rework.

How it reflects project health:

High resolution rate: BIM team is ahead of issues; the field is protected from conflicts.

Low rate or increasing backlog: Design and trade coordination are failing.

What poor performance means:
Low resolution rates usually reflect:

- Incomplete coordination model

- Trades not updating models promptly

- Late engineer approvals

- Poor BIM execution planning

- MEP subs short on qualified modelers

What leadership should do:
Enforce weekly BIM coordination sessions, track clash trends by system, and involve field supervisors early to validate install ability. Require model updates before coordination meetings.

Early warning threshold:
If the clash backlog grows **for two consecutive cycles**, field installation will soon be impacted.

38. Coordination Drawing Completion (Trade Coordination Progress)

What it measures:
Assesses the progress of coordinated shop drawings or "Coord Drawings" (MEP, structural embeds, architectural interfaces), which must be completed before installation begins.

Why it matters:
Inadequate coordination results in rework, change orders, delays, and increased installation costs. Coordination drawings are prerequisite documents for layout, fabrication, and field installation.

How it reflects project health:

High completion (>80% ahead of installation): Field is well supported.

Low completion (<60%): Installations are proceeding without proper coordination creates high rework risk.

What poor performance means:
Incomplete coordinate drawings typically stem from:

Late engineering decisions

BIM delays or clash resolution issues

Subcontractors not producing drawings on time

Insufficient integration with structural/architectural drawings

What leadership should do:
Tie coordination completion to pay applications, hold weekly progress reviews, and update sequencing by system or zone. No installation should begin without approved coordination drawings.

Early warning threshold:
If **coordination completion drops below 70%** for areas scheduled to start installation, rework risk is imminent.

39. Preconstruction Estimate Accuracy (Concept → DD → CD)

What it measures:
Evaluates the accuracy of estimate forecasts across design stages (Concept, Schematic, Design Development, Construction Documents), comparing predicted costs to actual contract values or buyout results.

Why it matters:
Accurate estimating protects the owner from budget shocks and protects contractors from underpriced contracts that lead to loss or claims. Estimating accuracy is one of the strongest indicators of preconstruction quality.

How it reflects project health:

High accuracy (±5–10% across phases): Preconstruction is disciplined and informed by reliable market data.

Low accuracy (>15–20% swings): Significant gaps in design assumptions, market intelligence, or scope definition.

What poor performance means:
Inaccuracy often reflects:

- Incomplete design documents

- Incorrect quantities or assumptions

- Poor subcontractor input

- Outdated market pricing

- Value engineering was not captured

- Owner scope shifts not reflected in estimates

What leadership should do:
Mandate estimating checklists, engage subcontractors early, perform quantity verification audits, and include escalation allowances. Leadership should also require detailed basis-of-estimate narratives.

Early warning threshold:
Any estimate phase-to-phase deviation >**15%** signals breakdown in the preconstruction discipline.

40. Buyout Savings vs. Budget (Procurement Performance)

What it measures:
Compares subcontractor buyout values to the budgeted amounts established during preconstruction, showing whether the project realizes savings or overruns during procurement.

Why it matters:
Buyout performance directly impacts contingency, profitability, and the ability to absorb design growth or owner changes. Strong buyout results provide a financial buffer; poor results create immediate cost pressure.

How it reflects project health:

Positive variance (savings): Good scope packaging, strong market pricing, competitive bidding.

Negative variance (over budget): Scope creep, incomplete design, poor estimate accuracy, or unfavorable market conditions.

What poor performance means:
Negative buyout usually results from:

- Underestimated scopes during preconstruction

- Trades expanding scope during bid

- Market price escalation

- Ambiguous bid instructions

- Incomplete design requiring allowances

What leadership should do:
Conduct scope alignment meetings, ensure apparent bid leveling, negotiate aggressively early, and split packages strategically to improve competition. Validate preconstruction assumptions with subcontractors.

Early warning threshold:
If the cumulative buyout exceeds the budget by >**5%**, escalation and contingency pressure will increase significantly.

41. Contingency Burn Rate (Owner or Contractor Contingency Usage)

What it measures:
Tracks how quickly the project is using its allocated contingency funds—either owner contingency, design contingency, or contractor contingency relative to progress and remaining scope.

Why it matters:
Contingency protects the project from normal design development, coordination gaps, minor scope clarifications, and market uncertainty. A healthy contingency profile enables the project to absorb unknowns without escalating to claims or budget shocks.

How it reflects project health:

Healthy burn: Contingency is used gradually and proportionally to design maturity.

High burn rate: Project is compensating for poor design quality, late changes, or failures in preconstruction assumptions.

No burn early in project: A red flag that issues may be underreported or improperly buried in trade budgets.

What poor performance means:
High burn rate typically results from:

- Inaccurate early estimates

- Excessive design changes

- Discovery of scope gaps during buyout

- Poor RFI and submittal quality

- Owner indecision triggering redesign

What leadership should do:
Require formal contingency logs, categorize usage by root cause, and predict remaining exposure with trend analysis. Leadership must ensure contingency is not used to band-aid systemic performance failures.

Early warning threshold:
If **more than 50% of contingency is consumed before 30% construction completion**, the project is at significant cost risk.

42. Allowance & Allowance Drawdown Accuracy

What it measures:

Evaluates how accurately allowances (undefined items carried as budget placeholders) are forecast, drawn down, and reconciled during the project.

Why it matters:

Allowances help manage incomplete design at GMP or contract execution. Poor allowance tracking is a significant cause of cost overruns and disputes with the owner.

How it reflects project health:

Healthy: Allowances convert to final costs within ±10% of the placeholder.

Unhealthy: Allowances repeatedly exceed budget due to unknown scope, design gaps, or poor assumptions.

What poor performance means:

Common causes include:

- Allowances set too low during preconstruction

- Incomplete specifications or late selections

- Missing details requiring expensive field-built solutions

- Unclear owner expectations on finish level or equipment

What leadership should do:

Push for early owner selections, tie allowances to detailed scope statements, and require reconciliation at each design milestone. Track allowance burn as part of the overall contingency strategy.

Early warning threshold:

Allowances trending **20%+ above placeholder values** signal a forecasting problem.

43. Open Issues Log Aging (Action Item Aging)

What it measures:

Monitors how long action items—issues, decisions, commitments—remain open on the project's issue log. Includes design decisions, owner approvals, clarifications, procurement actions, and coordination tasks.

Why it matters:

The issues log is the heartbeat of project decision-making. Aging items are early indicators of bottlenecks that can spill into major schedule or cost impacts.

How it reflects project health:

Healthy: Majority of action items closed within 1–2 weeks.

At risk: Growing backlog of open items with high aging.

Critical: Key decisions older than 30 days are delaying procurement or installation.

What poor performance means:
Aging issues arise due to:

- Owner indecision (e.g., color selections, equipment changes)

- Designer overload

- Contractor not escalating appropriately

- Poor documentation or unclear next steps

- Slow approval paths

What leadership should do:
Implement weekly issue review meetings, categorize issues by owner, design team, contractor, and trade responsibility—flag items tied to critical-path activities. Escalate owner or A/E delays without hesitation.

Early warning threshold:
If **30% of issues exceed 21 days open**, the project is functionally stuck.

44. Owner Decision Turnaround Time

What it measures:
Tracks how long the owner takes to make decisions needed to maintain schedule flow—finish selections, equipment approvals, design direction, pricing approval, and change order authorization.

Why it matters:
Construction cannot progress without timely owner decisions. Owner delays cause cascading schedule impacts, stalled procurement, extended general conditions, and increased change costs.

How it reflects project health:

Healthy: Owner decisions made within contractual timeframes (typically 7–21 days).

Unhealthy: Owner decisions aging out past need dates and delaying field progression.

What poor performance means:
Slow owner decisions usually stem from:

- Unclear owner expectations

- Internal approval layers

- Poor design completeness

- Budget constraints forcing redesign

- Lack of understanding of schedule urgency

What leadership should do:
Provide owners with a decision matrix showing urgency and impacts, schedule weekly decision review meetings, and present "good/better/best" options to simplify choices. Document impacts to protect against delay claims.

Early warning threshold:
If owner decisions exceed **14 days on critical items**, procurement delays are imminent.

45. PM/Engineer Response Time (Internal Team Responsiveness)

What it measures:
Evaluates how quickly the project management team responds to critical internal requests—RFI drafts, submittal reviews, contract clarifications, change pricing, schedule updates, and field inquiries.

Why it matters:
Internal responsiveness drives field productivity. Slow PM/engineering response times cause bottlenecks, idle time, low morale, and frustrated subcontractors.

How it reflects project health:

Responsive team: updates are timely, questions are answered quickly, and the workflow is smooth.

Slow team: frequent last-minute fire drills, missed dates, poor communication.

What poor performance means:
Slow response time reflects:

- Overloaded project staff

- Too many responsibilities per individual

- Excessive administrative tasks

- Lack of clarity on priorities

- Inefficient document control or routing

What leadership should do:
Rebalance workloads, assign clear responsibility matrices (e.g., RASCI charts), shorten internal approval loops, and enforce turnaround targets. Leadership should track response via dashboards.

Early warning threshold:
Response time > **three business days** on operational items is a major workflow threat.

46. Cost Forecast Accuracy (Monthly EAC Variance)

What it measures:
Tracks how accurately the project team forecasts the final cost (EAC) each month by measuring month-to-month changes and comparing predicted cost to actual trends.

Why it matters:
Forecast accuracy is one of the strongest indicators of project financial control. Large swings in EAC—even if the project ultimately finishes on budget—signal that forecasting is reactive, superficial, or not aligned with real field performance.

How it reflects project health:

High accuracy (low variance): disciplined forecasting, strong cost tracking, proactive management.

Low accuracy (large swings): unstable estimates, poor cost coding, or weak understanding of productivity trends.

What poor performance means:
KPI deterioration often stems from:

- Incorrect cost coding or inaccurate actuals

- Lack of timely subcontractor forecasting

- Poor quantity tracking or productivity understanding

- Hidden rework or unreported changes

- Overreliance on "to-complete" optimism

What leadership should do:
Perform bottom-up EAC reviews monthly, validate assumptions behind remaining work, require subcontractor EACs, and compare actual productivity to planned productivity using measured-mile analysis.

Early warning threshold:
If the monthly EAC variance exceeds ±3%, forecasting discipline is breaking down.

47. Cash Flow Performance (Actual vs. Planned Billings)

What it measures:
Compares actual monthly cash inflow (billings collected) against planned billing curves to determine whether the project is maintaining the necessary cash position.

Why it matters:
Cash flow sustains labor, materials, and subcontractors. Poor cash performance leads to delayed payments, strained subcontractor relationships, and financial instability for both owner and contractor.

How it reflects project health:

Healthy cash flow: billings align with work performed and as planned in the schedule of values.

Unhealthy cash flow: delayed billings, slow approvals, or unbilled work backlog.

What poor performance means:
Cash flow shortfalls typically arise from:

- Late owner approvals

- Incomplete documentation (backups, lien releases, inspections)

- Underbilling vs. earned value

- Unpriced or unsubmitted change orders

- Work performed out of contract scope without formal notice

What leadership should do:
Accelerate aging COs, improve pay app accuracy, negotiate progress billing milestones, and ensure subcontractors provide timely documentation. Leadership should also enforce alignment between WIP, schedule progress, and billing.

Early warning threshold:
If **two consecutive months fall >10% below planned billings**, liquidity risk is rising.

48. Claims and Disputes Frequency

What it measures:
Tracks the number of formal claims, notices of delay, contractual disputes, or potential disputes raised by the owner, contractor, or subcontractors.

Why it matters:
Frequent disputes are a leading indicator of poor project health, broken communication, deteriorating relationships, and unresolved issues that will ultimately escalate into costly claims.

How it reflects project health:

Low frequency: Issues are resolved informally and proactively.

High frequency: Parties are documenting to protect themselves rather than collaborating.

What poor performance means:
High dispute frequency usually comes from:

- Poor contract interpretation

- Lack of timely decisions

- Unresolved RFIs or submittals

- Schedule compression or acceleration

- Financial strain on subcontractors

- Hostile owner-contractor dynamics

What leadership should do:
Establish early resolution meetings, emphasize collaborative behaviors, clarify contractual rights and obligations, and resolve issues before they crystallize into claims. Maintain a real-time issues log with accountability.

Early warning threshold: More than **three formal dispute notices per month** indicates a deteriorating project environment.

49. Closeout Readiness Index (Documentation, O&M, Turnover Prep)

What it measures:
Evaluates how prepared the project is for turnover by assessing completeness of closeout documentation. O&M manuals, as-builts, warranties, training plans, commissioning reports, attic stock, and punch list status.

Why it matters:
Closeout is one of the costliest and most painful phases when not managed early. Poor closeout readiness delays final completion, extends general conditions, and damages relationships with owners.

How it reflects project health:

High readiness: documentation and training prepared early in construction.

Low readiness: scramble at the end, missing manuals, incomplete as-builts, untrained staff.

What poor performance means:
Poor readiness often comes from:

- Delayed submittals (especially O&M-related)

- Trades not updating as-builts during installation

- Commissioning delays

- No early closeout plan

- Late punch list accumulation

What leadership should do:
Create a closeout matrix early, tie closeout deliverables to subcontractor pay apps, and require monthly updates. Track O&M and as-built status concurrently with installation.

Early warning threshold:
If **closeout documentation is less than 50% complete by 80% project completion**, turnover will be delayed.

50. Customer Satisfaction Score (Owner & Stakeholder Feedback)

What it measures:
Captures owner and stakeholder satisfaction through surveys, interviews, meeting feedback, and turnover evaluations. Includes perceptions of communication, professionalism, quality, safety, and problem resolution.

Why it matters:
Construction is a relationship-driven industry. Customer satisfaction influences repeat business, future opportunities, reputation, and even claim potential. Dissatisfied owners file more claims.

How it reflects project health:

High score: trust, transparency, proactive issue management.

Low score: strained relationships, perceived mismanagement, or unmet expectations.

What poor performance means:
Low satisfaction generally comes from:

- Missed commitments or missed milestones

- Poor communication or responsiveness

- Unresolved change issues

- Repeated quality problems

- Inadequate turnover preparation

What leadership should do:
Hold regular expectation-alignment sessions, document commitments, be transparent about risks, and actively seek feedback before dissatisfaction escalates. The best projects solve issues before the owner brings them forward.

Early warning threshold:
Any major stakeholder scoring below **7/10** indicates relationship risk that could turn into a dispute.

Chapter Conclusion

Bringing KPI's to Life on a Construction Project

Key Performance Indicators are more than numbers on a dashboard they are the early warning system, the pulse check, and the decision compass for a construction project. When used correctly, KPI's transform what would otherwise be reactive management into a proactive, predictive, and stable operating system. They allow project leaders to see the truth early, intervene decisively, and steer the work away from risks that could become costly or catastrophic.

Across cost, schedule, procurement, safety, logistics, quality, and stakeholder engagement, KPI's reveal whether a project is progressing as intended or quietly drifting off course. No single metric tells the whole story. But together when monitored consistently and interpreted by experienced leaders they form a complete picture of project health.

Strong teams don't wait for the building to take shape to discover the story. They use KPI's to *write* the story. They detect patterns early, challenge assumptions, test forecasts, and convert complex field activity into simple, measurable indicators that drive better decisions. When project managers, engineers, superintendents, and executives share a common KPI language, they share a common understanding of truth, risk, and priority.

At its core, construction management is about controlling outcomes in an environment full of uncertainty. KPI's give you clarity in the chaos, discipline under pressure, and confidence in the face of constant change.

And if all else fails, remember this:

***"Metrics don't prevent claims. Ignoring them creates them."*- Risk Audit Principle**

CHAPTER 18

Construction Monthly Risk Audits

Chapter Foreword

The Importance of Monthly Construction Risk Audits

Construction is a business defined by uncertainty. Designs evolve, conditions change, supply chains shift, and decisions must be made with imperfect information. In this environment, risk is not a theoretical concept it is a daily operational reality that influences cost, schedule, safety, quality, and client trust. What separates successful projects from struggling ones is not the absence of risk, but the discipline to identify, measure, and manage it consistently.

Monthly construction risk audits provide that discipline.

A structured monthly audit forces the project team to step back from the pace of day-to-day activity and evaluate the project with clarity and intention. It shines a light on emerging issues long before they escalate into claims or crises. It evaluates whether previously identified risks were actually mitigated, whether new exposures have surfaced, and whether assumptions made at the beginning of the project still hold true.

These audits uncover the blind spots that naturally appear when teams become accustomed to operating under pressure. They reveal misalignments between cost forecasts and field reality, delays that are developing quietly behind the scenes, procurement bottlenecks, safety or quality trends, subcontractor performance concerns, and breakdowns in communication or coordination. Most importantly, they create a consistent, repeatable structure for anticipating problems not reacting to them.

Monthly audits also build accountability. They unify the project team around a shared understanding of priorities and elevate issues to the level where decision-makers can actually resolve them. They reinforce transparency and help owners, contractors, and designers maintain alignment throughout the entire construction lifecycle.

A project with strong monthly risk audits is a project that never gets surprised. It may encounter challenges as all projects do but those challenges are managed early, with intent and intelligence, rather than with panic and blame.

"What you audit monthly, you rarely litigate later." – **Construction Risk Maxim**

Monthly Risk Audit Process and Procedures

1. Executive Summary and Background

The purpose of this Project Risk Audit Report is to manage, control, and document our current assessed risks associated with the construction of the **Project Name located at Address**. A risk audit was conducted on **Date by Persons Name**.

2. Safety

Introduction

The goal of this project is to provide a safe and healthy working environment. This is achieved by eliminating or minimizing all known and potential hazards. To achieve this goal, everyone on the project is responsible for eliminating or correcting at-risk behavior or unsafe conditions. Safety is every individual's responsibility. Production and schedule never supersede safety.

The Project Health and Safety Plan and Emergency Response Plan (HASP) for the Project Name has been written to establish general safety requirements and procedures for the protection of personnel and to prevent and minimize personal injuries, illnesses, and physical damage to equipment, supplies, and property. A copy of this HASP is placed in a prominent place in the site trailer and, per the HASP, has been distributed to project-based staff, including Subcontractors.

Safety Concerns and Mitigations

- Excavation

- Demolition

- Confined Spaces

- Lock out Tag out

- Crane and Pick Plans

- Laydown

- Site Access

- Fall Protection

- Material Handling

3. Schedule

- Compression Index

- Schedule Issues

- Delays

4. Cost and Budget

5. Quality

6. Subcontractors

7. Material Procurement

- Critical Materials

- Submittal Log

- Procurement Log

8. Self-Perform Craft Labor and Equipment

9. Stakeholders

- Owners

- Designers

- Engineers

10. Organizational Chart

11. Staffing

12. Owner Disputes

13. Change Orders

- External Change Orders

- Owner Change Orders

- Change Order Log

14. Claims

15. Submittals

- Unapproved Submittals

- Submittal Log

16. RFI's

- Open RFI's

- RFI Log

17. Design and Specifications

18. Scope Gaps

19. Constructability Issues

20. Permits

21. Weather and Environmental

22. Bonds and Insurance

23. Key Performance Indicators

24. Risk and Opportunity

- Schedule Delays

- Errors and Omissions in the Contract Drawings and Specifications

- Change Management

- Subcontractor Performance and Default

- Productivity Inefficiencies

- Poor Quality and Workmanship

- Supply Chain Issues

- Poor Project Management

- Labor Shortages

- Poorly Defined Scope of Work

- Health and Safety Hazards

- Payment Disputes

- Estimating Errors and Omissions

- Scope Gaps between Trades

- Poor Project Coordination

- Poor Project Communication

- Environmental Impacts

- Financial Risks

- Legal Risks

25. Risk Mitigation Strategies

26. Other Issues

- Potential issues with Scope Gap / Overlap between contracts.

- Underground Obstructions

- Subcontractor Performance Issues

- Client Relationship Issues

27. Closing and Recommendations

28. Risk Log

28. Attachments

- Safety Incident Reporting

- RFI Log

- Change Order Log

- Submittal Log

- Procurement Log

- Billing and Payments

- Profit Loss Analysis

- Schedule of Remaining Work Activities and Narrative

- Schedule of Longest Path

- Cost and Budget Analysis Report

- Key Performance Indicators and Risk Review

- Project Risk Logs

Chapter Conclusion

Why Monthly Construction Risk Audits Matter

Monthly construction risk audits are not simply a reporting exercise; they are a disciplined evaluation of the project's true condition. In a fast-moving, high-stakes environment, risks evolve weekly, sometimes daily. What was harmless last month may be a critical threat today.

A monthly audit forces the project team to pause, recalibrate, and realign. It brings transparency to cost exposures, schedule vulnerabilities, procurement bottlenecks, quality deficiencies, safety concerns, and coordination gaps. It reveals whether mitigations are actually working not just promised. Most importantly, it provides executives and owners with early visibility into problems while they are still controllable rather than costly.

The discipline of monthly audits creates consistency, and consistency reduces chaos. It elevates accountability across all trades and departments. It reinforces proactive thinking over reactive scrambling and ensures that the project's strategy, operations, and communication remain tightly connected from groundbreaking to turnover.

Construction will always involve uncertainty. But risk audits turn uncertainty into manageable information, and information into more intelligent decisions.

And as every project manager eventually learns:

"We control our actions, but the consequences that flow from those actions are controlled by principles."
– Stephen Covey

CHAPTER 19

SCHEDULE, DELAY, AND ACCELERATION RISK

Chapter Foreword

Time is money, particularly in construction. Schedule delays do not merely escalate construction costs; they also ripple across financing arrangements, resource planning, subsequent projects, and company reputation. Despite its critical importance, schedule risk is frequently underestimated or poorly managed, leaving companies vulnerable to costly disputes and compromised performance.

This chapter provides essential knowledge and practical strategies to identify, manage, and mitigate schedule risks effectively. By proactively addressing scheduling issues, project teams can protect their margins, uphold project timelines, and strengthen client relationships.

"Time is the one resource you never get back." – **Project Controls Principle**

Types of Construction Delays

Effective schedule risk management begins with recognizing delay types and their entitlements clearly:

- Excusable Delay: Delays beyond the contractor's control, such as severe weather or unforeseen permitting issues, generally entitle contractors to a time extension.

- Non-Excusable Delay: Delays directly attributable to contractor actions like late mobilization or inefficient sequencing, providing no relief.

- Compensable Delay: Delays caused by the owner's actions or omissions (late responses, access issues), entitling contractors to both time extensions and additional compensation.

- Concurrent Delay: Delays simultaneously caused by multiple parties, typically resulting in a time extension without additional compensation.

Understanding and clearly categorizing delays is crucial for defending against liquidated damages or substantiating claims.

Clarifying Float Ownership

Float, the time a task can be delayed without affecting the overall project completion, is frequently contested. Establishing float ownership explicitly within the contract or Project Execution Plan (PEP) is best practice:

- Contractor-owned Float: Allows the contractor flexibility to optimize sequences and reduce risk.

- Owner-owned Float: Enables the owner to utilize float for added scope or to mitigate their own delays.

- Project-owned Float: Equitably allocates float on a "first-come, first-served" basis, most commonly accepted in litigation.

In the absence of explicit language, the "first to delay, first to use float" principle is commonly applied by courts.

Time Impact Analysis (TIA): A Crucial Tool

A TIA remains the standard method for quantifying schedule impacts of delays. A rigorous TIA involves:

1. Precisely identifying and timing the delay event.

2. Introducing a fragnet (logical sequence) into the baseline schedule.

3. Analyzing the resulting impact on the critical path.

4. Assessing concurrent delays and available mitigations.

Ensure baseline schedules are detailed and accurate, as TIAs depend heavily on the quality of the initial schedule. Specific instructions on creating TIA's can be found in **Chapter 26** of this book ***"Delay Analysis Standards and Methodology in Creating a TIA"***

Managing Acceleration Risk

Acceleration, whether directed or constructive, creates significant risk, including labor inefficiencies, safety hazards, and subcontractor disputes:

- Directed Acceleration: Explicit instruction by the owner to expedite work.

- Constructive Acceleration: Occurs when a contractor accelerates due to a denied justified time extension.

To mitigate acceleration risk, always secure clear written directives, document additional costs meticulously, and formally notify owners immediately upon recognizing constructive acceleration.

Liquidated Damages and Delay Claims

Liquidated Damages (LDs) represent pre-agreed sums for project delays, typically upheld by courts unless proven punitive. Strategies to mitigate LD exposure include:

- Documenting concurrent or excusable delays.

- Maintaining thorough records of owner-driven delays.

- Arguing for a waiver if owners have historically overlooked late completion.

Clearly defined LD provisions, including caps and reasonable daily rates, significantly reduce exposure.

Avoiding Schedule Manipulation and Maintaining Integrity

Schedule integrity is essential to credible delay claims or defenses. Red flags signaling manipulated schedules include:

- Activities lacking logical ties.

- Excessive constraints or artificially reduced float.

- Frequent, unjustified calendar modifications.

Maintain schedule integrity through enforced monthly narratives, regular health audits, and tie schedule updates directly to payment applications.

Case Study: The Cost of Poor Delay Claim Management

On a university laboratory project, the contractor experienced 90 days of permitting delays but failed to:

- Provide timely notice within the contractually stipulated 7 days.

- Maintain accurate schedule updates.

- Submit a robust TIA.

Consequently, the contractor faced enforced liquidated damages totaling $234,000. Timely documentation and rigorous claim management could have prevented this loss.

Schedule Risk Management Controls

Adopting disciplined controls greatly mitigates scheduling risks:

- Critical Path Method (CPM): Ensures logic-driven and transparent sequencing.

- Detailed Schedule Specifications: Mandate precise schedule updates, detailed narratives, and recovery plans.

- Three-week Lookahead Schedules: Provide practical day-to-day alignment with master schedules.

- Delay and TIA Tracking Logs: Maintain clear, contemporaneous records of delays, causes, and impacts.

- Formal Acceleration Protocols: Ensure clarity and agreed-upon compensation before accelerating.

Checklist: Schedule and Delay Risk Readiness

Confirm readiness by addressing these critical points:

- Is the CPM schedule updated monthly with accurate logic?

- Are all delays documented clearly, including their cause and duration?

- Have RFIs and submittal delays been clearly linked to schedule impacts?

- Are formal TIAs consistently conducted for all significant delays?

- Are time extensions promptly requested per contract stipulations?

- Is float ownership clearly defined or reasonably interpreted?

Chapter Conclusion

Mastering Time Management is Mastering Risk

Most construction claims revolve around schedule delays due to their broad impact on cost, cash flow, relationships, and project success. Teams must be proactive and disciplined in managing schedule risk. Documenting delays promptly, performing thorough TIAs, protecting float, and maintaining rigorous scheduling practices are essential.

By mastering time management, construction professionals not only reduce their exposure to claims and disputes but also enhance their capacity to deliver projects efficiently, profitably, and successfully.

***"Delay claims are built one missed day at a time."* – Delay Analyst Maxim**

CHAPTER 20

CHANGE ORDERS AND COST CONTROL RISK

Chapter Foreword

In construction, change is inevitable, but unmanaged change is catastrophic. Change orders frequently cause friction between owners, contractors, and subcontractors, driving cost overruns, schedule delays, and litigation. Poorly handled changes erode profit margins, destroy trust, and risk project success.

This chapter offers strategies to manage change proactively. It details identifying changes early, documenting clearly, pricing accurately, and negotiating strategically. Understanding the owner's perspective and implementing best practices for cost control can ensure that changes do not escalate into damaging disputes.

"The strength of a contract lies not in what it says – but in what it avoids." – **Construction Contracting Handbook**

Understanding Change Orders

A change order formally adjusts the original contract's scope, schedule, or price. Typical reasons include:

- Additional or deleted work

- Material substitutions

- Revised schedule milestones

- Shifting risk responsibilities

Change orders can originate from owners, contractors, designers, Authorities Having Jurisdiction (AHJs), or unforeseen conditions.

Risks from Poor Change Management

Without effective change management, projects face:

- Reduced margins from uncompensated scope changes

- Scope creep from undocumented directives

- Payment disputes and prolonged conflicts

- Legal claims over entitlements, notice, or pricing

- Strained stakeholder relationships

Research shows inadequate change management can decrease gross margins by 25–50% from original estimates.

Common pitfalls include:

- Performing work without written approval

- Late notification of changes

- Insufficient documentation and pricing backup

- Missing schedule impact assessments

- Unclear cost segregation

Contractual Notice Requirements

Contracts typically require written notice within specific timeframes (usually 7 to 14 days) after identifying a potential change. Immediate notice protects your rights to compensation.

Recommended standard clause:

"Contractor shall provide written notice of potential changes in scope, schedule, or cost within seven calendar days from the event's occurrence."

Categories of Change Orders

1. Owner-Directed Changes

- Clear entitlement, typically documented formally by the owner.

- General based on modifications to the construction documents.

2. Constructive Changes (Field-Directed Work)

- Verbal field instructions are often disputed if not documented.

- Always secure written Field Change Authorization (FCA).

3. Unforeseen Conditions

- Issues like hidden debris or groundwater.

- Requires prompt notification and detailed documentation.

4. Design Errors and Omissions

- Missing scope or conflicts in design documents.

- Frequently leads to negotiations with owner/design teams.

5. Schedule Delays

- Can be caused by the Owner, Contractor, Subcontractors or Vendors.

- Impacts the critical path of the schedule.

Change Order Waiver Language

Utilize for final change orders to reduce Owner risk against future time or cost impact claims related to the change.

Final and Complete Agreement – Release and Waiver of Claims:

Contractor acknowledges and agrees that this Change Order constitutes full and final settlement for all time, cost, and other impacts associated with the change described herein, including all direct, indirect, consequential, and cumulative impacts to unchanged work, project schedule, extended overhead, and any other effect on the Work under the Contract through the effective date of this Change Order.

By executing this Change Order, Contractor:

(1) **Affirms that the compensation and time adjustments stated herein are full and complete**, and that no further claims, equitable adjustments, or modifications of any kind shall be made by the Contractor for any matter arising from, related to, or impacted by the change described.

(2) **Expressly waives all rights to assert any further claim, dispute, or request for equitable adjustment** for any matter that is **known or reasonably foreseeable** to the Contractor as of the effective date of this Change Order, including without limitation claims for cumulative impacts, ripple effects, delay, acceleration, or disruption resulting from the change described; and

(3) **Releases Owner from any and all known or reasonably foreseeable claims** arising out of or related to the Work performed under the Contract through the effective date of this Change Order.

Pro Tip: Contractors can revise this language and apply to subcontractor change orders.

Pricing Strategies for Change Orders

Approaches:

- Time and Materials (T&M): Suitable for urgent or minor changes; requires rigorous documentation.

- Unit Pricing: Effective for repetitive scopes.

- Lump Sum: Best for defined scopes; must incorporate contingency and overhead.

- Pre-negotiated Rate Sheets (Cost-Plus): Simplifies frequent changes in pricing.

Avoid:

- Vague pricing without detailed backup

- Omitting overhead, profit, insurance, and bonds

- Proceeding without written directives

Maintain a standardized Change Event Pricing Template to ensure comprehensive documentation.

<table>
<tr><td colspan="5">POTENTIAL CHANGE ORDER</td></tr>
<tr><td colspan="3"></td><td>PCO NUMBER</td><td>0001</td></tr>
<tr><td colspan="5">PROJECT NAME</td></tr>
<tr><td colspan="5">CHANGE ORDER DESCRIPTION</td></tr>
<tr><td colspan="5">CHANGE ORDER DESCRIPTION AND DETAIL</td></tr>
<tr><td colspan="5"></td></tr>
<tr><td colspan="2">The duration for the additional work outlined in this proposal is</td><td>0</td><td colspan="2">working days</td></tr>
<tr><td colspan="2">The Contract Time Extension due to this Change Order Request is</td><td>0</td><td colspan="2">calendar days</td></tr>
<tr><td>LABOR</td><td></td><td>HRS</td><td>AVG $ / HR</td><td>TOTAL</td></tr>
<tr><td></td><td></td><td>0.0</td><td>$ -</td><td>$ -</td></tr>
<tr><td></td><td></td><td>OH&P</td><td>15.00%</td><td>$ -</td></tr>
<tr><td></td><td></td><td></td><td></td><td>$ -</td></tr>
<tr><td>MATERIALS</td><td></td><td></td><td></td><td>TOTAL</td></tr>
<tr><td></td><td></td><td></td><td></td><td>$ -</td></tr>
<tr><td></td><td></td><td>OH&P</td><td>15.00%</td><td>$ -</td></tr>
<tr><td></td><td></td><td></td><td></td><td>$ -</td></tr>
<tr><td>EQUIPMENT</td><td></td><td></td><td></td><td>TOTAL</td></tr>
<tr><td></td><td></td><td></td><td></td><td>$ -</td></tr>
<tr><td></td><td></td><td></td><td></td><td>$ -</td></tr>
<tr><td></td><td></td><td></td><td></td><td>$ -</td></tr>
<tr><td>SUBCONTRACTORS</td><td colspan="3">DESCRIPTION</td><td>TOTAL</td></tr>
<tr><td></td><td colspan="3"></td><td>$ -</td></tr>
<tr><td></td><td colspan="3"></td><td></td></tr>
<tr><td></td><td colspan="3"></td><td></td></tr>
<tr><td></td><td colspan="3"></td><td></td></tr>
<tr><td></td><td colspan="3"></td><td></td></tr>
<tr><td></td><td colspan="2">Subtotal</td><td></td><td>$ -</td></tr>
<tr><td></td><td colspan="2">OH&P</td><td>10.00%</td><td>$ -</td></tr>
<tr><td></td><td colspan="2"></td><td></td><td>$ -</td></tr>
<tr><td>OTHER</td><td>QTY</td><td></td><td>REFERENCE</td><td>TOTAL</td></tr>
<tr><td>Extended Project Overhead</td><td></td><td>Days * Cost Per Day</td><td>$ -</td><td>$ -</td></tr>
<tr><td>Builder's Risk Extention</td><td></td><td>Days * Cost Per Day</td><td>$ -</td><td>$ -</td></tr>
<tr><td>Standard Insurances</td><td></td><td></td><td>$ -</td><td>$ -</td></tr>
<tr><td>Additional Bond</td><td></td><td></td><td>$ -</td><td>$ -</td></tr>
<tr><td></td><td></td><td></td><td>SUBTOTAL</td><td>$ -</td></tr>
<tr><td colspan="3"></td><td>TOTAL</td><td>$ -</td></tr>
</table>

Potential Change Order Pricing Worksheet

Effective Use of Change Order Logs

Keep a regularly updated log that tracks:

- Change Order Number

- Description and Cause

- Entitlement and Pricing

- Approval Status

- Schedule Impact

Logs improve internal forecasting, facilitate regular owner discussions, and provide strong documentation for potential disputes.

Change Order Log														
Creation Date	PCO #	PCO Title	PCO Type	PCO Scope Description	Cost Range (Hi-Level)	Status	Schedule Impact (Hi-Level)	Funding Need By Date	Approval Date	Date of PCO Submission	Actual Cost	Actual Schedule Impact	PO Received Date	PO Number
	1					Quoted								
	2					Performed								
	3					Approved								
	4					In Review								
	5					Awaiting Pricing								
	6					Other								
				Total	$						Total	$		

Change Order Log Template

Case Study: The Cost of Undocumented Change

On a school construction project, the architect verbally approved additional audiovisual rough-ins not shown on the plans. The contractor proceeded without formal documentation. Later, the architect rejected the change, resulting in a $120,000 loss absorbed by the contractor.

Lesson: Always secure written approvals. Verbal directions are insufficient.

Managing Owner Resistance

Owners often resist change orders due to:

- Budget constraints

- Approval and accountability concerns

- Perception of contractor overreach

- Uncertainty about entitlement

Mitigate resistance by:

- Issuing early "Potential Change Notices" to avoid surprises

- Providing thorough pricing backup and comparative quotes

- Demonstrating the necessity and impact clearly

- Avoiding inflated markups and maintaining transparency

Cost Control Systems and Tools

Implement the following to mitigate change-order risk:

- Committed Cost Forecasts (aligned with approved changes)

- Pending Change Risk Ledger (categorized by likelihood)

- Integrated Subcontractor Change Order Logs

- Real-time budget tracking via ERP systems

- Contingency burn rate reports

Checklist: Change Order Management Readiness

- Are notice requirements clearly communicated to all staff?

- Are all potential changes documented immediately?

- Are T&M tickets reviewed, signed, and backed up daily?

- Do price proposals include all relevant costs and markups?

- Is schedule impact consistently tracked?

- Is contingency usage forecasted accurately?

- Are change order discussions held weekly with the owner?

Chapter Conclusion

Proactive Management of Change

Changes do not have to harm your project. Disciplined documentation, timely communication, accurate pricing, and strategic negotiations can transform change management into a controlled, even profitable aspect of construction.

Failure to manage change effectively leads to margin erosion, damaged relationships, and costly claims. Adopt a systematic approach to change orders.

"Change is inevitable. Chaos is optional." **– Systems Engineering Saying**

CHAPTER 21

QUALITY ASSURANCE AND DEFECT RISK

Chapter Foreword

In construction, quality is not merely the finished product. It is a ticking time bomb if not appropriately managed. A seemingly flawless building can hide critical workmanship issues, material defects, or overlooked inspections. Quality issues do not simply appear as punchlist annoyances; they evolve into warranty claims, reputational damage, and costly legal disputes long after occupancy.

This chapter will clearly distinguish Quality Assurance (QA) from Quality Control (QC), explore the root causes of defects, provide proven strategies for reducing latent defect exposure, and offer best practices to safeguard your projects from future risk proactively.

"Experience is the name that everyone gives to their mistakes." – Oscar Wilde

Distinguishing Quality Assurance and Quality Control

- **Quality Assurance (QA):**

  - Proactive approach designed to prevent defects.

  - Involves planning, training, and clearly defined procedures.

  - Managed by project managers and superintendents.

- **Quality Control (QC):**

  - Reactive approach aimed at detecting and fixing defects.

  - Includes inspections, testing, and verification processes.

  - Conducted by field crews, inspectors, or third-party specialists.

Key Insight: You cannot rely solely on inspections to achieve quality. Effective quality must be built proactively into your project's processes, team training, and leadership accountability.

Primary Causes of Quality Defects

Quality problems commonly arise from:

- Untrained or Unqualified Labor

- Substandard or Improperly Substituted Materials

- Incomplete Submittals and Shop Drawings

- Improper Sequencing of Construction Activities

- Skipped Inspections or Testing Protocols

- Failure to Follow Manufacturer's Installation Guidelines

- Unreviewed or Deferred Submittals

Example: Installing fire-rated doors without verifying submittal compliance, leading to failed inspections and costly rework.

Documentation: Your First Line of Defense

Effective documentation helps mitigate liability and supports quality control. Essential documents to maintain include:

- Approved submittals and shop drawing logs.

- Inspection and test reports (internal and external).

- Pre-installation and pre-pour checklists.

- Clarifying RFIs and responses.

- Material delivery logs with verification checklists.

- Photographic records of concealed conditions (e.g., rebar placement, waterproofing details).

- Concrete and pressure test result reports.

Consistent, real-time documentation can substantially reduce the risk of litigation related to defects.

Effective Deficiency Tracking and Punchlists

Unstructured punchlists or late-stage corrections can result in overlooked defects. To manage this risk effectively:

- Initiate rolling punchlists mid-project.

- Utilize digital platforms (Procore, Bluebeam, Fieldwire) to streamline tracking.

- Clearly assign responsibilities and deadlines for resolution.

- Identify recurring trade-specific issues for targeted corrective action.

Third-Party Inspection and Testing Risks

Special inspections and independent tests are frequently required but carry inherent risks:

- Missed or infrequent tests.

- Delayed or undocumented test results.

- Ambiguous inspector feedback.

- Lack of clear linkage between failures and corrective actions.

Mitigation Strategies:

- Maintain a comprehensive Testing and Inspection Log.

- Assign a dedicated coordinator for inspector scheduling and result monitoring.

- Ensure immediate correction and re-testing of failed items.

Case Study: The High Cost of Hidden Defects

A Texas luxury condominium project discovered water intrusion issues one year after completion, caused by improperly lapped vapor barriers concealed behind stucco finishes. The result included:

- $2.8M in warranty repairs.

- Litigation involving subcontractors and general contractors.

- Insurance disputes due to failure to comply with manufacturer instructions.

Key Lesson: Quality Control procedures must be thorough, documented, and verified during installation. Hidden defects often create severe financial and reputational repercussions.

Latent Defects and Warranty Risks

Latent defects: problems not detectable during standard inspections pose significant long-term liability. Key areas prone to latent defects include:

- **Roofing Systems:** Improper flashing or waterproofing.

- **Concrete Work:** Weak cylinder strength, premature cracking, or spalling.

- **Fireproofing:** Improper thickness or coverage.

- **HVAC Systems:** Inadequate balancing, ventilation issues.

- **Life Safety Systems:** Faulty alarm systems or wiring defects.

Latent defects can trigger expensive claims years after completion, especially when linked to negligence or regulatory non-compliance.

Warranty Management Practices

Warranty periods represent ongoing risk exposure. Standard practices for reducing warranty-related liability include:

- Clearly defining warranty periods for workmanship, roofing, MEP, and waterproofing.

- Transferring warranty requirements explicitly to subcontractors.

- Organizing and storing O&M manuals and warranty documentation securely.

- Conducting proactive warranty walkthroughs (typically 10–11 months post-occupancy).

Checklist: Quality Risk Readiness

Before finalizing project turnover, ensure you have addressed:

- Submission, review, and adherence to a comprehensive QA/QC plan.

- Timely logging of all inspections and tests.

- Adequate photographic documentation of concealed installations.

- Identification and escalation of recurring issues.

- Completion and documentation of required special inspections.

- An organized and actively managed punchlist process.

- Clear communication of warranty responsibilities to all stakeholders.

Contractor Quality Control Plans

Quality does not occur by accident in construction. It is the direct result of deliberate planning, disciplined execution, and consistent verification in the field. One of the most effective tools for reducing defect risk, minimizing rework, and protecting both schedule and reputation is a well-defined Contractor Quality Control Plan. A project without a CQCP is not managing quality. It is hoping for it.

A Contractor Quality Control Plan establishes the framework by which work is planned, executed, inspected, and accepted. It aligns project teams around clear quality objectives, defines responsibilities, and creates accountability at every stage of construction. More importantly, it shifts quality management from a reactive inspection activity to a proactive risk prevention process.

At a minimum, every CQCP should include the following core components.

The plan should begin with an **Executive Summary** that provides a concise overview of the project, its quality objectives, and the key elements of the quality control approach. This section sets the tone for the entire project by making it clear that quality is a leadership priority, not an administrative afterthought.

Next, the CQCP must **clearly define the project scope and quality objectives**. This includes identifying which areas of work are governed by the plan, what standards apply, and where the limits of responsibility lie. Clearly stating what is included and excluded eliminates ambiguity, reduces finger-pointing, and ensures that all parties understand the quality expectations before work begins.

The plan must also establish clear **Quality Control Procedures**. These procedures define how nonconforming work is identified, documented, corrected, and prevented from recurring. They also outline the process for project completion inspections and the method for managing quality issues as they arise. Well-defined procedures ensure consistency, transparency, and defensibility if disputes or claims later occur.

Central to every effective CQCP is the use of a structured **three-step inspection process**. This process embeds quality directly into the workflow rather than relying solely on end-of-task inspections.

- **The first step is pre-inspection**. Before work begins, the contractor verifies that prerequisites are in place, including approved submittals, qualified personnel, proper materials, calibrated equipment, and clear work instructions. This step prevents defects before they are built into the work.

- **The second step is inspection during execution.** As work progresses, inspections are performed to confirm that installation methods, workmanship, and materials conform to the contract requirements. Continuous verification during construction allows issues to be corrected immediately, when they are least costly and least disruptive.

- **The final step is post-inspection.** Once work is complete, the contractor evaluates the finished product to confirm it meets the specified quality standards and performance criteria. Any deficiencies are identified, corrected, and verified before the work is turned over or concealed.

When properly implemented, this three-step inspection process transforms quality control into a disciplined risk management system. It reduces rework, minimizes disputes, improves safety, protects margins, and strengthens the contractor's credibility with owners and regulators.

Ultimately, a Contractor Quality Control Plan is not just a compliance document. It is a leadership tool. Projects that embrace CQCPs consistently outperform those that do not because they understand a fundamental truth of construction risk management. Defects are far easier to prevent than they are to defend.

Chapter Conclusion

Managing Quality, Your Most Persistent Risk

You cannot eliminate every possible defect. However, you can significantly mitigate quality risks through proactive processes, rigorous documentation, and clear accountability at every project phase.

Successful contractors embed quality management into daily operations, not just final punchlists. By systematically addressing quality risks, you protect your firm financially, legally, and reputationally, long after the final coat of paint dries.

***"Quality is never an accident."* – John Ruskin**

CHAPTER 22

SAFETY AND ENVIRONMENTAL RISK

Chapter Foreword

Safety is more than a regulatory or moral imperative; it is a core element of construction risk management. A single incident can halt a project, void insurance coverage, trigger litigation, and irreparably harm a firm's reputation. Environmental risks, though often less visible, can be just as destructive, resulting in fines, delays, and public backlash.

This chapter presents a field-tested framework to manage safety and environmental risks proactively. From daily field behaviors to systemic leadership practices, the message is clear: safety is not an obligation; it is a strategic advantage.

"Safety is not a gadget, but a state of mind." – **Elenor Everet**

The Real Cost of an Unsafe Jobsite

A major safety incident exposes your project to:

- Medical and workers' compensation costs

- OSHA fines and regulatory citations

- Insurance rate increases or denied claims

- Site shutdowns and schedule delays

- Productivity disruptions

- Third-party claims or subcontractor lawsuits

Industry Stat:

- The direct cost of a serious injury is ~$50,000.

- Indirect costs, lost productivity, legal defense, and project delays can reach 4–10x more.

From Lagging to Leading: Predictive Safety Indicators

Too many firms only react to accidents. High-performing teams monitor ***leading indicators***, the signs that reveal risk before it turns into injury.

Best Practice: Treat near-miss reports with the same urgency as actual injuries. They are statistically predictive of future accidents.

Core Safety Systems Every Jobsite Needs

- Site-Specific Safety Plan (SSSP)Tailored to the project's scope and risks, must include evacuation maps, fall protection, and fire response protocols.

- Job Hazard Analysis (JHA)Task-specific assessments are updated weekly or daily to reflect changing site conditions.

- Routine Safety Audits Conducted internally or by third-party experts. Results should be reviewed weekly with the project team.

- Verified Training Records Maintain up-to-date documentation for confined space entry, rigging, trenching, aerial lifts, and more.

- Stop-Work Authority Empower all personnel to halt unsafe work without fear of reprisal.

Root Cause Analysis: Looking Beyond the Surface

Do not just assign blame, diagnose system failures. A meaningful investigation includes:

- Securing the site and attending to injuries

- Gathering objective documentation (photos, statements, weather reports)

- Assembling a cross-disciplinary investigation team

- Tracing breakdowns in planning, training, or supervision

- Issuing corrective actions tied to procedural or cultural improvements

Common Root Causes:

- Compressed schedules override safety

- Poorly sequenced scopes of work

- Communication breakdowns across trades

- Inadequate language-specific training

Safety Culture = Project Discipline

Companies with weak safety cultures also experience:

- More change orders

- Increased disputes

- Higher turnover

- More QA/QC rework

- Lower client satisfaction

Signs of Strong Safety Culture:

- Field leaders actively model safe practices

- Foremen, not just safety officers, own toolbox talks

- Reporting of hazards is encouraged, not penalized

- Safety data drives coaching and recognition

- No distinction between "production" and "safety" teams

Legal and Insurance Exposure

Poor safety compliance can expose your firm to:

- **OSHA Fines**: Up to $15,625 per violation; more for repeat or willful violations

- **Insurance Exclusions**: Denied coverage for non-compliance with safety protocols

- **Third-Party Lawsuits**: Vendors or site visitors injured due to unsafe conditions

- **Criminal Liability**: Particularly in fatality cases linked to gross negligence

Case Insight: A GC faced criminal charges after a subcontractor laborer died in a trench collapse. No shoring, no trench box, no competent person on-site.

Environmental Risk: Silent But Severe

Construction sites often trigger environmental liabilities:

Best Practice: Assign a dedicated environmental compliance coordinator for large or high-risk projects.

Managing the SWPPP (Stormwater Pollution Prevention Plan)

A SWPPP is required on nearly all job sites over a certain size or risk profile. It includes:

- Best Management Practices (BMPs)

- Rain event inspection protocols

- Perimeter and erosion control

- Dewatering and silt fencing methods

Mitigation Checklist:

- Embed photo verification into inspection logs

- Conduct walkthroughs before/after rain events

- Pre-stock erosion control materials

- Train all subcontractors on stormwater requirements

Checklist: Safety & Environmental Risk Readiness

- Is a current Site-Specific Safety Plan (SSSP) in place and enforced?

- Are toolbox talks and JHAs held regularly and documented?

- Are near-miss logs maintained and used for corrective actions?

- Are safety violations tracked, addressed, and escalated appropriately?

- Is SWPPP compliance up to date with real-time photo logs?

- Is a qualified environmental compliance lead assigned?

- Do all field supervisors understand their individual risk responsibilities?

Chapter Conclusion

Safety Is Profit Protection

Safety is not just compliance; it is risk control. A safe job site reduces injuries, delays, rework, legal costs, and reputational harm. It also reflects the level of operational discipline that predicts success across every construction phase.

Firms that treat safety as a strategic lever, not a burden, consistently outperform their competitors.

***"Safety doesn't happen by accident."* – Safety Engineering Maxim**

CHAPTER 23

INSURANCE RISKS: COVERAGE, PITFALLS, AND LEGAL LEVERAGE

Chapter Foreword

Construction projects are built on contracts but protected by insurance. When defects, delays, or injuries occur, insurance becomes the first and sometimes last line of financial defense. However, treating insurance as a "set-it-and-forget-it" safety net is dangerous. A policy you do not understand is no protection at all.

This chapter explores the essential link between construction claims and insurance coverage. We break down key policy types, outline common gaps and pitfalls, and highlight how to use insurance as a tactical tool, before, during, and after a dispute. Competent contractors do not just buy coverage. They understand how to activate it strategically when it matters most.

"Insurance does not eliminate risk; it prices it." – **Risk Finance Principle**

The Role of Insurance in Construction Claims

Insurance is not just a legal requirement; it is a risk management instrument that can shape how a claim unfolds and whether your company survives it.

Insurance Can:

- Fund legal defense costs

- Indemnify parties for covered damages

- Influence early settlement

- Reduce financial exposure

- Satisfy contract or statutory requirements

But beware, coverage is often denied due to:

- Policy exclusions

- Late reporting

- Poor documentation

- Misclassified risk or policy gaps

Core Construction Insurance Policies and Claim Triggers

1. **Commercial General Liability (CGL)**

Purpose: Covers third-party bodily injury, property damage, and personal injury.

Trigger: A jobsite "occurrence" resulting in third-party harm.

Covers:

- Injuries to site visitors

- Damage to neighboring property

- Fires or structural damage caused by crews

Exclusions:

- Your Work

- Contractual Liability

- Subcontractor Fault (unless endorsed)

Pro Tip: Request "CG 20 10 11/85" or similar broad AI endorsements.

2. **Builder's Risk Insurance**

Purpose: Covers direct damage to the project during construction.

Trigger: Fire, theft, collapse, weather events.

Covers:

- Framing loss from fire

- Stolen equipment

- Water damage during installation

Exclusions:

- Design errors

- Faulty workmanship

- Delay-related losses

Pro Tip: Ensure coverage includes soft costs like financing and A/E services.

3. Professional Liability / E&O

Purpose: Covers claims related to design negligence.

Trigger: Financial loss from professional services, not physical damage.

Covers:

- Design miscalculations

- HVAC system flaws

- ADA violations

Exclusions:

- Construction defects (if not design-related)

- Bodily injury/property damage

Pro Tip: GCs on design-build jobs should carry separate E&O or require it contractually from design partners.

4. Workers' Compensation Insurance

Purpose: Covers employee injury or occupational illness.

Trigger: On-the-job injury or exposure.

Covers:

- Jobsite accidents

- Long-term health conditions

- Death benefits

Pitfalls:

- Hiring uninsured subs

- Labor misclassification

Pro Tip: Track compliance using a Subcontractor Insurance Tracker. No insurance certificate, no mobilization.

5. Pollution Liability Insurance

Purpose: Covers environmental damage caused by operations or materials.

Trigger: Pollution event or hazardous material release.

Covers:

- Asbestos release

- Diesel spills

- Mold caused by wet conditions

Exclusions:

- Gradual pollution

- Owned site contamination

Pro Tip: Never rely on your CGL policy to cover pollution, it will not.

6. Subcontractor Default Insurance (SDI)

Purpose: Protects GCs from sub non-performance or insolvency.

Trigger: Failure of a subcontractor to complete or deliver.

Covers:

- Replacement contractor costs

- Schedule impacts

- GC overhead and delays

Pro Tip: Strong documentation and notice protocols are critical. SDI is not "automatic money."

Common Insurance Pitfalls That Derail Claims

1. Late Notice

Most policies require early written notice, often within 30 days of a triggering event.

Fix: Always file a Notice of Potential Claim even if you have not calculated the loss yet.

2. Failure to Preserve Evidence

Claims are denied due to a lack of:

- Site photos

- Daily reports

- Incident records

- Material logs

Fix: Implement a Claims Incident Checklist. Document early and often.

3. COI Errors and Omissions

Many Certificates of Insurance contain:

- Incorrect additional insured language

- Expired policies

- Missing waivers of subrogation

Fix: Maintain a real-time Insurance Compliance Matrix. Cross-check every COI.

4. Uninsurable Contract Clauses

You may sign indemnity or warranty terms that your policy will not support.

Fix: Involve your broker *and* legal team before signing key contracts.

5. Assuming Insurance = Payment

Carriers pay when you meet policy terms, not just when loss occurs.

Fix: Follow notice procedures. Maintain documentation. Treat every claim like it is going to trial.

Using Insurance Strategically in Your Claims Program

Strategy 1: Early and Separate Filing

- Notify all carriers as soon as any demand, lawsuit, or loss emerges.

- Use carrier-specific forms and confirm claim number.

Strategy 2: Leverage Duty to Defend

- Even if a claim is denied, the carrier may still fund your legal defense.

- This creates negotiation leverage and preserves cash flow.

Strategy 3: Bring Carriers to Mediation

- In large disputes, include insurers at mediation.

- Their input shapes outcomes and can force resolution.

Strategy 4: Project-Based Coverage Charts

Maintain a live Coverage Matrix for each project showing:

- Coverage types

- Policy triggers

- Notice responsibilities

- Broker contact info

Chapter Conclusion

Know What You are Covered for and What You are Not

Insurance will not stop a construction claim, but it can contain the fallout if you manage it right.

To leverage insurance effectively:

- Understand what your policy covers and what it does not.

- Train your team to trigger coverage early.

- Document everything like the carrier is watching.

A policy is not a safety net; it is a risk strategy. Make sure yours is built to catch you when it counts.

"Insurance is not protection against loss; it is protection against ruin." – **Felix Kloman**

CHAPTER 24

PAYMENT AND PERFORMANCE BOND RISKS

Chapter Forward

Payment and performance bonds are the owner's and lower-tier vendors' safety net and the GC's license to build at scale. However, bonds only pay when the obligee (owner or GC) follows the letter of the bond. The most common failures are procedural: missed notices, premature payments, overbroad change orders, or unclear default/termination steps. Those mistakes hand sureties' ready-made defenses and can invalidate coverage even on meritorious claims.

"The cost of prevention is always less than the cost of correction." – **Atul Gawande**

What These Bonds Do

- **Performance bond:** guarantees completion or correction after a proper declaration of default and termination (or other conditions precedent in the bond form). Under the widely used AIA A312, the obligee must (i) declare default, (ii) terminate the principal, and (iii) notify the surety, in that order, before the surety's performance options are triggered. Skipping steps risks discharge.

- **Payment bond:** guarantees payment to subs/suppliers who preserve rights (e.g., 90-day notice and one-year suit windows on many public jobs and under the Miller Act for federal projects). Requirements and deadlines are strict and vary by statute.

Top Bond Risks You Can Control

- **Procedural missteps (conditions precedent).** Failing to give pre-default notice, not holding the required meeting, or terminating without proper notice can release the surety. Courts repeatedly enforce A312's conditions precedent as written. Treat the bond as a checklist.

- **Material alterations & scope creep.** Cardinal changes, uncontrolled change order growth, or unilateral schedule extensions can be argued as risk-increasing material alterations that prejudice the surety. Keep changes documented and within the bonded contract's mechanisms.

- **Overpayment / premature release of retainage.** Paying ahead of earned value or releasing retainage early can impair collateral and discharge the surety in whole or in part. Tie disbursements to verified progress and keep retainage intact until conditions are met.

- **Late or misdirected payment-bond notices.** Under the Miller Act and many state statutes, 90-day notices must be received (not just mailed) by the right party, and suit deadlines are rigid. Build automated ticklers into closeout workflows.

- **Wrongful termination/lack of default.** Terminating without building a clean default record (cure notices, substantiation, opportunity to meet) fuels surety defenses that no default existed or that the obligee caused the breach.

Owner / Developer Playbook (Performance Bond)

- **Before NTP:** Confirm bond form (A312 or equivalent), verify attorney-in-fact authority on the power of attorney, and capture the surety's claim contact.

- **During performance:** Track schedule and pay apps against physical progress; log every change through the contract mechanism; avoid side deals.

- **Pre-default**: Send the intent-to-declare-default letter required by the bond; demand a senior-level meeting with the surety; document cure windows.

- **If defaulting:** Terminate strictly per bond + contract, then notice the surety after termination (per A312 §3.2) and elect the completion path. Preserve all job-site materials/equipment and quantify the remaining scope.

GC / CM Playbook (Payment Bond)

- Publish precise flow-down notice requirements to subs and suppliers.

- Run monthly lien/notice audits (who sent prelims, who needs 90-day notice soon).

- Keep retainage and paid-to-date reconciled to earned progress; avoid advance payments.

- On federal work, brief lower tiers on Miller Act rights and calendars (90-day notice; suit within one year of last furnishing).

A/E and Owner's Rep: How You Help or Hurt

- Lock the scope baseline; when changes are unavoidable, process them under the bonded contract, not via informal directives.

- Avoid schedule promises or directions that bypass the GC's contract chain.

- Keep contemporaneous documentation so the obligee can prove proper default, termination, and tender to the surety.

Red Flags and "Surety-Friendly" Traps to Avoid

- Email-only terminations with no formal letter or cure window.

- Change orders that double the job cost without compensation/time relief classic material alteration argument.

- Early retainage release to ease cash flow (if that retainage would have covered claims, you may have discharged the surety).

- Paying for uninstalled materials without proper security (UCC filings, title passage) impairment of collateral risk.

- Miller Act notices sent to the wrong party or mailed on day 90 (received on day 92).

Case Studies

- **Conditions Precedent Enforced (Performance Bond).** A project owner declared default but skipped A312's termination sequence before demanding surety performance. The court held the obliges failure to meet conditions precedent barred recovery against the surety. Lesson: Follow A312 steps, in order, and paper the file.

- **Overpayment / Impairment of Collateral.** On a federal project, the owner's payment practices and handling of contract funds impaired the surety's collateral; the court awarded relief to the surety. Lesson: Do not advance pay; protect retainage and security interests.

- **Material Modifications & Schedule Extensions.** A surety pursued affirmative relief where the owner materially modified the bonded contracts and extended time contrary to express terms. Lesson: Route major changes through formal mechanisms and keep the surety looped in.

- **Payment Bond Timing (Miller Act).** The lower-tier claimant missed the 90-day notice and the one-year suit window. Claim dismissed despite undisputed work furnished. Lesson: Calendar statutory deadlines and verify receipt, not just mailing.

Checklists

Performance Bond Default & Tender (A312-style)

- Re-read the bond; extract all conditions precedent into a one-page checklist.

- Send intent-to-declare-default; demand the bond meeting.

- Document cure attempts and remaining defects/scope; quantify finish costs.

- Terminate per contract; secure site and materials; suspend further payments.

- Notify surety post-termination and request election of its completion option.

- Keep communications centralized; avoid side agreements.

Payment Bond Claims Control

- Track prelim notices; map last-furnishing dates for each lower tier.

- Send statutory 90-day notices early; confirm delivery.

- Preserve invoices, delivery tickets, and daily reports.

- File suit before statutory deadline; confirm venue/jurisdiction.

Clauses & Controls That Reduce Bond Risk

- No advance payments: payments tied to observed progress; robust stored-materials conditions (title transfer, insurance, UCC filings).

- Change management discipline: thresholds that trigger surety notice; monthly CO aging reports.

- Bond governance exhibit: names/addresses for surety notices; required pre-default conference; timeline chart copied from the bond form.

Chapter Conclusion

Payment and performance bonds do not replace judgment. They only reward contractors who manage risk before they need the bond.

Bonds are powerful but literal. Treat the bond form as a process instrument, not a backstop you can invoke informally. If you (i) follow conditions precedent precisely, (ii) keep money aligned with earned work (retainage intact, no advances), (iii) route significant changes through the contract, and (iv) calendar every statutory notice and suit date, you will preserve bond value and eliminate 90% of surety defenses before they are raised.

"Failure is rarely sudden; it is cumulative." – **James Reason**

PART VIII – IDENTIFYING RISKS DURING THE CLOSEOUT AND COMMISSIONING PHASE

CLOSEOUT, WARRANTY, AND TURNOVER RISK

Chapter Foreword

Closeout is not the end of the project; it is the beginning of your legacy. What should be a celebratory finish often becomes a chaotic scramble. Teams rush to demobilize, finalize paperwork, and satisfy occupancy deadlines, yet this final 5% of the project can generate 50% of the legal and payment risk.

Missed documents, unresolved punchlists, unpaid change orders, and unsubmitted warranties do not just jeopardize cash flow; they invite litigation and long-term liability. This chapter reframes closeout as a ***strategic risk phase*** that requires forethought, ownership, and execution discipline. Done right, it protects margin, reputation, and future business.

"How you finish matters." – John Wooden

The Closeout Risk Landscape

Key Insight: Risk does not end at substantial completion, but often begins there, as legal and operational obligations transition into the warranty period.

Substantial vs. Final Completion: Know the Difference

Understanding these two critical milestones prevents miscommunication and payment disputes:

Best Practice: Define both milestones explicitly in your contract. Track them separately with punchlists and progress-based payment triggers.

Punchlist Management: Do not Let Details Derail You

Standard punchlist failure modes:

- Vague or delayed punch generation

- Missing trade participation in final walkthroughs

- Covered work prior to inspection

- Disputes over quality or spec compliance

Mitigation Strategies:

- Begin a ***Rolling Punchlist*** 60–90 days before projected completion

- Conduct trade-by-trade pre-punch walks

- Assign each punch item an owner, deadline, and status

- Tie punchlist clearance to subcontractor final pay apps

- Use mobile tools (Procore, Bluebeam, PlanGrid) for tracking

Turnover Documentation: Your Final Deliverable

Turnover is not just paperwork; it is proof of contract performance. Many clients withhold payment until all closeout documentation is submitted.

Typical Closeout Package Requirements:

- As-built drawings (CAD/PDF and hard copy)

- O&M manuals, indexed and bound

- Warranty certificates (GC, sub, manufacturer)

- Testing and commissioning reports

- Final inspection sign-offs

- Equipment training logs and user guides

- Certificate of Substantial Completion

- Punchlist resolution documentation

Pro Tip: Closeout does not begin at substantial completion. It begins on day one with organized submittals, accurate as built tracking, and a turnover plan that is built into your schedule, your contracts, and your field routines from the first day of mobilization.

Best Practice: Start documentation early, not at the end. Assign a dedicated ***Closeout Coordinator*** on larger projects.

Lien and Payment Risk at Closeout

Closeout is prime time for payment-related conflicts, especially involving:

- Unpaid change orders

- Miscommunication about scope

- Late lien waivers

- Subcontractors asserting claims for withheld compensation

Protective Measures:

- Require ***Conditional/Unconditional Waivers*** with every pay app

- Maintain a ***Lien Risk Log*** to flag outstanding exposures

- Confirm lien-free status before submitting for final retention

- Fully document every CO, signed, dated, and priced

Industry Statistic: Lien filings spike in the final 60 days of projects, often due to poorly communicated closeout status.

Retention Release: No Documents, No Dollars

Retention is often the last 5–10% of project revenue and the easiest to lose due to incomplete closeout.

Common risks:

- Missing O&M's or as-builts

- Training logs never delivered

- Outstanding lien releases

- Disputed or pending change orders

- Incomplete punchlist

Retention Risk Mitigation:

- Break closeout into release milestones (e.g., 50% at substantial, 50% at final)

- Make subcontractor retention conditional on complete documentation

- Review retention status weekly with accounting and PM teams

Warranty Risk: The Next Chapter of Risk Exposure

The warranty phase introduces its own set of obligations and pitfalls:

- Latent defect claims from hidden workmanship issues

- Denied claims due to lack of documentation or improper installation

- Owner frustration from lack of support post-turnover

- Staff burnout when PMs remain stuck fielding warranty calls

Best Practices:

- Track warranty periods by system and vendor

- Conduct a ***10-month walkthrough*** after substantial completion to address issues before expiration

- Assign a ***Warranty Manager*** post-closeout

- Provide the owner with a formal **"Warranty Submission Guide"** including contacts and procedures

Case Study: Closeout Neglect Turns into Litigation

On a $40M healthcare project:

- The GC completed all work but failed to submit test reports, O&M manuals, and equipment training logs

- The owner withheld $1.2M in final payment and retention

- Subcontractors filed liens, triggering a cascading dispute

- The GC sued for non-payment; the owner countersued for breach of closeout obligations

Outcome: After 14 months of litigation, the GC settled at a ~$450,000 loss.

Lesson: Closeout is not optional; it is contractual. Missing deliverables means lost leverage and unpaid compensation.

Checklist: Closeout Risk Readiness

- Has Substantial Completion been documented and signed?

- Is the punchlist active, rolling, and updated daily?

- Are O&M manuals and as-builts logged and submitted?

- Have subcontractors provided all required warranties?

- Are all lien releases collected, verified, and filed?

- Has retention release status been reviewed with finance?

- Is there a dedicated post-turnover warranty contact?

- Are owners trained on how to submit warranty claims?

Chapter Conclusion

Finish Strong, it is the Lasting Impression

Closeout is not a formality; it is your final performance. Whether it earns applause or litigation depends on your planning, execution, and documentation.

Teams that treat closeout with the same urgency as mobilization secure their profit, avoid disputes, and build lasting client relationships. Teams that stumble lose far more than money; they lose momentum, reputation, and repeat business.

"The end of a project is where reputations are made permanent." – Peter Drucker

Part IX – Forensic Methods and Quantum: How to Prove Your Claim

CHAPTER 26

DELAY ANALYSIS STANDARDS AND METHODOLOGY IN CREATING A TIA

Chapter Foreword

In Chapter 19, we examined how schedule delay and acceleration risks arise. This chapter addresses the next and more consequential question: how those delays should be analyzed, demonstrated, and defended.

Delay analysis is not a software exercise. It is the disciplined application of recognized methods to contemporaneous records in order to answer three questions:

- What actually happened in time?

- Who is responsible for which portions of delay?

- What is the resulting entitlement to time and, where allowed, money?

Time Impact Analysis (TIA) is one of the most frequently cited, and most frequently misapplied, methodologies. When used correctly in the right context, it can provide clear, contemporaneous evidence of entitlement. When used in the wrong context, or with manipulated schedules, it becomes advocacy dressed up as analysis and is quickly dismantled under scrutiny.

This chapter explains how to select and apply delay analysis methods that are consistent with leading industry guidance, including:

- AACE International Recommended Practice 29R-03, "Forensic Schedule Analysis"

- AACE International Recommended Practice 52R-06, "Time Impact Analysis"

- The Society of Construction Law Delay and Disruption Protocol, Second Edition (2017)

The intent is not to teach specific software. The focus is on method selection discipline, modeling integrity, and evidentiary credibility. The examples are illustrative only. Actual application must always consider the governing contract, the quality of the project schedules, the jurisdiction, and the project specific facts, and should be reviewed with qualified scheduling and legal professionals.

"The devil is in the details." – **Gustave Flaubert**

When to Use What Method

Method	Best Used When	Data Requirements	Primary Output	Strengths	Risks / Caveats
Time Impact Analysis (TIA)	Prospective/near-real-time assessment of a discrete event; contract requires modeled evaluation before granting EOT	Accepted CPM update just prior to event; well-defined fragnet; correct logic; known durations/assumptions	Modeled EOT (days) and path change from inserting a fragnet into the unimpacted update	Forward-looking; transparent assumptions; suitable for change management and contemporaneous decisions	Garbage-in/garbage-out if baseline/update is weak; assumes reasonableness of fragnet; not ideal for long, multi-cause periods.
Windows Analysis (observational)	Retrospective or mid-project review across time 'windows' (e.g., monthly) to see who drove the critical path	Reliable sequence of schedule updates; actual progress data; logic change log	Attribution of delay by window; trend of critical path slippage and EOT basis	Uses actuals; captures shifts in criticality; handles multiple causes across time	Quality depends on update integrity; it can mask micro-events; it needs clear logic-change explanations.
Collapsed As-Built (but-for)	Retrospective forensic scenario testing ('but for' selected excusable/compensable delays, when would it have finished?)	Detailed as-built, robust logic mapping; ability to remove modelled delays without distorting remaining logic	Hypothetical finish date after removing identified causes; comparative EOT and responsibility allocation	Useful where contemporaneous schedules are poor or absent; can test scenarios.	Highly assumption-sensitive; can over-model; some protocols caution against misuse; transparency is critical.

Principles of Delay Analysis

At its core, delay analysis is about cause and effect over time. AACE and the SCL Protocol emphasize four fundamental principles:

Use contemporaneous data where possible

Analyses based on accepted contemporaneous updates are preferred over those reconstructed later from memory.

Choose the method to fit the facts

Method selection should be driven by the timing and nature of the delay, the quality of the baseline and updates, and the available records. It should never be driven by which result is more favorable to one party.

Maintain transparency and repeatability

A defensible analysis is clear, logically explained, and can be replicated by an independent reviewer using the same inputs.

Stay aligned with contractual entitlement
Time and money conclusions must tie directly to the contract's notice provisions, extension of time clauses, and definitions of excusable and compensable delay.

Method Selection Discipline

Not every delay warrants a TIA. Not every project is suited to a Windows analysis. Retrospective "but for" models are not a default; they are a last resort.

AACE and the SCL Protocol both stress that:

Prospective methods should be used when assessing the impact of a delay at or near the time it occurs.

Observational methods are appropriate when multiple, overlapping events unfold across several updates.

Retrospective methods should be used cautiously, and usually only when contemporaneous schedules are incomplete, unreliable, or nonexistent.

Method Selection by Situation

Single, discrete event, good schedule in place, analyzed contemporaneously
→ Use a **Time Impact Analysis** (prospective, additive model) on the last accepted update before the event.

Multiple events, shifting critical paths, reliable monthly updates
→ Use a **Windows (observational) analysis** that examines slippage period by period.

Project completed, limited or poor updates, need to approximate what would have happened without certain delays
→ Use a **Collapsed As Built (but for) analysis** or similar retrospective method with heightened transparency.

Method Selection Warning

Selecting a delay analysis method because it produces a preferred outcome, rather than because it fits the project facts, is one of the fastest ways to lose credibility. Once a tribunal concludes that method choice was driven by advocacy, the entire analysis becomes suspect, no matter how detailed the graphics or narrative may be.

Standards (AACE & SCL)

Topic	AACE RP 29R-03 (Forensic Schedule Analysis)	AACE RP 52R-06 (TIA)	SCL Delay & Disruption Protocol (2nd ed.)
General Stance	Group methods emphasize method selection matched to data quality and dispute context; caution on inputs and transparency.	Defines TIA as a prospective, modeled technique using an accepted update immediately prior to the event.	Does not endorse a single 'best' method; stresses good records, suitability, and explaining assumptions.
Use of TIA	Recognizes modeled approaches; stresses logical insertion and contemporaneous use where possible.	Core guidance requires a clean pre-event update and a reasoned fragnet, aimed at change/EOT decisions.	Accepts prospective analyses where appropriate; emphasizes clarity and contemporaneous programming.
Windows analysis	Treats windows as observational; attributes delay by periods using actual progress and changing the critical path.	Not the focus.	Considers observational approaches valid if updates are reliable and logic changes are explained.
Collapsed as-built	Permissible with caution; scenario testing must be transparent and justified; sensitivity matters.	Not the focus.	Warns about misuse; requires clear disclosure of removals/assumptions; avoids opaque 'black box' modelling.

Quick Glossary

- CCD/CO - Construction Change Directive / Change Order.

- DSC - Differing Site Condition.

- EOT - Extension of time.

- FF Relationship – Finish to Finish Relationship

- FOH/HOH - Field/Home Office Overhead.

- FS Relationship – Finish to Start Relationship

- Fragnet - Small schedule network modeling a discrete impact.

- Measured Mile - Compare productivity in unimpacted vs impacted work.

- SC – Substantial Completion

- SF Relationship – Start to Finish Relationship

- SS Relationship – Start to Start Relationship

- TIA – Time Impact Analysis

Example 1: Utilize a Time Impact Analysis (TIA)

Scenario

This scenario illustrates how a discrete delay event is evaluated prospectively using a Time Impact Analysis. The method relies on inserting a fragnet representing the delay into the last accepted schedule update immediately preceding the event. By recalculating the critical path before and after the insertion, the analysis isolates the net impact to project completion attributable to the event.

AACE 52R-06 and the SCL Protocol both recognize TIA as an appropriate method when:

- A discrete delay event occurs during the project

- There is an accepted CPM update immediately before the event

- The event can be reasonably modeled as a fragnet

- The analysis is done prospectively or near contemporaneously

- Typical examples include:

- A change order that adds new work to a defined portion of the schedule

- A late design decision that affects a specific path

- A single, well defined differing site condition

Simple TIA Example

Context

Accepted June update shows substantial completion on 30 October 2026.

Status date: 30 June 2025.

Mechanical riser path is on the longest path with zero total float.

On 5 July 2025, an RFI response requires a redesign and additional approvals for the mechanical riser.

Steps

Select the schedule
Use the last accepted update before the event. Here, the June 2025 update.

Build the fragnet
Create a small network representing the new RFI driven work:

Review and redesign

Revised submittal and review

Revised fabrication or installation start

Insert the fragnet
Tie the start of the fragnet to the affected activity on the mechanical path as of the data date. Tie the end of the fragnet back into the existing sequence.

Recalculate the schedule
Compare substantial completion and total float on the longest path before and after the fragnet insertion.

Activity	Original Duration (d)	Fragnet Duration (d)	Predecessors / Notes
A: Fabricate riser	10	10	Predecessor to B
B: Install riser	5	5	On the critical path
F1: Receive RFI answer	—	2	Inserted on 01 Aug
F2: Re-submittal	—	3	FS to F1
F3: Approval	—	5	FS to F2; FS to B

- Original Baseline Substantial Completion (SC) = 30 Oct. 2026

- Event occurred on 01 Aug. 2025 – RFI answer delay adds review/re-submittal/approval steps to the mechanical riser path.

- Method: Insert fragnet F1→F2→F3 into the accepted July 2025 update (status date 31 Jul. 2025). This is the accepted schedule prior to the impact.

- Recompute the longest path.

- Before: path float = 0d, SC = 30 Oct. 2026

- After: longest path extended by +10d; SC = 09 Nov. 2026 → Extension of Time (EOT) request = 10 days (subject to contract).

- Assumptions: The durations for F1–F3, have no resource limits, no out-of-sequence execution, and no ability to mitigate.

Result (illustrative)

- Before impact: substantial completion 30 October 2026

- After impact: substantial completion 9 November 2026

- Net delay: 10 calendar days

- If the contract allows time, but not necessarily money, for this type of change, the TIA supports an EOT claim of 10 days, subject to concurrency and mitigation review.

TIA procedure checklist

- Confirm the baseline and all updates are accepted and free of the analyzed event.

- Select the correct pre-event update.

- Build a realistic fragnet with justified durations and logic.

- Insert the fragnet at the correct data date.

- Before and after completion dates

- Changes in total float

- Any shift in the longest path

- Recalculate, and document:

- Address potential mitigation and alternative sequences.

- Tie the result back to specific contract clauses for notice and EOT.

Example 2: Utilize a Windows Analysis (Observational)

Scenario

This scenario demonstrates a Windows Analysis used when project delays evolve over time and critical path drivers shift between schedule updates. Rather than modeling a single event, the analysis observes contemporaneous updates to determine how responsibility for delay changes across defined time periods. This approach is particularly effective when impacts are cumulative, overlapping, or not readily modeled as a single fragnet.

When to use a Windows analysis

AACE 29R-03 and the SCL Protocol recognize observational (Windows) analyses as appropriate when:

- Multiple events occur over the course of the project

- The critical path shifts between updates

- Impacts are cumulative, overlapping, or difficult to model as a single fragnet

- Contemporaneous updates exist and are generally reliable

Simple Windows example

Context

Monthly updates are accepted and show shifting drivers.

The project runs from January 2025 to December 2026.

Two windows are examined:

Window 1: March to April 2025

Critical path shifts from structural steel to building envelope.

Structural redesign causes 5 days of excusable delay.

Contractor driven late mobilization adds 3 days of non-excusable delay.

Window 2: May to June 2025

Heavy rain and restricted site access add 8 days of excusable, non-compensable delay.

No contractor caused critical path delay in this period.

Analysis structure

For each window:

- Identify the longest path at the start and end of the window.

- Measure slippage in the completion date within that window.

- Attribute slippage to specific causes based on contemporaneous records.

- Distinguish excusable versus non-excusable, and compensable versus non-compensable, per the contract.

Window	Critical Driver Observed	Slip in Window (d)	Attribution (Excusable / Compensable?)	Notes
Jun-25	Abnormal rain halts civil works	5	Excusable, non-compensable (per contract weather clause)	Weather data attached; resequencing limited
Jul-25	Late-approved IFC drawings for duct riser	8	Excusable and compensable (Owner/AE info delay)	RFI trail shows the due date was missed

- Monthly updates show shifting drivers. Evaluate both June and July windows.

- Result: EOT basis = 5 + 8 = 13 days (compensation tied only to July's 8d if contract so provides).

- Provide logic-change narrative and path trace screenshots per update.

Result (illustrative)

- Window 1: 5 days of slippage

- 5 days excusable (weather)

- Window 2: 8 days excusable, compensable (owner delay)

Total EOT basis:

- 5 days excusable, non-compensable weather delay

- 8 days excusable, compensable owner delay

The tribunal sees each period in context, grounded in the contemporaneous updates.

Windows procedure checklist

- Confirm the sequence of updates is accepted and reflects actual progress.

- Define windows (for example, monthly) based on update dates and project phases.

- Starting and ending completion dates

- Drivers of the longest path

- Amount and cause of any slippage

- Any changes to logic or constraints, with explanations

- For each window, document:

- Summarize results in a table that rolls up total delay and allocation.

- Reconcile the analysis with contemporaneous notices and correspondence.

Example 3: Utilize a Collapsed As-Built ('But-For')

Scenario

This scenario presents a retrospective Collapsed As-Built analysis applied after project completion. The method evaluates what the completion date would have been "but for" specific delays by selectively removing modeled impacts from the as-built schedule. Due to its reliance on hindsight, this approach requires heightened transparency, careful logic preservation, and sensitivity testing to remain credible.

When to use a Collapsed As Built

AACE and the SCL Protocol caution that retrospective techniques should be used sparingly and with full transparency. They may be appropriate when:

- The project is complete

- Contemporaneous schedule updates are missing, incomplete, or unreliable

- The parties need a way to approximate "what would have happened" in the absence of certain delays

Simple Collapsed As Built example

Context

As built records show actual activity dates from start to finish.

Actual substantial completion: 18 November 2026.

Two major concurrent changes have been identified, with reliable records of their durations.

Contractor caused delays must remain in the model.

Basic steps

- Reconstruct an As-built logic network that matches actual sequence and dates.

- Identify discrete owner caused delays, with their start, finish, and logic ties.

- Shortening or deleting the delay activities

- Reconnecting the logic to preserve realistic sequencing

- "Remove" those delays from the as built model by:

- Recalculate the schedule to determine the hypothetical "but for" completion date.

Cause Removed	Days Removed	Revised Hypothetical SC	Comment
Owner info delay	12	11/18/2026	Compensable candidate, if causation is proven
Contractor crew shortage	6	11/12/2026	Non-excusable; not a basis for EOT

- Identify and remove modeled owner-caused delay (12d submittal cycle) and contractor internal delay (6d crew shortage).

- Caveat: Ensure removals do not distort remaining logic.

- Disclose all assumptions and run sensitivity (e.g., owner delay ±2d).

Result (illustrative)

- As built completion: 18 November 2026

- Collapsed As Built completion (without owner delay): 12 November 2026

- Collapsed As Built completion (with owner delay): 18 November 2026

- Net owner caused delay: 6 days – compensable

- Net concurrent delay: 6 days – concurrent and excusable

Because this method relies heavily on hindsight, the analysis must:

- Disclose all removed activities and assumptions

- Explain how logic was preserved

- Provide sensitivity tests to show the effect of reasonable changes in delay durations

Why Time Impact Analyses Fail Under Scrutiny

Most Time Impact Analyses fail not because the underlying delay is invalid, but because the analysis itself is methodologically flawed. Common failure points include inserting fragnets into a schedule update selected for convenience rather than acceptance, using hindsight-driven durations or logic, failing to disclose schedule logic changes between updates, and ignoring concurrency that materially affects entitlement. Over-modeling is another frequent error by adding unnecessary complexity that obscures rather than clarifies causation. Under cross-examination, these weaknesses are quickly exposed, often reducing the analysis to opinion rather than evidence. A defensible TIA must be simple, transparent, and repeatable. If the opposing expert cannot independently replicate the result using the same inputs, the analysis will not survive challenge.

Evidence Pack & Common Pitfalls

- Always align with contract notice and EOT provisions; tie each method output to entitlement language.

- Keep a logic-change log per update; unexplained changes undermine credibility.

- For TIA, use the last accepted pre-event update and avoid hindsight in durations/logic.

- For windows, do not rewrite updates retroactively; observe what the contemporaneous schedule shows.

- For collapsed as-built, disclose every removal and preserve the chain of logic; run sensitivities.

Minimal Math Cheat sheets (Transparency First)

- Float Change (ΔTF) = Total Float After − Total Float Before on the longest path activity

- EOT is justified when completion is pushed, and no recovery is contractually required or reasonably feasible.

- Measured-Mile Link: When delay causes disruption, pair time analysis with a simple productivity delta (qty/hr.) to inform cost, keeping time and money analyses consistent.

How Decision-Makers Evaluate Delay Methodologies

Dispute Review Boards, arbitrators, and courts tend to favor delay analyses that reflect **contemporaneous project reality** and align with recognized industry standards. Prospective methods such as Time Impact Analysis are generally viewed more favorably when supported by accepted schedule updates and proper notice. Observational (Windows) analyses are often accepted where project dynamics are complex or evolving, provided the updates are reliable and logic changes are explained. Retrospective methods, particularly Collapsed As-Built analyses, receive heightened scrutiny due to their susceptibility to hindsight bias and selective delay removal. The Society of Construction Law cautions that retrospective techniques should be applied conservatively and with full disclosure of assumptions and limitations. Ultimately, decision-makers are less concerned with which method is used than with whether the method was selected appropriately, applied consistently, and tied directly to contractual entitlement.

Chapter Conclusion

A TIA is not a crystal ball, it is a fragnet at the data date that shows exactly who pushed the finish line.

A Time Impact Analysis is not a prediction tool, a negotiation tactic, or a retrospective justification. It is a **prospective, contemporaneous test** that answers a single question: *did a discrete event, modeled at the correct data date, push the project's completion?*

Use a TIA **only** when you have a clean, accepted schedule update immediately preceding the event and a change that can be realistically modeled without hindsight. Build a disciplined fragnet, insert it at the data date, and recompute. Capture the before-and-after completion dates, total float changes, and longest-path shifts with objective screenshots, not narrative argument.

Where impacts smear across multiple updates, pivot to a **Windows Analysis**. Where damages hinge on lost productivity, pair time analysis with a **measured-mile** approach to costs. Above all, disclose assumptions, test reasonable mitigation, identify concurrency, and align every conclusion with contract entitlement.

A credible delay analysis reads like engineering, not persuasion. When method selection is disciplined, modeling is transparent, and documentation is contemporaneous, schedule analysis becomes evidence rather than opinion.

"To measure is to know. If you cannot measure it, you cannot improve it." **– Lord Kelvin**

CHAPTER 27

DAMAGES FOR DELAY AND DISRUPTION: PRACTICAL WORKSHEETS

Chapter Foreword

Home office overhead, field office overhead, and equipment standby costs are among the most frequently asserted and most frequently rejected categories of delay damages in construction claims. Methods such as Eichleay, Hudson, and Harmony are well known in theory, but routinely fail in practice when entitlement is not clearly established, prerequisites are misunderstood, or assumptions are inadequately disclosed.

This chapter addresses how time-related costs should be quantified **only after entitlement has been proven** through proper schedule analysis and notice compliance. It focuses on the disciplined application of accepted methodologies for allocating home office overhead, calculating extended field costs, and substantiating equipment idle or standby claims. The guidance presented aligns with recognized industry standards, including AACE International Recommended Practices and the Society of Construction Law Delay and Disruption Protocol, while acknowledging that outcomes remain highly dependent on contract language, governing law, and contemporaneous records.

The intent of this chapter is not to advocate for a particular formula, but to establish method-selection discipline, evidentiary rigor, and transparency. These damages are not theoretical constructs; they are mathematical allocations that will be scrutinized line by line. When applied correctly, they can withstand audit, expert challenge, and legal review. When applied casually, they collapse quickly and often undermine otherwise valid delay claims.

"In matters of judgment, credibility is everything." – Learned Hand

Home Office Overhead vs. Field Office Overhead: A Simple Distinction

Home Office Overhead and Field Office Overhead are fundamentally different costs and must never be treated interchangeably. **Home Office Overhead** consists of company-wide indirect expenses; executive management, accounting, legal, estimating, IT, and corporate facilities. It supports all projects and cannot be directly assigned to a single job. The **Eichleay formula** is a narrow allocation method used to apportion a share of those home-office costs to a specific project, but only when strict legal prerequisites such as owner-caused standby and inability to replace the work are met. **Field Office Overhead**, by contrast, consists of actual, project-specific costs incurred at the site – superintendents, project managers, trailers, temporary utilities, site security, and permits—that continue during project prolongation. Field overhead is proven using **actual costs and daily burn rates**, not allocation formulas. Confusing the two is a common and fatal error: Eichleay applies to corporate overhead in limited circumstances, while field office overhead is a direct, time-related project cost recoverable when delay entitlement is established.

How to Use This Chapter

- **Establish entitlement first** using a defensible schedule analysis (TIA, Windows, or equivalent) and confirm compliance with contractual notice provisions.

- **Select the cost method that fits your jurisdiction, contract, and available records**, not the method that produces the largest number.

- **Use the worksheets contemporaneously**, as management tools during delay, not as retrospective reconstructions built for litigation.

Overview: Time, Money, and Method

Question	Answer Framework	Where to Prove It
Is there an excusable delay?	CPM analysis (Windows/TIA) shows the owner-risk event drove Substantial Completion.	AACE 29R-03 methods; SCL Protocol (method selection, transparency)
Is it compensable?	Contract language: owner breach/change vs. weather/force-majeure.	AIA/other form; notices; directives
What money is recoverable?	Actual prolongation costs and, where allowed, unabsorbed HOOH via accepted formula.	Cost records, payrolls, invoices, and formula prerequisites

Home Office Overhead (HOOH): Three Common Approaches

Eichleay Formula (U.S. standby cases)

Use when an owner-caused delay of uncertain duration places the contractor in a standby and prevents taking on replacement work. Courts often require precise prerequisites before applying this allocation method.

- Determine contract's share of home office overhead during performance: (Total home-office overhead during contract period × Contract billings ÷ Total company billings).

- Divide by days of contract performance to get Daily Contract Overhead.

- Multiply Daily Contract Overhead × Days of compensable delay.

- Prerequisites to document (typical): owner-caused delay; uncertain duration; standby; inability to replace the work reasonably.

Strengths: Links to actual accounts; familiar with public-works disputes.

Risks: Fails without strict prerequisites; disputes over what counts as indirect expense.

Worked example:

Total HOOH during period $4,000,000

Total company billings $80,000,000

Contract billings $10,000,000

Contract days 400

Compensable delay 30 days → Daily Contract Overhead = (($4,000,000 × $10,000,000 ÷ $80,000,000) ÷ 400) = $1,250/day → Claim = $37,500.

Hudson Formula (tender-based percentage)

Use where jurisdictions accept a tender/allowance-based proxy for head-office overhead and profit (OH&P) contribution. The percentage typically comes from the bid or audited accounts.

- Allocable OH&P per day = (Head-office OH&P % × Contract sum) ÷ Original contract period (days).

- Claimed amount = Allocable OH&P per day × Compensable delay days.

- Guardrails: Show the need to hold resources on the project and limited ability to redeploy. Modern practice may prefer audited averages over raw tender percentages where evidence allows.

- Worked example: OH&P % 10%; contract sum $12,000,000; period 365 days; delay 20 days → per-day = (0.10 × $12,000,000) ÷ 365 ≈ $3,288/day → Claim ≈ $65,760.

Harmony Method (Canadian usage, scenario-based proxy)

Use in some Canadian matters as an alternative proxy when actuals are thin, but a reasonable contribution to head-office costs is provable. Often considered alongside Hudson/Emden, with emphasis on reasonableness and transparency.

- Start with the attributable head-office cost rate from financials (average contribution margin).

- Apply to the value of work affected over the delay span, adjusted to avoid double-counting direct field costs.

- Cross-check against productivity and schedule evidence; disclose all assumptions.

- Worked example (illustrative): Derived HOOH rate 6% of revenue; revenue foregone during delay window $1,200,000 → HOOH = $72,000 (subject to adjustments for saved costs).

Worksheet: Home Office Overhead

Item	Value	Notes
Total HOOH during the relevant period	$__________	From accounts
Total company billings during the period	$__________	
Contract billings during the period	$__________	
Contract performance days	__________	
Compensable delay days	__________	
Bid or audited OH&P % (Hudson)	__________ %	If using Hudson
Computed Daily Contract Overhead (Eichleay)	$__________	
Claim (method used: Eichleay/Hudson/Harmony)	$__________	Show calculation steps

Field Office Overhead (FOH): Extended Project Costs

FOH are the actual, project-site costs that continue during prolongation: supervision, trailers, temp utilities, site security, permits, project management, etc. SCL Protocol emphasizes actual cost for prolongation; tender allowances are not the measure for time-related site preliminaries.

FOH approach:

- Establish daily FOH burn rate from payrolls, rentals, and recurring site invoices.

- Multiply by compensable prolongation days (net of mitigated periods).

- Add discrete prolongation costs (e.g., extended insurance/bonds) with invoices.

- Worked example: FOH daily rate $6,800 (supervision, trailers, utilities); prolongation 25 days → FOH = $170,000; add extended builder's risk $4,200 → Total FOH = $174,200.

Worksheet: FOH

FOH Component	Daily/Monthly	Qty/Days	Amount	Notes
Superintendent + PE + Admin payroll	Daily $____	____ days	$__________	
Trailer/office rental & utilities	Monthly $____	____ months	$__________	
Site services (toilets, dumpsters, security)	Weekly $____	____ weeks	$__________	
IT/comm/site systems	Monthly $____	____ months	$__________	
Insurance/bonds (extended)	Lump $____	—	$__________	
Other (specify)	—	—	$__________	

Equipment Idle / Standby: Ownership vs. Operating

Idle equipment claims typically separate ownership (depreciation, interest, taxes, insurance) from 'operating' (fuel, maintenance, operator). Only the costs actually incurred during idle should be claimed; follow contract rate schedules or agreed pricing bases where available.

Approach:

- Identify impacted equipment, dates, hours, and whether operators were on standby.

- Apply contract/Blue-Book/agreed rates, removing saved operating components when equipment is idle without an operator.

- Corroborate with dailies, photos, delivery, and maintenance logs.

- Worked example: 60-ton crane ownership rate $150/hr., operating $70/hr. Idle without operator 24 hours → claim 24 × $150 = $3,600; if operator held on standby at $55/hr. for 16 hours → + $880 = $4,480.

Worksheet: Equipment Idle/Standby

Equipment	Idle Dates/Hours	Ownership $/hr	Operating $/hr	Operator $/hr	Idle Type	Amount
Crane (60-ton)	____ hrs.	$____	$____	$____	Idle w/o operator	$__________
Boom lift 60'	____ hrs.	$____	$____	$____	Idle w/ operator	$__________

Integration Rules: Keep Time and Money in Sync

- Tie every day of claimed cost to a window/TIA result; reconcile with concurrency findings.

- Mitigation: record what you tried, what was directed, and costs avoided, SCL stresses reasonableness.

- Avoid double recovery (e.g., do not stack FOH and HOOH for the same dollars); be explicit about overlaps.

- Disclose assumptions and include a logic-change log; transparency is a Protocol theme.

Cross-Walk to Standards

Topic	AACE Reference	SCL Reference	What to include in the Claim
Method transparency & schedule proof	RP 29R-03 (selection, inputs, transparency)	Protocol §4–§6 (method selection; records)	Explain method choice; keep logic-change and data-date notes.
Prospective TIA	RP 52R-06 (TIA practice)	Protocol (prospective programming)	Use accepted pre-event update; show fragnet; avoid hindsight.
Prolongation cost basis	RP guidance on cost tracking/forensics	Protocol §21 (actual cost for prolongation)	Price FOH from actuals, not tender allowances.
HOOH proxies (formulas)	Industry practice; jurisdictional acceptance varies	Protocol cautions on formulae vs. actuals	Disclose prerequisites; prefer actuals where required.

Chapter Conclusion

Delay damages are arithmetic, not advocacy

Delay damages are not awarded because a project felt prolonged; they are awarded because entitlement was proven, days were established, and costs were tied directly to those days with credible records. No days, no critical path, no documentation means no recovery.

Field office overhead should be calculated using actual, time-related site costs, net of mitigation and avoided expenses. Home office overhead should only be allocated using Eichleay, Hudson, Harmony, or similar proxies when their prerequisites are satisfied and assumptions are fully disclosed. Equipment standby claims must distinguish clearly between ownership and operating costs and be corroborated by contemporaneous field records.

Across all categories, double recovery must be avoided, concurrency must be reconciled, and mitigation must be documented. Every claimed dollar should trace back to a defined period of compensable delay established through schedule analysis. When time and money are aligned, assumptions are transparent, and calculations are auditable, these claims read less like negotiation positions and more like accounting exercises grounded in project reality.

In delay damages, precision matters. The standard is not whether the math is clever, but whether it is defensible.

"Facts are stubborn things." — John Adams

CHAPTER 28

MEASURED MILE: PROVING DISRUPTION WITHOUT GUESSWORK

Chapter Forward

Loss of productivity claims fail more often than they succeed, not because disruption did not occur, but because it is rarely proven with discipline. The measured mile method remains one of the most reliable and widely accepted ways to quantify productivity loss because it compares the contractor's own performance against itself, rather than relying on industry averages, bid assumptions, or theoretical models.

At its core, a measured mile asks a simple question: *how did the same contractor, using the same crew and methods, perform when work was unimpacted versus when it was disrupted?* When that comparison is properly selected, normalized, and documented, the resulting analysis converts disruption into defensible hours and dollars without speculation.

This chapter focuses on **how to apply measured mile correctly**, when it should be used, and—equally important—when it should not. It emphasizes comparator selection, normalization discipline, and evidentiary packaging rather than formulas or templates. The goal is not mathematical precision for its own sake, but credibility: an analysis that can withstand owner scrutiny, expert rebuttal, and legal challenge.

The guidance in this chapter aligns with AACE International Recommended Practices and the Society of Construction Law Delay and Disruption Protocol. As with all productivity claims, application must reflect the governing contract, jurisdictional standards, and project-specific facts.

"Proof, not possibility, is the foundation of recovery." – **Learned Hand**

Measured Mile: A Beginners Explanation

A measured mile is a way to prove lost productivity by comparing a contractor's own work to itself. You identify a period or area where the work was performed under normal, unimpacted conditions and measure how productive the crew was. Then you compare that performance to the same work performed later when conditions were disrupted by owner-risk events such as trade stacking, access restrictions, resequencing, or late information. The difference between those two productivity rates represents the loss caused by the disruption. Because the comparison uses the contractor's actual crews, methods, and records, it avoids speculation and industry averages, making it one of the most credible ways to quantify productivity loss when the comparison is fair and properly documented.

When to Use and When Not To

- Use when you can identify like-for-like work areas (same trade, methods, materials) with reliable quantity and hours data.

- Use when disruption, not just pure delay, drives cost (stacking of trades, access limits, late info, rework).

- Avoid when the only 'unimpacted' period is a learning-curve outlier, or when the scope changed materially between areas.

- If comparability is weak or causes smear across months, pivot to triangulated approaches (time-and-motion sampling, windows analysis for time + cost-based corroboration).

Minimum Data You Need

- Quantities installed by location/segment and date range (drawings with takeoff marks help).

- Direct labor hours by crew/day (and subcontractor daily reports where applicable).

- Crew composition and changes (classifications, supervision).

- Access/sequence records (look-aheads, area control, delivery logs).

- Photos/video, RFIs/directives, and schedule updates covering the comparison windows.

- Weather logs if exterior work may be affected.

Picking the Comparator (Unimpacted Segment)

- Start with the same **crew and means** on a similar quantity profile (e.g., same gauge studs, same floor plate).

- Prefer a segment **after** the learning curve but **before** significant disruption or a matched floor/zone executed in parallel by the same team.

- Document why the chosen segment is the best available comparator; note any compromises and their adjustments.

Normalize Before You Calculate

- Learning curve: exclude the first few days or adjust using a short warm-up factor.

- Material/spec differences: adjust quantities (e.g., heavier gauge, additional layers).

- Access and logistics: note hoist distances, laydown limits, working heights.

- Crew mix and overtime: keep the mix constant; separate OT productivity where necessary.

- Weather and inspections: exclude shutdown days or document as separate causes.

Step-By-Step Method (Field-Forward)

- Define the scope unit (LF, SF, EA) for a single trade and activity.

- Select the best unimpacted comparator and one or more impacted segments; map them on a plan.

- Collect quantities and direct hours per segment/period; confirm crew composition.

- Compute productivity for each: Qty ÷ Hours = Units per hour (or Hours per unit).

- Calculate the delta: Impacted productivity vs. Unimpacted baseline.

- Translate the delta into **extra hours** = (Impacted Qty × Hours/unit impacted) − (Impacted Qty × Hours/unit unimpacted).

- Price those extra hours at actual labor cost (wages, fringes, burden) plus allowed markups; add items directly tied to the disruption (rework materials, small tools).

- Run a sensitivity check (swap another plausible comparator or exclude suspect days); disclose results.

- Package with a one-page narrative, plan markup, photo set, data tables, and a cross-reference to the schedule analysis for time context.

Example 1: Interior Framing – Stacked Trades Disruption

A drywall framing crew completed Level 4 East using standard methods, identical crew composition, and unrestricted access. Over a seven-day period, the crew installed approximately 12,000 square feet with 480 direct labor hours, yielding a stable baseline productivity rate.

Two weeks later, the same crew performed the same scope on Level 3 East. During this period, MEP rough-in overlapped framing, limiting access, forcing resequencing, and increasing material handling. Quantities installed were comparable, but labor hours increased materially. After normalizing for a minor material difference and excluding an initial learning-curve day, productivity dropped by approximately 20 percent.

The difference between baseline and impacted productivity was translated into additional labor hours attributable solely to trade stacking. Those hours were priced using actual labor cost records and allowed contract markups, then cross-referenced to schedule windows showing the same disruption period. The claim relied entirely on contemporaneous dailies, photos, plan markups, and payroll records, no estimates, no assumptions beyond disclosed adjustments.

Example 2: Equipment-Intensive Work – Access Constraints

A concrete placing operation achieved consistent productivity during podium pours with unrestricted crane access and stable delivery windows. When owner-directed resequencing later restricted crane availability and forced off-peak placements, cycle times increased and crews were intermittently idle.

Rather than relying on industry production rates, the contractor compared its own unaffected pours to the disrupted pours. Equipment standby time, additional crew hours, and extended pour durations were isolated to the access-restricted period. Productivity deltas were calculated using actual quantities and hours, with weather and inspection shutdowns excluded.

The resulting measured mile demonstrated not only increased labor hours, but also equipment standby costs directly tied to the same disruption window identified in the schedule analysis.

Example 3: When Measured Mile Should Not Be Used

A contractor attempted to apply measured mile where the only "unimpacted" period occurred during early mobilization and learning-curve conditions. Later work involved design changes, different materials, and modified sequencing.

In this case, comparability was weak and adjustments would have required excessive assumptions. Rather than force a measured mile, the contractor pivoted to a hybrid approach: limited measured-mile sampling for discrete activities, supported by time-and-motion studies and schedule window analysis to establish causation. Credibility was preserved by choosing defensibility over convenience.

Key Judgment Rules

- Measured mile lives or dies on **comparability**, not math.

- Normalize inputs before calculating deltas; never after.

- If adjustments exceed explanation, your comparator is wrong.

- Pair measured mile with **schedule windows** to anchor causation.

- Disclose sensitivity checks; hiding them weakens credibility.

Common Pushbacks and How to Answer

- "Not comparable." → Show like-for-like scope, crew, and conditions; disclose and adjust for any differences.

- "Learning curve skew." → Exclude ramp-up, or use a stabilized period as baseline.

- "Other causes present." → Acknowledge and remove non-owner causes; pair with schedule windows for time context.

- "Global claim." → Present discrete tables by segment and cause; no lump-sum leaps.

Extended Overtime and Productivity Loss

In high-velocity projects such as semiconductor fabs and hyperscale data centers, extended overtime is often imposed deliberately. Owners accept increased labor cost in exchange for earlier revenue, market capture, or commissioning milestones. What is frequently overlooked is that sustained overtime does not merely increase cost, it degrades productivity.

Decades of empirical studies demonstrate that productivity declines materially once workweeks exceed approximately 50–60 hours, with losses compounding as fatigue, error rates, rework, and absenteeism increase. These effects are foreseeable, measurable, and widely recognized in construction management literature.

Pro Tip:

As construction work increases from 40 hours to 50 and then 60 hours per week, productivity per hour typically declines due to fatigue, reduced focus, and increased safety risks. At around 40 hours, workers are generally operating near their optimal productivity level. When hours rise to about 50 per week, studies in labor economics and construction management often estimate an effective loss of roughly 10–15% of productive time compared with staying at 40 hours, because the additional hours do not translate into proportional output. At 60 hours, the decline is more severe, with some research indicating that total weekly output may be similar to or only slightly higher than that achieved in 50 hours, implying an effective productivity loss of around 20–30% relative to a 40-hour baseline. Under current labor laws in many jurisdictions, employers are required to pay overtime premiums (for example, 1.5× the regular rate after 40 hours in the U.S.), but those laws generally do not adjust for diminished productivity – meaning contractors often pay more per hour precisely when each extra hour tends to produce less work, significantly increasing the cost per unit of output.

Within a measured mile analysis, extended overtime should not be used as an abstract multiplier or standalone claim. Instead, it functions as an **explanatory and normalization factor**. Where the unimpacted comparator reflects straight-time or limited overtime conditions, and the impacted period reflects sustained extended shifts, the productivity delta captured by the measured mile inherently reflects overtime fatigue. The measured mile quantifies the loss; overtime explains *why* the loss occurred.

To preserve credibility:

- Overtime must be documented contemporaneously (timecards, schedules, directives).

- The measured mile must still rely on actual productivity records.

- Industry studies may be cited only to corroborate foreseeability not to calculate damages.

- When overtime is owner-directed, schedule-driven, and sustained beyond normal thresholds, the resulting productivity loss is not inefficiency – it is a predictable consequence of acceleration.

Acceleration and Constructive Acceleration: More productivity loss to consider.

- Directed vs. constructive acceleration

- Overtime as a means and a consequence

- Productivity degradation curves

- Recovery vs. acceleration fallacy

- How owners knowingly trade productivity for time

For more information on this topic refer to NECA, MCAA, CII, AACE, and USACE as references.

Cross-Walk to AACE/SCL

Topic	AACE Pointer	SCL Pointer	What You Should Do
Method transparency	RP 29R-03 groups methods; choose based on data and context	Protocol stresses clarity and records	Explain why the measured mile fits; show data sources
Prospective vs retrospective	RP 29R-03 allows observational productivity methods	Protocol accepts measured mile where records permit	Use contemporaneous data; avoid after-the-fact reconstructions where possible
Adjustments/normalization	RP emphasizes input quality and adjustments	Protocol warns against untested assumptions	Document each adjustment and run sensitivity
Packaging evidence	RP on traceability of facts to conclusions	Protocol on transparency and auditability	Deliver plan markups, photos, dailies, and tables together

Chapter Conclusion

If the work is apples, your measured mile should not smell like oranges.

Measured mile is not a productivity formula, it is a credibility test. When the comparison is clean, the math is simple, and the documentation is contemporaneous, the method converts disruption into proof rather than argument.

The strongest measured mile claims rely on the contractor's own records to tell a restrained story: same trade, same means, similar conditions, different outcome. Normalization removes noise, not responsibility. The delta is translated into hours, those hours into dollars, and every dollar is tied to a documented disruption window supported by schedule analysis and entitlement clauses.

Measured mile fails when it is stretched beyond its limits when weak comparators are forced to fit, when learning curves are ignored, or when unrelated impacts are blended into a global number. Precision theater impresses no one. Transparency does.

When applied with discipline, measured mile does not ask decision-makers to believe you. It shows them.

"The weight of evidence depends not on quantity, but on coherence." – **Oliver Wendell Holmes Jr.**

Part X – Building, Defending, and Settling Claims

CHAPTER 29

HOW TO WRITE CLAIMS THAT WIN

Chapter Forward

Claims do not fail because entitlement is weak; they fail because the proof is disorganized, the narrative is buried, and the decision-maker cannot quickly see why "yes" is the rational answer. This chapter addresses that failure directly.

Think of a successful claim as an engineered system. Contract language establishes risk transfer. Facts establish breach. Schedule analysis establishes impact. Cost records establish quantum. Presentation determines whether all of that work results in recovery or stalemate. This chapter focuses on the last and most neglected element.

Here, we move beyond analysis for its own sake and into disciplined claim construction: building a submission that a neutral, an executive, or an owner's counsel can audit quickly and trust. The approach aligns with AACE and the Society of Construction Law's emphasis on transparency, contemporaneous evidence, and reproducibility, while reflecting the practical reality that most claims are resolved, not tried.

If your claim cannot be understood in minutes, it will be resisted for months. This chapter shows how to structure entitlement, time, and money into a concise, defensible package that invites settlement rather than argument.

"The art of persuasion consists in knowing what to leave out." – **Blaise Pascal**

Cross-References

- Chapter 26: Delay Analysis Standards and Methodology in Creating TIA

- Chapter 27: Damages for Delay & Disruption: Practical Worksheets

- Chapter 28: Measured Mile: Proving Disruption Without Guesswork

What "Winning" Looks Like

- Entitlement established in the contract language and facts (not rhetoric).

- Time impact proven on the **longest path** or near-critical path; concurrency addressed.

- Quantum built from contemporaneous **actuals** with transparent assumptions.

- Presentation brief, auditable, and settlement-oriented (decision-maker can say "yes" on one page).

The Claim Architecture™ Model

The structure used throughout this chapter follows what the author refers to as the *Claim Architecture™* Model. The premise is simple: if a claim cannot be traced step-by-step from contract language to factual breach to schedule impact to quantified cost, it will not survive scrutiny regardless of how real the disruption may have been.

This model is not a formula. It is an architecture. Each component of the claim must stand on its own, but also connect cleanly to the next, allowing a neutral or executive reviewer to validate conclusions without interpretation or advocacy.

Claim Structure That Works

1. Executive Summary (No More Than Half a Page)
Open with a concise summary that allows an executive or neutral to understand the entire claim in minutes. State what happened, identify the specific contract clause(s) that allocate risk or grant entitlement, and summarize the net result in time and money. Briefly note mitigation efforts undertaken and conclude with a clear, quantified request. If a decision-maker reads nothing else, this section should still lead them to the correct outcome.

2. Entitlement: Contract First, Facts Second
Establish entitlement by citing the governing contract provisions and explaining how the facts triggered the owner's contractual responsibility. Map each obligation to a corresponding act, omission, or directive, and include required notice dates and compliance. Avoid narrative argument; entitlement should read like a logical application of contract language to undisputed facts.

3. Chronology of Facts: A Dated, Traceable Timeline
Present a clean, bullet-style chronology that shows how the issue developed over time. Each bullet should contain one fact, one date, and a direct reference to a supporting exhibit. This section is not storytelling; it is orientation. A reviewer should be able to follow the sequence without interpretation or cross-checking emails.

4. Time Analysis: Proving Impact, Not Describing Delay
Demonstrate schedule impact using the appropriate methodology—Windows Analysis, Time Impact Analysis, or both, based on the nature of the delay. Show before-and-after schedule snapshots, identify float consumption,

document path migration, and address concurrency explicitly. The goal is to prove when and how the project completion date was affected, not merely that delays occurred.

5. Disruption Analysis: Measured Mile Where It Fits

Where disruption drives cost, quantify productivity loss using a measured-mile approach or other defensible observational method. Explain the selection of the unimpacted comparator, disclose all normalizations, and calculate the productivity delta in simple terms. Translate that delta into extra hours attributable to the disruption and tie the analysis to the same time windows established in the schedule analysis.

6. Quantum: Pricing the Net Impact with Actuals

Build damages from contemporaneous records. Calculate field office overhead using actual site costs over compensable prolongation periods. Apply home office overhead only where jurisdictional and factual prerequisites are satisfied. Separately account for equipment idle or standby costs, subcontractor impacts, and material-related costs. Apply contract-allowed markups and deduct credits or avoided costs. This section must be reproducible, not persuasive.

7. Mitigation and Resolution Options

Document what mitigation measures were attempted, what was directed, and what costs or time were avoided as a result. Present reasonable settlement options, including brackets or alternative relief scenarios, to demonstrate good faith and commercial awareness. This section signals that the claim is solution-oriented, not adversarial.

8. Relief Requested: Decision-Ready Language

Conclude with a precise statement of the relief sought. State the exact number of days and dollars requested and include draft change order or extension-of-time language that can be executed without revision. A claim that ends with signature-ready language shortens the path to approval.

1. CONTRACT ENTITLEMENT
Relevant clause + risk allocation

2. NOTICE & PRESERVATION
Timely notice, no waiver

3. FACT CHRONOLOGY
Dated events with exhibit hooks

4. TIME IMPACT
Critical path or near-critical path effect

5. CAUSATION LINK
Cause → effect → period

6. QUANTUM
Actual cost built from records

7. MITIGATION & CREDITS
What was avoided or reduced

8. DECISION PACKAGE
Signature-ready CO / EOT request

Claim Architecture™: From Contract Entitlement to Executable Decision

Failure Modes by Claim Architecture™ Stage

"What Happens If You Skip This Step"

1. Contract Entitlement (Clause Identification)

Failure Mode if skipped:
You argue fairness instead of rights.

What actually happens:

- Owner says: *"There's no contractual basis for this."*

- Your facts may be true, but **truth without entitlement is irrelevant**.

- Claim dies before schedule or cost is even reviewed.

Typical rejection language:

"The Contract does not provide for additional compensation under these circumstances."

2. Notice & Procedural Compliance

Failure Mode if skipped:
You win the facts and lose on a technicality.

What actually happens:

- Late or defective notice becomes a **complete bar to recovery**.

- Owner claims prejudice - even if they had actual knowledge.

- Courts and DRBs enforce notice strictly when contracts say they must.

Typical rejection language:

"The Contractor failed to comply with the condition precedent for notice."

3. Facts & Chronology (Cause → Effect)

Failure Mode if skipped:
Your claim reads like opinion, not evidence.

What actually happens:

- Reviewer cannot trace what happened, when, or why it matters.

- Facts feel cherry-picked or out of sequence.

- Opposing expert reframes the story before you ever finish telling it.

Typical rejection language:

"The record does not establish a clear causal link between the alleged events and the claimed impact."

4. Time Impact / Critical Path Proof

Failure Mode if skipped:
You claim cost without proving time.

What actually happens:

- Owner says: *"Even if this occurred, it didn't affect the critical path."*

- Delay damages are rejected wholesale.

- Your disruption claim is labeled "global" or speculative.

Typical rejection language:

"No demonstrable impact to project completion was shown."

5. Disruption / Measured Mile

Failure Mode if skipped:
You rely on averages, assumptions, or bid rates.

What actually happens:

- Productivity loss is dismissed as inefficiency or contractor risk.

- Owner expert substitutes industry norms to minimize damages.

- Court views the claim as **unquantified frustration**.

Typical rejection language:

"The claimed inefficiencies were not proven with reliable project-specific data."

6. Quantum (Cost Build-Up)

Failure Mode if skipped:
Your math cannot be trusted.

What actually happens:

- Double counting (FOH + HOOH) is exposed.

- Unsupported markups are stripped.

- Claimed dollars exceed demonstrated entitlement.

Typical rejection language:

"The quantum is overstated and unsupported by contemporaneous records."

7. Mitigation & Net Impact

Failure Mode if skipped:
You look unreasonable, even if you're right.

What actually happens:

- Owner argues you sat idle or failed to mitigate.

- Entire claim is reduced, not just the disputed portion.

- Decision-makers penalize you for appearing opportunistic.

Typical rejection language:

"The Contractor failed to take reasonable steps to mitigate its damages."

8. Relief Requested (Executable Ask)

Failure Mode if skipped:
No one knows what to approve.

What actually happens:

- Claim stalls in review cycles.

- Owner asks for "clarification" indefinitely.

- Settlement authority never triggers.

Typical rejection language:

"The submission does not clearly state the relief requested."

Pro Tip: Meta-Failure (When Multiple Steps Are Skipped)

What really happens:

- Claim is labeled **"global," "advocacy,"** or **"unsupported."**

- Owner hardens position.

- Lawyers and experts replace engineers and PMs.

- Cost of recovery exceeds value of recovery.

The Five Links of a Traceable Claim

- **Clause:** The contract language that allocates risk and establishes entitlement

- **Cause:** The specific act, omission, or directive that breached that clause

- **Time:** The demonstrated impact on the critical or near-critical path

- **Cost:** The quantified, contemporaneous dollars tied to that time impact

- **Ask:** A clean, net request that accounts for mitigation, concurrency, and credits

If any link is weak, the claim fails at that point.

Evidence Pack: What Makes a Claim Verifiable

1. Schedule Records: The Backbone of Time Proof

Include all accepted baseline and update schedules relevant to the claim period, along with a complete logic-change log. Provide the specific fragnet insertions or Windows Analysis snapshots relied upon, clearly labeled with data dates. These records must allow a neutral reviewer to replicate the time impact independently without inference or explanation.

2. Contemporaneous Field Narrative: Cause to Effect, Day by Day

Provide daily reports, superintendent logs, and running narratives that link the cause of the issue to its observed effects over specific periods. Entries should connect directives, access constraints, resequencing, or interruptions directly to impacted work activities. This documentation bridges the gap between schedule theory and jobsite reality.

3. Directional Documents: Authority and Control

Include all RFIs, written directives, change directives, CCDs, submittal logs, inspection records, gate logs, and access-control documentation that demonstrate owner involvement, delayed responses, or imposed constraints. These documents establish who controlled the conditions that caused the impact and when that control was exercised.

4. Visual Evidence: Orienting the Decision-Maker

Provide dated and labeled photo and video records showing work conditions, congestion, access restrictions, rework, or idle resources. Each image set should identify the date, location, and activity depicted. Include a marked-up plan or area map so the reviewer can immediately understand where the impact occurred without reading narrative text.

5. Cost Records: From Hours to Dollars

Support all claimed costs with contemporaneous financial records, including timecards, certified payrolls, T&M tickets, vendor invoices, equipment utilization logs, and rental records. Field office overhead and home office overhead calculations must be traceable to underlying records and reconciled to the periods established in the time analysis. No summaries without source data.

Standards Cross-Walk

Topic	AACE Pointer	SCL Pointer	What You Do in the Claim
Method transparency	RP 29R-03: choose method to fit data; show inputs/limits	Protocol: transparency, contemporaneous programming	State method choice; list data dates and any caveats
Time Impact Analysis	RP 52R-06: use pre-event update; insert fragnet; disclose assumptions	Protocol: prospective analyses where appropriate	Show before/after path, float change, and mitigation
Windows Analysis	RP 29R-03: observational, attribute slippage by window	Protocol: explain logic changes; no hindsight edits	One table per window: driver, slip, responsibility
Productivity / Disruption	RP 29R-03: input quality and adjustments matter	Protocol: measured-mile accepted with records	Pick clean comparator; normalize; run sensitivity
Prolongation Cost	Actuals preferred; traceability to records	Protocol §21: price prelims from actuals	Use FOH daily burn; avoid tender allowances

Time Proof

- Use windows analysis when delay causes span multiple periods or when critical path drivers shift over time. Use a Time Impact Analysis when a discrete, identifiable event can be modeled at the correct data date using the last accepted schedule update immediately preceding the event.

- Do not select a method based on outcome preference. The method selection must follow the facts and schedule quality.

- Keep the narrative minimal. Let before-and-after screenshots, float-delta tables, and longest-path traces demonstrate impact. Address concurrency explicitly by segregating responsibility by window or event; ignoring concurrency weakens credibility faster than losing days.

Disruption Proof

- Choose a like-for-like baseline using the same trade, crew, means, and scope under unimpacted conditions. Normalize differences such as learning curve, material specifications, access, sequencing, and overtime before calculating productivity deltas, not after.

- Compute a simple hours-per-unit delta and translate only the attributable loss into extra hours, priced at actual all-in labor rates.

- Disruption must be tied to documented causes and defined periods; measured mile proves *how much* productivity was lost, while schedule analysis establishes *why and when*. Avoid global productivity claims if causation cannot be isolated, credibility collapses

Quantum Principles: Turning Proven Time into Defensible Dollars

Field Office Overhead (FOH): Actual Cost of Prolongation

Field office overhead must be calculated using actual, recurring site costs that continued solely because the project duration was extended. This includes supervision, temporary facilities, site utilities, safety, site management staff, permits, and similar preliminaries. The calculation should apply a verified daily burn rate to the net compensable prolongation days, after accounting for mitigation or recovered time. Tender allowances are not evidence; invoices and payroll records are.

Home Office Overhead (HOOH): Use Only When the Law Allows It

Home office overhead recovery is not automatic and should be pursued only when the strict legal and factual prerequisites are met. Whether applying Eichleay, Hudson, or Harmony, assumptions must be disclosed, calculations must be reproducible, and the jurisdictional standard must be satisfied. HOOH is a last resort when actual allocation is impractical. It is not a substitute for weak field records.

Equipment Costs: Ownership vs. Operating

Equipment claims must clearly distinguish between ownership costs (depreciation, interest, insurance, taxes) and operating costs (fuel, maintenance, operators). Only costs actually incurred during idle or standby periods may be claimed, and saved operating costs must be credited where equipment was not working. Standby must be documented explicitly through daily reports, directives, or access restrictions. Implied idleness is not enough.

Credits and Avoided Costs: Show the Net, Not the Gross

A credible quantum analysis acknowledges what was avoided or mitigated. This includes deleted scope, resequenced work, demobilized crews, or recovered time. Credits must be shown transparently and applied consistently. Never stack field office overhead and home office overhead for the same dollars or periods. Net claims survive scrutiny; gross claims invite rejection.

Presentation & Negotiation - Make Approval Easy

Show, Don't Argue

Claims are not won with adjectives. Use tables instead of prose, dates instead of conclusions, and screenshots instead of summaries. Let the evidence carry the argument. Each section should visually demonstrate causation and impact without requiring interpretation.

Close Each Section With a Clear Ask

Every major section should end with a one-line conclusion that states exactly what relief is requested. For example: *"Grant an extension of eight (8) calendar days and $245,000 in compensable costs as detailed above."* If the reader has to infer the ask, the claim is incomplete.

Offer Options, Not Ultimatums

Present structured settlement brackets: full entitlement, partial split (time and/or money), and a time-only fallback where appropriate. Note any reservations of rights clearly and identify follow-up actions required to close remaining issues. This signals reasonableness and accelerates resolution.

The Negotiation One-Pager - Executive-Level Decision Tool

The Three Points That Matter Most

- The one-pager should distill the claim to its essentials:

- The governing contract clause and the controlling fact.

- The resulting slip to the longest or near-critical path.

- The dollars calculated from contemporaneous records tied to that slip.

Settlement Brackets With Guardrails

Present a clear progression of options, from full change order approval to partial compromise, to a time-only resolution. Each with defined impacts and reservation language. This allows decision-makers to choose a path forward without reopening entitlement debates.

Authority and Timing

Include a simple authority chart identifying who has approval power for each option. Propose a specific decision date. Indecision thrives in ambiguity; closure requires a calendar.

Document the Close

Before adjourning any negotiation meeting, confirm agreements, open items, and next steps in writing. Issue meeting minutes and an action list the same day. Verbal alignment without documentation is not alignment.

Five Brutal Tests Before You File

Traceability Test

Can a neutral reviewer trace every conclusion directly to a dated document, schedule update, or cost record, without explanation?

Concurrency Test

Does the claimed relief survive a window-by-window concurrency analysis, with net days clearly stated?

Math Integrity Test

Would you personally sign the calculation knowing it contains no double-counts, no hidden assumptions, and no arithmetic shortcuts?

Executive Test

Could a senior executive approve this claim after a five-minute skim of the executive summary and exhibits?

Adjective Test

If every adjective were removed, would the claim still succeed on facts alone?

If the answer to any is "no," the claim is not ready.

Pre-Empt Common Owner Defenses Before They Raise Them

Notice and Prejudice

Include date-stamped notices and demonstrate actual owner knowledge of the issue. If notice timing is challenged, explain clearly why no prejudice occurred.

No Critical Path Impact

Lead with the windows analysis or TIA table. Show before-and-after path screenshots and float deltas upfront, do not bury them.

Concurrency Allegations

Segregate impacted periods carefully. Address concurrency explicitly and state only net, compensable days.

"Global Claim" Accusations

Break disruption into discrete measured-mile threads tied to specific activities, periods, and causes. Avoid lump-sum assertions without lineage.

Release and Waiver Language

Identify carve-outs and define the temporal scope of any partial agreements. Never allow silence to be interpreted as release.

For expanded treatment of these defenses and rebuttal strategies, refer to Chapter 31.

Failed Claim Sidebar: *Why a Technically Valid Claim Still Lost*

Sidebar: Claim Autopsy, When Entitlement Isn't Enough

The Claim

The contractor submitted a $3.4 million delay and disruption claim supported by hundreds of pages of correspondence, schedules, and cost records. The owner did not dispute that delays occurred.

What Went Wrong

- The submission opened with narrative instead of the governing contract clauses.

- Delay impacts were discussed generally, but no single schedule update showed a net critical-path shift attributable to a specific event.

- Costs were presented as cumulative totals without tying each dollar to a defined delay window.

- Field office overhead, home office overhead, and productivity loss were blended into a single global number.

- Mitigation efforts were mentioned but not quantified.

The Result

The owner rejected the claim as "unsubstantiated and global." In mediation, the neutral agreed that disruption likely occurred but could not determine *how much* or *when*. The claim settled for less than 15% of its original value after significant legal expense.

The Lesson

The claim failed not because the contractor was wrong, but because the decision-maker could not quickly trace a clean line from:

contract clause → breach → schedule impact → time window → cost delta → net ask.

A claim that requires interpretation invites rejection. A claim that performs its own proof invites payment.

Chapter Conclusion

If your proof fits on one page, your check might too.

Claims that succeed are not louder, longer, or more aggressive. They are clearer. They present entitlement without drama, impact without exaggeration, and cost without inflation. Most importantly, they respect the reality that decision-makers are time-constrained and risk-averse.

A winning claim follows a disciplined sequence: contract clause to factual breach; breach to schedule impact; impact to quantifiable cost; cost to a clean, auditable ask. Every step is supported by contemporaneous records. Every assumption is disclosed. Every number can be re-performed by someone else. When those conditions are met, the discussion shifts from "whether" to "how much."

This chapter's structure reflects that reality. It blends the evidentiary rigor demanded by AACE and the SCL Protocol with the practical presentation discipline that drives real-world settlements. The goal is not to posture for litigation, but to create a submission so credible that litigation becomes unnecessary.

Strip away adjectives. Lead with exhibits. Offer options. Reserve rights. And never forget: a claim that reads like a solution is far more likely to be paid than one that reads like a grievance.

***"What convinces is not force, but clarity."* -Aristotle**

CHAPTER 30

CONTRACT ADMINISTRATION AND THE NEW PROJECT MANAGER

Chapter Foreword

Most construction disputes do not begin with a claim. They begin with a missed response deadline, an unclear RFI, or a direction given in a meeting that was never documented. Contract administration is where projects quietly succeed or quietly fail.

This chapter is written for the project manager who has just been handed a live job and told to "take over." It bridges the gap between contract language and daily field decisions. The focus is not legal theory or formal claims strategy, which are addressed elsewhere, but the daily habits that protect schedule, cost, and credibility long before lawyers are involved

You will not find templates, charts, or clause citations here. Instead, you will find practical guidance on how to manage RFIs, submittals, approvals, notices, and risk in real time. If you do these few things consistently and early, many disputes never form. If you do not, even strong positions become difficult to defend.

This chapter is a field manual. It is designed to help new project managers orient themselves quickly, stabilize a troubled job, and understand how daily contract administration decisions shape risk allocation.

"The best time to fix a problem is before it becomes one." – Peter Drucker

What Contract Administration Really Is

Contract administration is not paperwork. It is the process of controlling time, responsibility, and decision making using the tools the contract already gives you.

Every contract answers the same basic questions:

Who decides

- How long do they have to decide?

- What happens if they do not?

- Who pays when things change?

Your job as a project manager is to make sure those answers stay clear in practice, not just on paper.

RFIs: How Small Questions Become Big Problems

An RFI is not a design critique, and it is not a venting mechanism. It is a formal request for direction when the contract documents do not clearly answer a specific question.

Good RFIs share three traits. They are narrow, documented, and time aware.

State one problem in plain language. Avoid bundling multiple issues into one request. Attach a marked up plan or detail and a photo if one exists. Show exactly where the problem occurs.

Whenever possible, offer reasonable solutions. Presenting two constructible options with basic time or cost implications helps decision makers respond faster and shows good faith.

Always identify the affected drawing, specification section, and schedule activity. If the issue may affect the critical path, say so clearly. Track the date sent, the response due date, and every follow up. If the response is late, that delay belongs to someone else only if you documented it.

Most claims fail because RFIs were treated casually early and urgently late.

Submittals: The Quiet Schedule Driver

Submittals are one of the most common hidden causes of delay. Late reviews, serial resubmittals, and unclear comments can quietly move the schedule long before anyone notices.

The discipline here is simple. Every submittal needs an owner, a due date, and a status. Tie submittals to the sequence of work, not just to specification sections. If a late return forces resequencing or rework, document it immediately.

If a submittal comes back with comments that change scope, means, or sequencing, treat it as direction. That is when notice obligations often begin.

Certifications, Tests, and Inspections

Missed inspections and late testing approvals are a common source of unplanned downtime.

Know what certifications and tests are required before work begins. Understand lead times and who controls scheduling. Track requests, results, retests, and approvals. Keep lab reports and inspector sign offs organized and accessible.

If an inspection or test delays work, document the date, the area affected, and what work could not proceed. These details matter later.

Notices: The Most Forgiving Mistake Until It Is Not

Most contracts require notice. Some are forgiving. Some are not. None can be ignored safely.

A notice is not a claim. It is a warning flag that something may affect time or cost. The purpose is to preserve rights and prompt direction.

Notices typically arise from design changes, access restrictions, late approvals, differing conditions, suspensions, acceleration, or defective work by others. A good notice states what happened, when it happened, what clause applies, what work is affected, what mitigation is underway, and what direction is requested.

Late notice is one of the easiest defenses for an owner. Timely notice is one of the easiest protections for a contractor.

Understanding Risk Allocation Without Becoming a Lawyer

Every contract allocates risk, whether it says so clearly or not. Some risks belong to the owner. Some belong to the contractor. Some are shared.

As a new project manager, you do not need to memorize contract forms. You need to recognize patterns.

Design risk usually follows design responsibility. Approval delays usually sit with the party responsible for review. Unknown conditions often depend on notice and investigation requirements. Schedule float ownership and delay compensation vary widely and must be confirmed.

When something goes wrong, ask three questions:

- Who caused it?

- Who controls it?

- Who does the contract say pays for it?

If you cannot answer all three, slow down and document.

The First Thirty Days on a Troubled Job

The first month matters more than most people realize.

Start by freezing the facts. Secure the last accepted schedule, existing logs, photos, and correspondence. Begin a running narrative that records what happens each day and why it matters.

Meet early with the superintendent, scheduler, and project accountant. Agree on where records live and who controls them.

Identify what approvals or information are blocking progress. Track response clocks. Issue notices where required, even if impacts are still developing.

Choose the right analysis approach early. If delays are spreading across time, windows analysis may be appropriate. If a discrete event occurs, preserve the option for a time impact analysis later.

By the end of the first month, you should be able to explain what is happening, why it matters, and what decisions are needed next.

What follows is a stripped-down survival kit for new project managers when problems escalate faster than experience.

The Rapid Claims Kit for New Project Managers

A Field Survival Guide When Things Go Sideways

Most new project managers freeze when they hear the word "claim." They assume it means lawyers, expert reports, and years of dispute. In reality, most successful claims are built quietly and early by project managers who know what to capture and when.

This Rapid Claims Kit is not about writing a formal claim. It is about **preserving the building blocks** so that if a claim becomes necessary, the work is already done.

If you do nothing else in this chapter, do these five things.

1. Capture the Event Immediately

Do not wait for certainty.

When something unusual happens, late information, restricted access, resequencing, stacked trades, unexpected conditions, write it down the same day.

Record:

- What happened

- Where it happened

- When it started

- What work was affected

This can be as simple as a daily narrative entry or a dated email to the project file. Perfect wording does not matter. Timing does.

If you wait until impacts are obvious, you are already late.

2. Tie the Event to the Contract Early

You do not need to quote clauses. You need to **identify ownership**.

Ask yourself:

- Is this design related

- Is this access or sequencing

- Is this approval delay

- Is this owner direction or third-party interference

Once you can answer that, you know whether notice is required. Issue a short notice even if impacts are still developing. You can always refine later. You cannot backdate notice.

3. Anchor the Event to the Schedule

Every claim lives or dies on time.

You do not need to perform a full delay analysis. You do need to identify:

- Which activity or work area is affected

- Whether it sits on or near the critical path

- Whether work was stopped, slowed, or resequenced

Take screenshots of the schedule before and after the event if possible. Save them. Schedules change. Memory does not hold up.

4. Preserve Cost Evidence as It Happens

Claims fail when cost records are recreated instead of preserved.

When an event causes inefficiency, standby, or extra effort:

- Keep daily labor hours separate if possible

- Flag overtime and extended shifts

- Retain time and material tickets

- Note idle equipment or crews waiting on direction

You are not pricing the claim yet. You are protecting the evidence.

5. Keep the Story Simple and Linear

Good claims tell a short story.

- Cause

- Leads to effect

- Over a defined period

- With measurable time or cost impact

If you cannot explain the issue in five sentences, it is not clear yet. Do not embellish. Do not argue. Just record.

The One-Page Rapid Claims Summary

What Every New PM Should Be Able to Produce

At any point, you should be able to summarize an issue on one page:

- **What happened:** one paragraph

- **When and where:** dates and work area

- **Why it matters:** schedule or cost exposure

- **What you did:** mitigation and notices

- **What is needed:** direction, time, or money

If you can produce this page, you are doing contract administration correctly, even if the issue never becomes a formal claim.

What This Kit Is and Is Not

This Rapid Claims Kit is:

- A preservation tool

- A discipline guide

- A confidence builder for new PMs

It is not:

- A legal argument

- A final damages calculation

- A substitute for expert analysis

Its job is to keep options open.

For a new project manager, a claim can be reduced to five elements:

- A contract clause

- A cause

- A schedule impact

- A defined period

- A cost or time outcome

If any one of those is missing, the claim struggles.

Your daily job is not to build claims. It is to protect these five elements so that if a claim becomes necessary, the foundation already exists.

The Language You Will Hear Every Day

You will quickly become fluent in a small set of terms. RFI, submittal, extension of time, time impact analysis, windows analysis, measured mile, field overhead, home office overhead.

Do not be intimidated by the terminology. Each represents a practical concept already covered in this book. Use the language precisely and consistently and confusion drops fast.

Chapter Conclusion

Good contract administration is not about winning arguments. It is about avoiding them.

For new project managers, claims should not be feared or avoided. They should be understood as a natural extension of disciplined contract administration. When events are captured early, tied to the contract, anchored to the schedule, and supported by real records, claims stop being confrontational and start becoming factual.

Clear RFIs, disciplined tracking of approvals, timely notices, and an understanding of who owns which risks do more to protect a project than any after the fact claim. For new project managers, the learning curve is steep, but the fundamentals are simple. Document early. Track time. Tie direction to the contract. Say what you need and say it on time.

When contract administration is done well, disputes shrink, decisions come faster, and projects move forward with fewer surprises. When it is done poorly, even strong positions become hard to prove.

The habits you build in your first months on a project will follow you for your entire career.

"Excellence is not an act. It is a habit." – Aristotle

CHAPTER 31

THE CONSTRUCTION CLAIM DEFENSE PLAYBOOK

Chapter Foreword

Owners do not invent defenses at the end of a project. They recycle the same ones because they work. Late notice. No critical path impact. Concurrency. Failure to mitigate. Release language. When contractors are unprepared, these defenses end the discussion before it begins.

This chapter exists to make those defenses ineffective.

The objective is not advocacy after the fact. It is preparation before the claim is ever submitted. Claims rarely fail because the underlying event was weak. They fail because notice was delayed, schedule proof was incomplete, records were thin, or defenses were allowed to mature quietly over time. Once that happens, even a valid claim becomes expensive to recover.

What follows is a practical owner defense playbook. Each defense is stated the way it actually appears in rejection letters and reservation-of-rights responses. Each is followed by the discipline required to neutralize it through records, schedule proof, and pricing built during the job, not reconstructed later.

This chapter is not about winning a hearing. It is about preventing the owner from saying no in the first place.

Side Note: *Although this chapter is written as defenses against the Owner these are equally applicable to Owners, Contractors and Subcontractors.*

"Preparation is the difference between persuasion and surprise." **– Louis Brandeis**

The Defense System: How Owners Evaluate Claims

Owners do not evaluate claims chronologically. They evaluate them defensively. Read this chapter while building the claim, not after rejection. Identify which defense will be raised, then verify your file neutralizes it before submission. Almost every rejection fits into one of four categories:

1. Procedural Defenses

Did you comply with the contract's notice, timing, and release requirements?

2. Time Defenses

Did the event actually delay Substantial Completion on the longest path?

3. Cost and Causation Defenses

Can you prove cause and effect, quantify impacts, and separate responsibility?

4. Legal Bars

Do clauses or doctrines eliminate or limit recovery regardless of impact?

Each defense below fits into one of these categories. The goal is not to argue against them later, but to remove them from consideration before the claim is reviewed.

Procedural Defenses

"Your claim is untimely and therefore waived."

Owner position (as actually stated):
The contractor failed to provide timely and proper notice as required by the contract. Because notice was late, incomplete, or sent to the wrong party, the claim is barred regardless of merit.

Effective response:
Notice provisions exist to prevent prejudice, not to create forfeiture traps. The response begins by demonstrating that the owner had actual knowledge of the event through RFIs, meeting minutes, directives, emails, or daily coordination. When the owner knew what happened, when it happened, and continued to direct the work, lack of formal notice rarely causes prejudice.

Where the contract does not make notice an express condition precedent, substantial compliance is often sufficient. Even where notice was imperfect, owner direction, acceptance of continued performance, or control over the information undermines this defense.

Field example:
On a municipal wastewater project, late structural details forced resequencing of pours. The PM documented the issue in RFIs and weekly meetings but did not issue a formal notice letter until impacts became clear. The owner rejected the claim as untimely. Meeting minutes and engineer emails showed repeated acknowledgment and interim direction. The board found no prejudice and allowed the claim.

Rule:

The earlier the paper trail begins in any form, the weaker this defense becomes.

"You released this claim."

Owner position:

The contractor executed change orders or payment applications containing release language that extinguished the claim.

Effective response:

Release language is interpreted, not assumed. Ambiguities, carve-outs, and reservations preserve rights. Impacts that were not known or quantifiable at the time of execution are often outside the scope of a release. Consistent reservation language in pay applications and correspondence matters more than boilerplate language buried in exhibits.

Field example:

A contractor executed partial change orders to maintain cash flow. Later impacts became measurable. Reservation language in monthly pay applications preserved the claim, and the arbitrator ruled the releases did not bar later discovered impacts.

Rule:

Releases end claims only when they clearly say so.

Time Defenses

"There is no critical path impact."

Owner position:

The alleged event did not delay the project's critical path. Without longest path impact, there is no entitlement to time or money.

Effective response:

Critical path impact is proven through logic, not opinion. Contemporaneous schedule updates are used to show path migration, float erosion, or extension of Substantial Completion. Windows analysis or a properly executed time impact analysis demonstrates when and how the event affected completion.

Before-and-after schedule screenshots, float deltas, and logic relationships carry more weight than narrative explanations.

Field example:

On a hospital expansion, delayed equipment approvals were initially noncritical. Later updates showed the affected rooms migrated onto the longest path. A windows analysis using accepted updates demonstrated a nine-day extension. The owner's defense failed because the impact was visible in the CPM model.

Rule:

If the schedule tells the story, the defense ends quickly.

"Concurrency eliminates your entitlement."

Owner position:

Contractor delay overlapped owner delay. At most, the contractor is entitled to time only, if anything at all.

Effective response:

True concurrency requires two independent delays driving completion during the same window. Noncritical contractor inefficiency does not offset critical owner delay. Concurrency must be evaluated window by window, not blended into a global condition.

Where responsibility shifts over time, impacts are apportioned rather than conceded.

Field example:

On a data center project, manpower issues overlapped owner-directed resequencing. The contractor separated the analysis into two windows. Contractor delay consumed float in the first window. Owner access restrictions drove the critical path in the second. Time and money were recovered for the owner-controlled period.

Rule:

Precision defeats concurrency.

"You failed to mitigate."

Owner position:

The contractor did not take reasonable steps to reduce delay or cost.

Effective response:

The duty is reasonableness, not self-sacrifice. Contractors are not required to incur unrecoverable costs without direction or assurance of compensation. Effective mitigation is proven through documented proposals, resequencing attempts, and owner responses.

Where mitigation was infeasible, records must explain why.

Field example:

Late permitting delayed coastal work. The owner argued the contractor should have accelerated elsewhere. Emails showed resequencing proposals rejected due to owner operational limits. Daily reports showed crews reassigned where feasible. The defense failed.

Rule:

Mitigation is proven by records, not hindsight.

Cost and Causation Defenses

"This is a global claim."

Owner position:
The contractor presents a lump sum claim without discrete cause-and-effect proof.

Effective response:
Break the claim into individual threads by event, work area, and period. Avoid pure total cost. Use measured mile or modified total cost only with documented adjustments. Corroborate each component with contemporaneous records.

Field example:
A refinery claim was initially rejected as global. The contractor restructured it into discrete measured mile analyses for piping, steel, and electrical work. Once causation was isolated, settlement followed.

Rule:
Granularity creates credibility.

"Your measured mile is not comparable."

Owner position:
The baseline and impacted work differ in crew, scope, or conditions, making the analysis unreliable.

Effective response:
Demonstrate like-for-like conditions. Disclose and adjust for learning curve, access, or specification differences. Where no clean comparator exists, triangulate with other evidence rather than forcing the method.

Field example:
An owner challenged a drywall measured mile by alleging different crews. Payroll records showed identical crews, floor plates, and materials. Minor differences were disclosed and adjusted. The owner's challenge failed.

Rule:
Transparency strengthens analysis.

"Home office overhead is not recoverable."

Owner position:

Eichleay prerequisites are not met, so home office overhead is barred.

Effective response:

Demonstrate owner-caused delay of uncertain duration, standby, and inability to take replacement work. If Eichleay prerequisites are not met, apply an alternative method consistent with the contract and governing law.

Field example:

Multiple stop-start owner delays kept crews idle on a federal project. Daily logs showed standby and inability to reassign resources. Recovery was allowed.

Rule:

Eichleay is a test, not the only path.

Legal Bars

"No damages for delay applies."

Owner position:

The contract allows time extensions only and bars monetary recovery for delay.

Effective response:

Delay clauses do not exist in isolation. Owner-directed changes, suspensions, interference, or acceleration often trigger change provisions rather than pure delay clauses. Recognized exceptions preserve recovery.

Field example:

Late design revisions caused rework and extended supervision. The tribunal found the damages arose from changes, not delay, and allowed recovery.

"Liquidated damages apply as written."

Owner position:

Substantial Completion occurred late. Liquidated damages are enforceable regardless of alleged impacts.

Effective response:

Liquidated damages apply only if the contractor caused the delay. Establish entitlement to an Extension of Time through schedule analysis. Eliminating the trigger is usually more effective than challenging enforceability.

Field example:

By proving excusable delay, a contractor eliminated LD exposure without litigating the clause.

"Consequential damages are waived."

Owner position:

The contract waives consequential damages, barring recovery of delay costs.

Effective response:

The waiver applies to downstream business losses, not direct time-related project costs. Frame claims around extended field supervision, site facilities, and project management tied to defined delay periods.

Field example:

An owner argued lost productivity was consequential. The contractor reframed the claim as direct time-related costs. Recovery was allowed.

Chapter Conclusion

Owner defenses are not personal. They are structural.

They are raised because the contract allows them to be raised, and because the file allows them to succeed. When notice is thin, when the schedule is reactive instead of analytical, when releases are signed without discipline, when pricing lacks causation, the defense does not defeat the claim. The file does.

This chapter is not about arguing better. It is about building differently.

Strong claims are engineered the same way strong projects are engineered. With structure. With logic. With documentation that anticipates resistance. The best claims are assembled quietly during performance, long before they are labeled as claims. They are built in daily reports, in schedule updates, in reservation language, in cost codes that separate cause from consequence.

By the time the formal submission is made, the defense should already be neutralized.

When an owner opens your claim package, the first question in their mind is not "Is this fair?"
It is "How do we defend this?"

Your objective is to remove the available defenses before they are ever written.

If notice is timely, waiver language is reserved, the CPM tells the story, concurrency is dissected window by window, mitigation is documented, and pricing is transparent and event-specific, the conversation shifts. The file speaks. The defense narrows. Resolution accelerates.

This is not advocacy. It is architecture.

And like all good construction, the outcome is determined long before the inspection.

When preparation replaces reaction, owner defenses stop being barriers and start becoming confirmation that the claim was built correctly.

"Facts are stubborn things." – **John Adams**

"Facts are stubborn things." – **John Adams**

CHAPTER 32

CLAIMS GONE WRONG: WHAT FAILED, WHY, AND HOW TO FIX IT

Chapter Foreword

Owners do not reject claims randomly. They reject them using the same defenses described in the prior chapter. When claims fail, it is almost always because those defenses were allowed to stand unanswered.

This chapter is the mirror image of the Owner Defense Playbook. Where the prior chapter explains how owners say no, this chapter shows why claims give them the opportunity to do so. It is not a catalogue of mistakes. It is a diagnostic guide.

Weak claims fail long before they reach a hearing. Notice is late. The schedule is dirty. Logic edits are hidden. Concurrency is ignored. Pricing is blended. Each flaw aligns neatly with a defense owners already know how to use.

The purpose here is simple. If you understand how claims fail against owner defenses, you can redesign them before submission so those defenses never gain traction.

Good claims are not aggressive. They are defensively complete.

"Confidence comes from preparation, not position." – Colin Powell

How Claims Fail Inside the Owner Defense System

Owners evaluate claims through four lenses, as described in the **Chapter 32 – The Construction Claims Defense Playbook:**

1. **Procedural compliance**

2. **Time and critical path proof**

3. **Cost causation and responsibility**

4. **Legal bars and contractual limits**

Every failed claim in this chapter collapses in at least one of these categories. Most collapse in more than one.

This chapter follows that same structure, so the failure and the fix are unmistakable.

Procedural Failures

How Claims Invite Procedural Defenses

Failure Pattern

- Notice is late, informal, or incomplete

- Releases are signed without reservations

- Claims are assembled after the fact instead of preserved contemporaneously

Why Owners Win

These failures allow the owner to assert waiver, release, or forfeiture before the merits are ever discussed.

What Tribunals Punish

Not imperfect paperwork, but silence. When the record shows no timely warning, no reservation, and no escalation, decision makers infer acquiescence.

How to Fix It

- Document events immediately, even imperfectly

- Reserve time and money consistently

- Treat notice as preservation, not argument

If the paper trail exists early, procedural defenses weaken quickly.

"Once procedural defenses are neutralized, owners shift to time."

Time Analysis Failures

How Claims Collapse Under Critical Path Scrutiny

Failure Pattern

- No accepted baseline

- Dirty data dates

- Hidden logic repairs

- TIA or windows built on unaccepted updates

Why Owners Win

Owners argue there is no reliable proof of critical path impact. Without an accepted schedule foundation, they are usually correct.

What Tribunals Punish

Hindsight modeling. Any analysis that appears engineered to produce a result rather than observe reality loses credibility immediately.

How to Fix It

- Use the last accepted update

- Freeze logic before analysis

- Disclose all changes

- Let the CPM model tell the story

When the schedule is clean, time defenses collapse fast.

"When time defenses fail, cost and causation become the next line of resistance."

Concurrency Failures

How Claims Invite the Concurrency Defense

Failure Pattern

Full entitlement claimed without netting contractor delay

Overlapping periods blended into a single assertion

Why Owners Win

Concurrency becomes an easy hammer when claims fail to isolate responsibility window by window.

What Tribunals Punish

Assertions that ignore overlap. They do not punish shared responsibility. They punish untested responsibility.

How to Fix It

- Analyze concurrency by discrete windows

- Identify the driver in each period

- Claim only the net result

Precision removes concurrency from the conversation.

Cost and Causation Failures

How Claims Become "Global" by Accident

Failure Pattern

- Estimate versus actual pricing

- No segregation by event or period

- No tie between cost, time, and cause

Why Owners Win

Owners argue the claim lacks causation. Without segmentation, they are right.

What Tribunals Punish

Math without lineage. Numbers that cannot be re-performed are discounted or rejected.

How to Fix It

- Break claims into threads

- Tie each cost to a period and driver

- Use measured mile only with valid comparators

- Deduct credits and avoided costs

Granularity restores trust.

Legal Bar Failures

How Valid Claims Get Blocked Contractually

Failure Pattern

- No damages for delay clauses ignored

- Liquidated damages triggers misunderstood

- Consequential damage waivers misread

Why Owners Win

Claims are framed improperly, inviting contractual bars that could have been avoided.

What Tribunals Punish

Overreaching. Claims that seek barred damages instead of allowable ones lose credibility even where entitlement exists.

How to Fix It

- Separate time entitlement from cost entitlement

- Frame costs as direct time-related impacts

- Eliminate LDs through EOT rather than enforceability fights

Legal bars are navigated, not argued away.

Three Mini Cases Revisited Through the Construction Claims Defense Lens

The examples in this chapter are not anecdotes. They are diagnostic tools. Each accepted claim succeeds because it was built to survive predictable owner defenses. Each rejected claim fails because it triggered those defenses and left them unanswered.

Seen through the Owner Defense System, the outcomes are not surprising.

Mini-Case One: Time Impact Analysis

Defense Tested: No Critical Path Impact

Rejected Version

The contractor submitted a Time Impact Analysis built on an unaccepted schedule update. Logic had been quietly repaired to reflect how the team believed the work should have flowed, not how it actually flowed at the time. Concurrency was asserted but never netted. The owner rejected the claim on the ground that there was no reliable proof of critical path impact, and the tribunal agreed. The analysis appeared engineered, not observational.

Accepted Version

The contractor rebuilt the analysis using the last accepted update at the data date. All fragnet logic was disclosed. Before and after screenshots showed path migration clearly. Concurrency was tested window by window, with contractor delay netted out. The owner's "no critical path impact" defense collapsed because the CPM model, not narrative explanation, demonstrated the extension.

Lesson

This claim did not win because the event was larger. It won because it eliminated the time defense before it could be raised.

Mini-Case Two: Windows Analysis

Defense Tested: Concurrency Eliminates Entitlement

Rejected Version

The contractor alleged a continuous owner delay across several months and claimed the full period as compensable. Overlapping contractor inefficiencies were never segregated. The owner asserted concurrency broadly and denied compensation. The tribunal rejected the claim because the contractor failed to test overlap by discrete periods.

Accepted Version

The contractor divided the same period into three windows aligned with schedule updates. In each window, the delay driver was identified, and contractor delay was netted where present. Two windows produced zero entitlement. One produced a net owner delay. The owner's concurrency defense failed because it was answered directly, period by period.

Lesson

Concurrency is not defeated by argument. It is defeated by segmentation.

Mini-Case Three: Mixed Delay and Disruption

Defense Tested: Global Claim and Cost Causation

Rejected Version

The contractor compared estimated labor hours to actual hours across the project and claimed the difference as disruption. No attempt was made to separate access restrictions, late design information, or contractor inefficiency. The owner rejected the claim as global and speculative. The tribunal agreed.

Accepted Version

The contractor split the claim into phases. Access restrictions were analyzed using windows and claimed as time only. Late design directives were analyzed using a discrete TIA. Productivity loss tied to those directives was quantified using a measured mile with disclosed normalizations. Contractor inefficiency was carved out. Credits were deducted. The owner settled.

Lesson

Global claims fail because they ignore defenses. Partialized claims succeed because they anticipate them.

Pre-Filing Defense Audit

The Owner Defense Checklist Applied

Before filing any claim, ask:

- Can the owner credibly argue waiver or release

- Can the owner challenge the schedule foundation

- Can the owner assert concurrency without rebuttal

- Can the owner characterize pricing as global

- Can the owner invoke a contractual bar

If the answer is yes to any, the claim is not ready.

Chapter Conclusion

The previous chapter explained how claims are rejected.

This chapter explained why those rejections succeeded.

Claims do not fail because owners are unreasonable. They fail because predictable defenses are left unanswered. Late notice invites waiver. Dirty schedules invite time defenses. Blended pricing invites global claim attacks. Misframed costs invite contractual bars.

Strong claims are not aggressive. They are complete.

- They anticipate the defense before it is written.

- They remove objections before they are raised.

- They leave decision-makers with facts instead of positions.

When a claim is defensively engineered, it rarely reaches a hearing. It reaches a decision.

Build claims so that when the owner opens their defense playbook, each page has already been addressed. When nothing is left to argue, the answer tends to arrive quickly.

"Luck favors the prepared." **– Louis Pasteur**

CHAPTER 33

DOCTRINES AND REMEDIES: TURNING PROOFS INTO RECOVERABLE RELIEF

Chapter Foreword

By the time a claim reaches this chapter, the hard work should already be done. The delay has been analyzed. The longest path has been proven. Concurrency has been tested and netted. The numbers are built from contemporaneous records.

What remains is translation.

Courts, boards, and decision makers do not award relief because a project went poorly. They award relief because facts align with recognized doctrines and contractual remedies. If the issue cannot be mapped to a doctrine and tied to an available remedy, it will not be compensated no matter how disruptive it felt in the field.

This chapter is the bridge between proof and recovery. It converts delay analysis and disruption evidence into legally recognized paths for time and money. It also shows the limits. Some impacts earn time only. Some costs are barred unless strict prerequisites are met. Some claims fail not because they are untrue, but because they are framed under the wrong doctrine.

Read this chapter the way an owner or tribunal does. Start with the issue. Identify the governing doctrine. Apply the test. Select the remedy the contract allows. Then assemble the minimum evidence required to survive defenses.

If the prior chapters taught you how to prove what happened, this chapter teaches you how to get paid for it.

"The law does not reward effort. It rewards alignment." – **Oliver Wendell Holmes, Jr.**

How This Chapter Fits the System

This chapter sits between **delay and disruption analysis** and **claim drafting**.

- Delay analysis chapters answer: *Did the event affect the longest path and by how much?*

- The Owner Defense Playbook explains: *How owners say no.*

- This chapter answers: *What doctrine converts proven impact into recoverable relief, and what remedy is actually available.*

Think of this as a **doctrine selector**, not a legal treatise.

The Doctrine-to-Remedy Framework

This section introduces what I refer to as the **Doctrine-to-Remedy Translation Framework**. It is a practical system for converting proven project impacts into recoverable relief by aligning facts with the doctrines and remedies decision makers actually recognize. Too many claims fail because they skip this translation step. The impact is proven, the delay is real, the disruption is documented, but the remedy requested does not match the governing doctrine or the contract's limits. This framework forces discipline. It requires the claimant to identify the issue, select the correct doctrine, apply the applicable test, and pursue only the remedies that doctrine supports. When that alignment exists, claims become defensible, auditable, and far more likely to be resolved without escalation.

You may also think of this as a **Claim Alignment Framework**. Its purpose is to eliminate **Remedy Misalignment Risk**, the most common and least discussed reason otherwise valid claims are rejected, discounted, or settled for pennies on the dollar.

Every compensable claim follows the same progression:

1. **Issue**
   What actually went wrong in the field?

2. **Doctrine**
   What legal or contractual concept governs that issue?

3. **Test**
   What must be proven in plain English?

4. **Remedy**
   Is the relief time, money, both, or neither?

5. **Evidence**

What records defeat the predictable owner defense?

If any link in that chain is missing, the claim weakens immediately.

From Proof to Consequences

This chapter is the natural pivot point of the book. Up to this point, the focus has been on proving what happened, when it happened, and how it affected the project. From here forward, the focus shifts to what those facts actually mean. Courts and boards do not reward disruption in the abstract. They award remedies defined by doctrine, constrained by contract language, and filtered through precedent. The chapters that follow examine how these doctrines are applied in real cases and how small framing decisions lead to dramatically different outcomes. Read this chapter carefully before moving on. From here on, we are no longer talking about theory. We are talking about consequences.

Core Doctrines and Remedies (Practitioner Matrix)

Rather than memorizing doctrine names, focus on **what problem each doctrine solves** and **what it pays**.

Issue	Doctrine / Concept	Typical Test (Plain English)	Remedy Angle	Evidence to Win	Watch-outs
Owner-caused hindrance	Prevention Principle	Owner action/inaction made performance on time impossible/near impossible	EOT; cost is compensable under the clause	Notices, directives, access logs, windows/TIA	Waiver by conduct; concurrent contractor delay
Design info gaps	Constructive Change / Spearin concepts	Contractor relied on the owner's design; info errors/omissions required extra work.	Change order; time + cost	RFI chain, submittals, redlines, time analysis	Betterment disputes; spec vs drawing conflicts
No-Damages-for-Delay (ND4D)	Clause-based bar with exceptions	Delay money barred unless an exception (e.g., active interference, bad faith, not contemplated)	Time only unless exception proven	Exception facts, emails, directives, and schedule proof	State-specific; burden high; keep to facts
Force majeure	Excusable non-compensable events	Unforeseeable events outside control; notice + mitigation	EOT only	Weather logs, supplier notices, mitigation steps	Document normal vs abnormal; avoid double-counting
Differing site conditions	Type I/II conditions	Site materially differs from contract indications or is unusual	Time + cost	Pre-bid docs, as-found photos, daily reports	Notice timing; pre-bid inspection duties
Acceleration	Directed or Constructive	Owner's direction to finish earlier or denial of justified EOT	Acceleration costs	EOT request, denial, overtime/stacking records	Proof of denial; voluntary acceleration is not compensable
Suspension	Suspension of Work	The owner ordered stop/slow; within the clause	EOT + cost if allowed	Order letters, idle logs, and equipment standby	Duty to mitigate; restart inefficiency proof
Concurrency	Apportionment of delays	Overlapping owner and contractor delays	Net EOT; cost limited	Windows/TIA, cause mapping	Jurisdictional views differ; disclose method
Waiver/estoppel	Rights waived by conduct	The owner's conduct is inconsistent with the strict enforcement relied upon by the contractor.	Avoided forfeiture; equitable relief	Emails, course of dealing	Do not rely on this alone; keep notices flowing
Liquidated damages	Agreed daily rate	The owner may deduct if the contractor is late without EOT	Defend via EOT/concurrency	Windows/TIA; notice trail	LD reasonableness is seldom re-litigated at claim time
Home office overhead	Eichleay / Hudson / Harmony	Prerequisites met; allocation method fits jurisdiction	Unabsorbed OH	Accounts, billings, and delay period linkage	Strict prerequisites; avoid overlap with FOH
Quantum meruit	Unjust Enrichment	Work outside the contract or after termination; benefit conferred	Reasonable value recovery	Invoices, scope proof, acceptance	Contract may control; the measure differs
Termination for convenience	Owner's unilateral right	Proper notice; settlement per clause	Close-out costs; profit on work done	Inventory, demob, settlement proposals	Release language traps; timing
Termination for default	Cause termination	Material breach; cure notice; opportunity to cure	Defend; convert to convenience if wrongful	Cure notices, performance proof	Surety, schedule, and quality records are critical

Why Claims Fail Here, Not in Delay Analysis

Most failed claims do not fail in delay analysis. They fail here. The longest path is proven. The schedule logic is sound. Concurrency has been netted correctly. Yet the claim still collapses because the relief sought does not fit the doctrine that governs the issue, or because barred costs are mixed with allowable ones. Tribunals do not repair misaligned claims. They reject them. Owners do not separate good money from bad. They discount the entire submission. This chapter exists because proof alone is not enough. Claims must be translated into the correct legal and contractual language of recovery. When that step is skipped, even excellent technical analysis produces disappointing results.

Owner-Caused Hindrance

When owner action or inaction makes timely performance impossible or impractical.

- **Typical remedy:** Extension of time, often with compensable cost

- **Key evidence:** Notices, directives, access logs, windows or TIA

- **Watch-out:** Concurrent contractor delay will be netted

Design Information Gaps

When the contractor reasonably relies on owner-furnished design that proves incomplete or defective.

- **Typical remedy:** Change order for time and cost

- **Key evidence:** RFIs, submittals, redlines, design revisions, schedule impact

- **Watch-out:** Betterment arguments and spec-drawing conflicts

No-Damages-for-Delay Clauses

When the contract limits delay compensation unless an exception applies.

- **Typical remedy:** Time only unless an exception is proven

- **Key evidence:** Facts showing active interference, bad faith, or uncontemplated delay

- **Watch-out:** Jurisdictional differences and high proof burden

Force Majeure

When unforeseeable events outside either party's control delay the work.

- **Typical remedy:** Extension of time only

- **Key evidence:** Weather data, supplier notices, mitigation records

- **Watch-out:** Distinguish abnormal from anticipated conditions

Differing Site Conditions

When subsurface or latent conditions materially differ from contract indications.

- **Typical remedy:** Time and cost

- **Key evidence:** Pre-bid documents, as-found photos, daily reports

- **Watch-out:** Strict notice and pre-bid inspection duties

Acceleration

When the contractor is required to recover delay without proper time relief.

- **Typical remedy:** Acceleration costs

- **Key evidence:** EOT request, denial, overtime and stacking records

- **Watch-out:** Voluntary acceleration is not compensable

Suspension of Work

When the owner orders a stop or slow-down.

- **Typical remedy:** Time and, if allowed, cost

- **Key evidence:** Suspension directives, idle logs, restart inefficiency proof

- **Watch-out:** Mitigation and remobilization efficiency

Concurrency

When owner and contractor delays overlap.

- **Typical remedy:** Net extension of time, limited cost

- **Key evidence:** Window-by-window delay attribution

- **Watch-out:** Jurisdictional views vary

Liquidated Damages

When the contract sets a daily rate for late completion.

Typical remedy: Avoidance through EOT

Key evidence: Windows or TIA proving excusable delay

Watch-out: LD enforceability is rarely re-litigated at claim stage

Home Office Overhead

When owner-caused delay prevents absorption of fixed corporate costs.

- **Typical remedy:** Unabsorbed overhead under jurisdictional method

- **Key evidence:** Billing history, standby proof, delay linkage

- **Watch-out:** Strict prerequisites and overlap with field overhead

The Remedies Chooser: A Practical Filter

Before claiming any dollar, walk through this sequence:

1. **Is there entitlement?**
   Clause plus facts plus timely notice. If not, stop.

2. **Is time impacted on the longest path?**
   If yes, pursue extension of time and net days.

3. **Is the cost compensable under the clause?**
   If yes, price from contemporaneous actuals only.

4. **Do prerequisites apply?**
   If they are not met, do not claim that bucket.

5. **Are there bars or releases?**
   Adjust the ask rather than fighting the contract.

Strong claims are selective. Weak claims are greedy.

Owner Defenses and the Exhibits That Defeat Them

Every doctrine above corresponds to a predictable defense. Your job is to answer it before it is raised.

- **Late notice** → Date-stamped emails and logs showing actual knowledge

- **No critical path impact** → Before-and-after schedule shots with driver callouts

- **Concurrency** → Window-by-window net delay tables

- **Global claim** → Measured mile analyses with exclusions and credits

- **Scope risk** → Clause excerpts plus RFIs showing direction or change

If the exhibit exists, the defense rarely survives.

Real-World Case Examples

Why Proven Claims Still Fail

Field Example: Remedy Misalignment

A contractor proved a twelve-day owner-caused delay through a clean windows analysis. The claim sought extended field overhead, lost productivity, and home office overhead. The contract contained a no-damages-for-delay clause with narrow exceptions that were not supported by the record. The owner rejected the claim in full. When the submission was reframed to seek time only, supported by the same schedule proof, the extension was granted immediately. The claim failed not because the delay was unproven, but because the remedy sought exceeded what the governing doctrine and contract permitted.

Field Example: Underpriced Settlement

On an industrial project, a contractor proved owner-directed acceleration and recovered only partial costs in settlement. The original claim blended acceleration costs with general inefficiency and barred delay damages. During negotiation, the owner discounted the entire quantum due to overreach. A later forensic review showed that a properly isolated acceleration claim, aligned to the correct doctrine, would likely have recovered significantly more without litigation.

Field Example: Avoidable Litigation

A project reached arbitration over extended overhead. The underlying delay was undisputed. The dispute centered entirely on whether the claimed costs were direct or consequential under the contract. Had the claim been framed initially around time-related direct costs tied to prolongation, the dispute likely would have resolved at the executive level. Instead, misalignment forced the parties into a legal fight over classification rather than facts.

The Claim Storyboard

Each of these failures could have been avoided by forcing the claim through a disciplined alignment check before submission.

A defensible claim can be summarized on one page:

1. Clause and risk allocation

2. Cause and dates

3. Longest path proof

4. Disruption method and comparator

5. Quantum built from actuals

6. Draft change order or EOT language

If it cannot be told in this sequence, it is not ready.

Chapter Conclusion

Claims are rarely rejected because they lack effort.

They are rejected because they ask for the wrong remedy, seek barred costs, or ignore the doctrine that governs the issue. Others are not rejected outright but quietly underpriced in settlement because owners see the misalignment and discount the risk accordingly. Still others escalate into unnecessary litigation, not because the facts are disputed, but because the claim was framed in a way that left no defensible middle ground.

Most claims are not lost on the facts. They are lost on framing.

This chapter is meant to prevent all three outcomes. When issues are mapped to the correct doctrine, remedies are selected with discipline, and evidence is tailored to defeat predictable defenses, claims stop being arguments and start becoming decisions.

Precision here does not weaken a claim. It protects it.

"In matters of proof, clarity beats force." - Learned Hand

CHAPTER 34

Global Claims Admissibility, Partialization, Causation, and Pricing

Chapter Foreword

By the time a claim reaches this chapter, the technical work should already be complete. The delay has been analyzed. The longest path has been established. Concurrency has been tested and netted. Costs have been built from contemporaneous records.

What remains is judgment.

This chapter addresses one of the most misunderstood and most frequently misused tools in construction claims: the global claim. Used properly, it can be an efficient and defensible way to present recovery where owner-risk events overlap and cannot be meaningfully separated. Used improperly, it is one of the fastest ways to lose credibility, invite rejection, or underprice a settlement.

Courts and boards do not reject global claims because they dislike consolidation. They reject them because consolidation is used to avoid proof. This chapter exists to draw that line clearly.

It is not legal advice. It is a practitioner-aligned framework informed by accepted themes in AACE recommended practices, the Society of Construction Law Delay and Disruption Protocol, and decades of tribunal treatment of delay and disruption claims. Always defer to your contract and governing law.

Read this chapter as a gate. If your claim cannot pass through it cleanly, it does not belong in front of a tribunal.

From this point forward in the book, theory gives way to consequences.

What a Global Claim Is, And What It Is Not

A global claim is a consolidated presentation seeking time and or money for the combined effect of multiple owner-risk events where pricing each micro-event separately would be unreliable, arbitrary, or disproportionate.

- It is not a total cost claim.

- It is not an estimate versus actual reconciliation.

- It is not a substitute for causation.

A defensible global claim still proves entitlement and quantum using accepted methods. Time is demonstrated through windows analysis or a targeted time impact analysis tied to accepted schedule updates. Disruption is quantified through measured mile or another recognized method using disclosed comparators and normalizations. Contractor-caused and neutral impacts are expressly excluded, and credits or avoided costs are shown.

Global presentation is a packaging choice, not a shortcut.

When a Global Claim May Be Appropriate

A consolidated presentation may be justified where:

- Owner-risk events overlap in the same period, area, or workstream, producing indivisible effects

- Accepted schedule updates exist and can support windows analysis or a short TIA

- Path migration can be explained clearly without speculation

- A credible measured mile or equivalent method exists and normalizations are disclosed

- Contractor-risk and neutral causes can be excluded transparently

- The contract and jurisdiction allow consolidated presentation when proven rigorously

The justification is not convenience. It is impracticability of reliable segregation.

When a Global Claim Should Not Be Used

A global claim is not appropriate where:

- Discrete events can reasonably be segregated and priced

- Accepted schedule updates are missing or unreliable

- Longest path impact cannot be demonstrated

- No valid disruption comparator exists

- Contractor-caused issues dominate the period

- Consolidation would undermine notice or time-bar compliance

If the proof is weak, consolidation magnifies the weakness. In those cases, carve the claim smaller or do not file it.

The Impracticability Test: What You Must Be Able to Show

Tribunals do not accept global claims because segregation is inconvenient. They accept them when segregation is unreasonable or unreliable under the circumstances.

Supporting indicators include:

- Disproportionate effort where forensic segregation would exceed the value of the claim

- Sensitivity swings where reasonable allocation methods vary results materially without a non-arbitrary basis

- Record structures tracking costs by area, phase, or crew rather than by micro-event

- Shared impacts such as stacked trades or access limits affecting the same resources

- High overlap of RFIs, submittals, and directives driving the same critical path within narrow windows

You do not need all of these. You need enough to show that atomization would be artificial.

Admissibility Gate: Five Tests Every Global Claim Must Pass

Before presenting a consolidated claim, it must survive five threshold tests:

1. **Causation Narrative**
   A single, coherent explanation linking owner-risk events to critical path delay and measured disruption.

2. **Impracticability of Segregation**
   A documented explanation of why micro-event pricing would be unreasonable.

3. **Recognized Methods and Transparency**
   Windows analysis, TIA, and measured mile applied openly with disclosed inputs and assumptions.

4. **Exclusion of Contractor and Neutral Causes**
   Learning curve, inefficiencies, weather within norms, and trade errors removed.

5. **No Total Cost Shortcut**
   Quantification based on attributable deltas, not estimate versus actual gaps.

If any one of these fails, the claim should not be presented globally.

Partialization: How Strong Global Claims Survive

Even where global presentation is justified, partialization is essential. Breaking the claim into coherent slices reduces risk and increases credibility.

Common partialization approaches include:

- By period, separating early design information impacts from later access constraints

- By area, such as process zones versus utilities

- By trade stream, isolating framing, MEP, or finishes

- By cause family, separating design lag from owner-directed resequencing

Partialization does not weaken the claim. It makes it auditable.

Causation Scaffolding: How the Story Is Told

A defensible global claim follows a consistent structure:

- Start with the last accepted update before the central cluster of events

- Show float status and longest path before impact

- Lay RFIs, submittals, and directives against the windows timeline

- Explain path migration in plain language

- Bridge time to money using measured mile within the same windows

- Close with net days and net dollars after exclusions and credits

If the bridge from time to money is unclear, the claim will fail regardless of facts.

Pricing Hygiene: Where Global Claims Often Collapse

Global claims are often rejected not on entitlement, but on math.

Pricing discipline requires:

- Actual field overhead burn rates, not tender allowances

- Home office overhead only where jurisdictional prerequisites are met

- Clear separation of owned versus operating equipment costs

- Explicit standby documentation

- Full subtraction of avoided costs and concessions

- Rounding only at the final step

Transparency beats aggression every time.

Worked Mini-Cases: Accepted and Rejected

Design Information Lag (Accepted)

Repeated revise and resubmit cycles drove path migration to riser approvals. Windows analysis across three months, a short TIA for a discrete directive, and a normalized measured mile supported disruption. Contractor inefficiencies were excluded. The claim was accepted because segregation by period and cause remained credible.

Stacked Trades and Access Constraints (Rejected)

Crowding and access limits were priced as a single total cost delta. No accepted baseline existed. No comparator was used. No exclusions were shown. The claim was rejected as a global total cost presentation lacking method and transparency.

Late Design and Owner-Directed Resequencing (Accepted After Partialization)

Initial submission blended resequencing and design lag. After splitting into two phases, time only for resequencing and time plus disruption for design lag, the claim was accepted. The facts did not change. The framing did.

Chapter Conclusion

If your claim cannot survive a flashlight, it does not belong in a courtroom.

A global claim is not a shortcut. It is a disciplined packaging decision made only after segregation becomes unreasonable and only when proof remains transparent.

Most global claims fail not because the impacts were unreal, but because the presentation asked the tribunal to trust arithmetic instead of evidence. When methods are disclosed, exclusions are explicit, and the time-to-money bridge is visible, consolidation can work. When any of those are missing, it invites rejection.

This chapter is the last checkpoint before the case law that follows. From here forward, you will see how courts and boards respond when these rules are followed and what happens when they are ignored.

"Excellence is the result of caring more than others think is wise, risking more than others think is safe, and doing more than others think is practical." **– Vince Lombardi**

CHAPTER 35

PUTTING IT ALL TOGETHER: RISK, PROOF AND OUTCOME

Chapter Foreword

This book did not begin with claims.

It began with risk. How risk is created, misunderstood, transferred, and ignored long before a project ever slips. Claims are not anomalies in construction. They are the predictable byproduct of unmanaged risk, unclear allocation, and human behavior under pressure.

Volume One has followed that lifecycle deliberately.

From foundational risk theory and company culture, through contract administration and procurement, into schedule control, cost management, and forensic proof, each chapter has built toward a single objective: **preventing disputes where possible and resolving them decisively where they are unavoidable**.

This final chapter pulls those threads together.

It explains how early decisions echo forward, how technical proof only works when the groundwork is laid, and why most claims fail not in arbitration or court, but months or years earlier when risk was mismanaged or documentation was neglected.

What follows is not a summary. It is a systems check.

If you understand how the parts of this book interlock, you understand why claims succeed, why they fail, and how to control the outcome.

"The best time to solve a problem is when it is still small." **- Henry Kissinger**

The Construction Risk Lifecycle: One System, Not Separate Chapters

Part I – Foundations: Risks, Causes, Culture

Chapters 1 through 3 established the uncomfortable truth most organizations resist: **claims are cultural before they are contractual.**

Projects that normalize ambiguity, tolerate late decisions, or discourage early escalation create the conditions where disputes thrive. Claims do not originate in the field alone; they originate in leadership behavior, incentive structures, and communication norms.

If risk is not openly acknowledged and deliberately managed, it will surface later as cost, delay, and conflict, whether labeled as a claim or not.

Part II – Contract Administration and Project Manager Discipline

Chapters 4 through 9 translated risk into daily behavior.

Risk allocation checklists, early warning signs, psychology of disagreement, and contract administration fundamentals all reinforce one principle: **claims are prevented, or preserved, by routine project management habits**.

Late RFIs, undocumented directives, informal approvals, and ignored notice clocks are not administrative oversights. They are future defenses being handed to the other side.

This part of the book explains why many claims are already lost before a scheduler or lawyer ever sees them.

Parts III–VI – Risk Before the First Shovel Hits the Ground

Chapters 10 through 15 addressed the most underestimated phase of all: **pre-commitment risk**.

Pre-bid assumptions, proposal language, owner contract terms, design development gaps, procurement choices, and subcontractor risk flow-down all determine:

- Who owns which risk

- Whether recovery is contractually possible

- How hard proof will be later

By the time construction begins, most of the financial and legal boundaries are already set. These chapters explain why strong claims often fail despite good facts because the contract and procurement structure made recovery difficult from day one.

Part VII – Risk During Construction Execution

Chapters 16 through 24 examined the pressure cooker.

Construction phase risk is dynamic. Schedules compress. Costs rise. Safety, quality, insurance, and bonding exposures converge. Monthly risk audits, KPIs, and disciplined change management are not bureaucratic exercises. They are **early dispute resolution tools**.

Projects that monitor risk continuously adapt. Projects that do not accumulate exposure silently until claims become unavoidable.

Part VIII – Closeout Is Not the End of Risk

Chapter 25 addressed a common myth: that risk ends at Substantial Completion.

Closeout, commissioning, warranties, and turnover frequently determine whether disputes close cleanly or metastasize into litigation. Releases, final payments, and unresolved punch items often decide the fate of claims more than technical merit.

Part IX – Forensic Proof: Turning Experience into Evidence

Chapters 26 through 28 shifted the book from management to measurement.

Delay analysis, disruption quantification, and measured mile methodology convert lived experience into defensible proof. These chapters explain how time and money are demonstrated, not asserted.

But proof alone is not enough.

Part X – Claims Are Won or Lost Before They Are Filed

Chapters 29 through 32 made that explicit.

Winning claims are not aggressive. They are **disciplined.**

- They anticipate owner defenses.

- They isolate responsibility.

- They avoid overreach.

Claims fail when notice is late, schedules are dirty, logic edits are hidden, concurrency is ignored, or quantum is blended. These are not technical failures—they are system failures.

Part XI – Doctrine: Turning Proof into Recovery

Chapters 33 and 34 explained the final translation.

Courts and boards do not pay for disruption because it was painful. They pay because facts align with recognized doctrines and permitted remedies. Proof that is misaligned with doctrine does not disappear, it is discounted.

This is where underpriced settlements, rejected claims, and unnecessary litigation are born.

The System in Three Parts

- Risk unmanaged becomes dispute.

- Dispute undocumented becomes defense.

- Defense unanswered becomes rejection.

Volume I exists to break that chain.

Why Volume Two Exists

From here forward, the discussion changes.

Volume Two does not explain **how** claims should be built.
It shows **what actually happened** when claims met decision makers.

Each case illustrates one or more of the system failures described in Volume I, or demonstrates what happens when the system is applied correctly.

- They are not academic.

- They are consequential.

Where Volume One Ends and Volume Two Begins

Volume One ends here.

- It ends with method, discipline, and structure.

- It equips you to predict outcomes before they happen.

Volume Two begins with results.

It documents how tribunals, courts, boards, and arbitrators responded when theory met reality across the 9 most common categories of construction claims.

Read Volume Two with Volume One in mind.
Every case will make more sense.

Chapter Conclusion

Claims do not fail because construction is difficult.

They fail because risk was misunderstood, proof was incomplete, or remedies were misaligned.

Volume One has shown how to control each of those variables.

If you manage risk early, document consistently, prove time and cost cleanly, align claims to doctrine, and neutralize defenses before they are raised, disputes lose their leverage.

What remains is judgment.

Volume Two will show how that judgment was exercised by others, sometimes wisely, sometimes not, and what it cost them.

"In the end, facts are what matter – but only when they are properly framed." - **Justice Benjamin N. Cardozo**

Disclaimer

The legal content in this book is intended for educational and informational purposes only. It does not constitute legal advice and should not be relied upon as such. Readers should consult qualified construction counsel regarding any specific legal matters.

REFERENCES AND CITATIONS: VOLUME I AND VOLUME II

AACE International Recommended Practice (RP) 25R-03, Estimating Lost Labor Productivity in Construction Claims (2004).

AACE International Recommended Practice 29R-03: Forensic Schedule Analysis.

AACE International Recommended Practice 52R-06: Time Impact Analysis.

ABA TIPS, Retainage and the Potential Defense to the Surety for Early Release of Retainage.

AIA Document A201-2017

AIA Document A312, Performance Bond (2010 ed.).

Ali D. Haidar, Global Claims in Construction (2011).

Allied Materials & Equip. Co. v. Parsons, 572 F. Supp. 558 (D. Kan. 1983).

Allied Materials & Equip. Co. v. United States, 569 F.2d 562 (Ct. Cl. 1978).

AMB Contractors, Inc. v. United States, 707 F.2d 809 (Fed. Cir. 1983).

Appeal of C.J. Mahan Constr. Co., ENG BCA No. 6198 (1992).

Appeal of Fruin-Colnon Corp., ASBCA No. 22093 (1981).

Appeal of M.A. Mortenson Co., ASBCA No. 40750 (1992).

Appeal of Nicon, Inc., ASBCA No. 27595 (1984).

Appeal of Peter Kiewit Sons' Co., ENG BCA No. 3717 (1983).

Appeal of Sw. Welding & Mfg. Co., ASBCA No. 18072 (1975).

Atlantic Basin Iron Works v. United States, 390 F.2d 634 (Ct. Cl. 1968).

Barry B. Bramble & Michael T. Callahan, Construction Delay Claims (7th ed. 2021).

Beacon Residential Cmty. Ass'n v. Skidmore, Owings & Merrill LLP, 327 P.3d 850 (Cal. 2014).

Bell BCI Co. v. United States, 570 F.3d 1337 (Fed. Cir. 2009).

Betterment & economic waste: defect/change jurisprudence; expert valuation where appropriate.

Biltmore Constructors, Inc. v. Twin City Fire Ins. Co., 572 So. 2d 912 (Fla. Dist. Ct. App. 1990).

Blake Constr. Co. v. C. J. Cochran & Co., 232 F.2d 503 (D.C. Cir. 1956).

Blake Constr. Co. v. United States, 987 F.2d 742 (Fed. Cir. 1993).

Blinderman Constr. Co. v. United States, 695 F.2d 552 (Fed. Cir. 1982).

Bovis Lend Lease LMB, Inc. v. N.Y.C. Dep't of Envtl. Prot., OATH Index No. 546/05 (2005).

Brandt Constr. Co. v. City of Houston, 401 S.W.3d 166 (Tex. App. 2011).

Brock v. L.E. Myers Co., 818 F.2d 1270 (6th Cir. 1987).

Bruce Constr. Corp. v. United States, 163 Ct. Cl. 97 (1963).

Burlington Ins. Co. v. N.Y.C. Transit Auth., 79 N.E.3d 477 (N.Y. 2017).

C. Norman Peterson Co. v. Container Corp. of America, 172 Cal. App. 3d 628 (Cal. Ct. App. 1985).

Caffall Bros. Forest Prods., Inc. v. State, 725 P.2d 815 (Or. Ct. App. 1986).

Cates Constr., Inc. v. Talbot Partners, 980 P.2d 407 (Cal. 1999).

CIlam Parithi, Construction Contract Claims for Beginners (entry-level roadmaps).

City Inn Ltd. v. Shepherd Constr. Ltd., [2010] CSIH 68 (Scot.).

City of Beverly Hills v. Five Star Grading & Paving, Inc., 181 Cal. Rptr. 3d 106 (Ct. App. 2010).

City of Columbia v. Paul N. Howard Co., 707 S.E.2d 639 (S.C. 2011).

City of Omaha v. CBS Corp., 917 F.3d 686 (8th Cir. 2019).

Clark Constr. Co. v. United States, 5 Cl. Ct. 659 (1984).

Cleveland Constr., Inc. v. United States, 102 Fed. Cl. 774 (2012).

Clover Constr. Co. v. City of Pontiac, 351 N.W.2d 286 (Mich. Ct. App. 1984).

ConsensusDocs 260.

Corinno Civetta Constr. Corp. v. City of New York, 493 N.E.2d 905 (N.Y. 1986).

Council of Co-Owners v. Whiting-Turner Contracting Co., 517 A.2d 336 (Md. 1986).

Crawford v. Weather Shield Mfg., Inc., 187 P.3d 424 (Cal. 2008).

D.C. McClain, Inc. v. Arlington Cnty., 452 S.E.2d 659 (Va. 1995).

Dave Gustafson & Co. v. State, 156 N.W.2d 185 (S.D. 1968).

DBIA Standard Forms (e.g., 700-series) and Guide (design-build responsibilities).

Delay Analysis in Construction Contracts — Patrick J. Keane & A. F. Caletka (2d ed. 2015).

Dillingham Constr. N.A. Inc. v. City of Chi., 778 F.2d 1431 (7th Cir. 1985).

Downey v. D.R. Allen & Son, Inc., 302 N.J. Super. 570 (1997).

Dravo Corp. v. United States, 428 F.2d 1147 (Ct. Cl. 1970).

East River S.S. Corp. v. Transamerica Delaval Inc., 476 U.S. 858 (1986).

Ecological Rts. Found. v. Pac. Lumber Co., 230 F.3d 1141 (9th Cir. 2000).

Edelweiss Gardens Condo. Ass'n v. Edelweiss Gardens, L.P., 946 A.2d 103 (Pa. Super. Ct. 2008).

Edward R. Marden Corp. v. United States, 442 F.2d 364 (Ct. Cl. 1971).

Eichleay prerequisites: Federal Circuit/board precedent; alternative HOOH approaches where Eichleay is not met.

Equipment Watch, Rental Rate Blue Book (ownership/operating/standby guidance).

Evans v. Hebert Constr., LLC, 174 So. 3d 1222 (La. Ct. App. 2015).

F.D. Rich Co. v. United States ex rel. Indus. Lumber Co., 417 U.S. 116 (1974).

FIDIC, Conditions of Contract for Construction (2017).

Fireman's Fund Ins. Co. v. Structural Sys. Tech., Inc., 436 F. Supp. 2d 882 (S.D. Tex. 2006).

Foster Constr. C.A. & Williams Bros. Co. v. United States, 435 F.2d 873 (Ct. Cl. 1970).

Fraser Constr. Co. v. United States, 384 F.3d 1354 (Fed. Cir. 2004).

FTR Int'l, Inc. v. Rio Sch. Dist., 182 Cal. Rptr. 3d 865 (Ct. App. 2015).

Fullerton & Knowles, 50-State Summary of Payment Bond Law on Public Projects.

Ganton Techs., Inc. v. Quadion Corp., 834 F. Supp. 1018 (N.D. Ill. 1993).

Gen. Builders Supply Co. v. United States, 409 F.2d 246 (Ct. Cl. 1969).

Geoffrey Trickey & Jeremy Hackett, The Presentation and Settlement of Contractors' Claims (2d ed. 2002).

Gilbane Bldg. Co. v. R.I. Airport Corp., 909 A.2d 829 (R.I. 2006).

Global Claims in Construction — Ali D. Haidar (Routledge 2011).

Green Int'l, Inc. v. Solis, 951 S.W.2d 384 (Tex. 1997).

Gurtler, Hebert & Co. v. Orleans Parish Sch. Bd., 346 So. 2d 1335 (La. 1977).

Hackett, Jeremy, Construction Claims: Current Practice and Case Management (2000).

Henry Boot Constr. (UK) Ltd. v. Malmaison Hotel (Manchester) Ltd., [1999] C.P. Rep. 38 (TCC).

Herman v. Markham Air Rifle Co., 329 F.2d 457 (6th Cir. 1964).

Howard Contracting, Inc. v. G.A. MacDonald Constr. Co., 85 Cal. Rptr. 2d 590 (Ct. App. 1999).

Interstate Gen. Gov't Contractors, Inc. v. West, 12 F.3d 1053 (Fed. Cir. 1993).

Jacob & Youngs, Inc. v. Kent, 129 N.E. 889 (N.Y. 1921).

John Doyle Constr. Ltd. v. Erith Contractors Ltd., [2021] EWCA Civ 1452.

John M. Wickwire, Thomas J. Driscoll, Stephen B. Hurlbut & Michael T. Groff, Construction Scheduling (2018).

Johnson Controls, Inc. v. City of Cedar Rapids, 713 N.W.2d 491 (Iowa 2006).

JPS Constr. Grp. v. Cnty. of Essex, 284 A.3d 953 (N.J. App. Div. 2023).

Kajima/Ray Wilson v. L.A. Cnty. Metro. Transp. Auth., 1 P.3d 63 (Cal. 2000).

Krygoski Constr. Co. v. United States, 94 F.3d 1537 (Fed. Cir. 1996).

L&A Contracting Co. v. S. Concrete Servs., Inc., 17 F.3d 106 (5th Cir. 1994).

Len Co. & Assocs. v. United States, 385 F.2d 438 (Ct. Cl. 1967).

Lichter v. Mellon-Stuart Co., 305 F.2d 216 (3d Cir. 1962).

Merritt-Chapman & Scott Corp. v. United States, 429 F.2d 431 (Ct. Cl. 1970).

Metcalf Constr. Co. v. United States, 742 F.3d 984 (Fed. Cir. 2014).

Miller v. Constr. One, Inc., 796 N.E.2d 1104 (Ohio Ct. App. 2003).

Milner Hotels, Inc. v. Norfolk & W. Ry., 226 N.E.2d 639 (Ill. App. Ct. 1967).

MW Erectors, Inc. v. Niederhauser Ornamental & Metal Works Co., 115 P.3d 41 (Cal. 2005).

Nat'l Union Fire Ins. Co. v. City Sav. F.S.B., 28 F.3d 376 (3d Cir. 1994).

Neal & Co. v. City of Dillingham, 923 P.2d 89 (Alaska 1996).

NEC, Engineering and Construction Contract (NEC4, 2017).

Nicon, Inc. v. United States, 331 F.3d 878 (Fed. Cir. 2003).

Norair Eng'g Corp. v. United States, 666 F.2d 546 (Ct. Cl. 1981).

P.J. Dick, Inc. v. Principi, 324 F.3d 1364 (Fed. Cir. 2003).

Paschall's, Inc. v. Dozier, 407 S.W.2d 150 (Tenn. 1966).

Patco Constr. Co. v. People's United Bank, 684 F.3d 197 (1st Cir. 2012).

Patrick J. Keane & A. F. Caletka, Delay Analysis in Construction Contracts (2d ed. 2015).

Pearlman v. Reliance Ins. Co., 371 U.S. 132 (1962).

Peevyhouse v. Garland Coal & Mining Co., 382 P.2d 109 (Okla. 1962).

Perini Corp. v. Greate Bay Hotel & Casino, Inc., 610 A.2d 364 (N.J. 1992).

Pickering v. Barker, 192 N.W. 227 (Mich. 1923).

Prairie State Bank v. United States, 164 U.S. 227 (1896).

Preparing Construction Claims — Stephen Hall (Routledge 2014).

Prestressed Concrete, Inc. v. United States, 403 F.2d 123 (Ct. Cl. 1968).

Priebe & Sons, Inc. v. United States, 332 U.S. 407 (1947).

Raytheon Constructors, Inc. v. Asarco Inc., 368 F.3d 1214 (10th Cir. 2003).

Restatement (Second) of Contracts § 348(2) (Am. L. Inst. 1981).

Rickard v. F.M. Chiles, Inc., 173 S.W.3d 713 (Tenn. Ct. App. 2004).

S.S.D.W. Co. v. Brisk Waterproofing Co., 565 N.E.2d 1259 (N.Y. 1990).

Sec'y of Labor v. Ames Constr., Inc., 16 O.S.H.C. 1805 (OSHRC 1993) (OSHA willful; excavation).

Sec'y of Labor v. R & R Builders, Inc., 22 O.S.H.C. 1807 (OSHRC 2009) (fall protection; multi-employer).

Servidone Constr. Corp. v. United States, 931 F.2d 860 (Fed. Cir. 1991).

Severin v. United States, 99 Ct. Cl. 435 (1943).

Society of Construction Law, Delay & Disruption Protocol (2d ed. 2017).

Southwest Eng'g Co. v. United States, 341 F.2d 998 (Ct. Cl. 1965).

St. Paul Fire & Marine Ins. Co. v. City of Green River, 93 F.3d 1245 (10th Cir. 1996).

Summers-Taylor, Inc. v. Sec'y of Labor, 765 F.3d 447 (6th Cir. 2014).

Sverdrup/Parsons Brinckerhoff v. Metro. Wash. Airports Auth., 251 F.3d 173 (4th Cir. 2001).

Sweetwater Constructors v. Town of Apex, 402 S.E.2d 493 (N.C. Ct. App. 1991).

Thomas & Marker Constr. Co. v. Wal-Mart Stores, Inc., 2008-Ohio-1492.

Tidewater Constr. Corp. v. United States, 39 Fed. Cl. 66 (1997).

Travelers Indem. Co. v. Crown Corr, Inc., 98 N.E.3d 984 (Ind. Ct. App. 2018).

United Contractors v. United States, 368 F.2d 585 (Ct. Cl. 1966).

United States ex rel. Aurora Painting, Inc. v. Fireman's Fund Ins. Co., 832 F.2d 1150 (9th Cir. 1987).

United States v. BDH Corp., 356 F. Supp. 2d 129 (D. Me. 2005).

United States v. Brooks-Callaway Co., 318 U.S. 120 (1943).

United States v. Carter, 353 U.S. 210 (1957).

United States v. Hensel Phelps Constr. Co., 413 F.2d 701 (10th Cir. 1969).

United States v. Munsey Tr. Co., 332 U.S. 234 (1947).

United States v. Sci. Applications Int'l Corp., 626 F.3d 1257 (D.C. Cir. 2010).

United States v. Spearin, 248 U.S. 132 (1918).

Universal Concrete Prods. Corp. v. Turner Constr. Co., 595 F.3d 443 (2d Cir. 2010).

Walter Lilly & Co. v. Mackay, [2012] EWHC 1773 (TCC).

Walton Constr. Co. v. MGM Grand Hotel, Inc., 137 F.3d 964 (7th Cir. 1998).

Weedo v. Stone-E-Brick, Inc., 405 A.2d 788 (N.J. 1979).

Weeks Marine, Inc. v. United States, 575 F.3d 1352 (Fed. Cir. 2009).

White v. Edsall Constr. Co., 296 F.3d 1081 (Fed. Cir. 2002).

William R. Clarke Corp. v. Safeco Ins. Co., 938 P.2d 372 (Cal. 1997).

WRB Corp. v. United States, 183 Ct. Cl. 409 (1968).